Praise for *Triple Crown Leadership*

"A rare combination of deep insight and helpful research, and an important book. Relevant and timely. Smart and helpful guidance for leaders about today's pressing problems."
—**Stephen R. Covey** and **Stephen M. R. Covey,**
Bestselling Authors and Father and Son
(from the Foreword)

"It's been more than thirty years since the sport of kings last saw a Triple Crown. We can't wait that long for the triple crown of leadership—the stakes are too high and the need too urgent. It's time to embrace this vision of lasting, ethical leadership."
—**Daniel H. Pink,** Bestselling Author of
Drive and *A Whole New Mind*

"The Vanoureks have written the new leadership manifesto. There is nothing more essential for leaders today than to lead with their head and heart, and they explain exactly how to do this. It is a gift to all of us who believe in the power of purposeful leadership."
—**Richard Leider,** Bestselling Author of
Repacking Your Bags and *The Power of Purpose*

"A clarion call for anyone striving to create an enduring organization with lasting positive impact. Bob and Gregg Vanourek have written an illuminating book that we can't afford to ignore."
—**David Gergen,** Director of the Center for Public
Leadership at the Harvard Kennedy School and
CNN Senior Political Analyst, and **Christopher
Gergen,** Founder and CEO, Forward Ventures,
Father and Son

"A powerful case for leaders who combine ethics and excellence to create enduring organizations. Fed up with failed leaders, the Vanoureks describe successful leaders who achieve superior results over the long term by focusing on values and performance. Following their wise counsel will enable you to inspire your team to peak performance using your head and your heart."

—**Bill George,** Harvard Business School
Professor and Former CEO, Medtronic

"Bob and Gregg Vanourek have written a timely and practical book about the complex art and practice of leadership. They skillfully relate traditional problems all leaders face to the current crop of challenges that recently have brought all institutional leadership under greater public scrutiny. They speak directly to leaders in plain language, providing useful examples and backing it up with research. Every leader of tomorrow must read this book today."

—**James O'Toole,** Leadership Author and Daniels
Distinguished Professor of Business Ethics at the
Daniels College of Business, University of Denver

"An inspiring call to action, a challenging mandate, and a compelling road map for leaders across the public, private, or nonprofit sector. It is a must-read if you have the courage to aspire to be the best you can be."

—**Marty Linsky,** Harvard Kennedy School Faculty
and Co-founder, Cambridge Leadership
Associates

"In a crowded marketplace of books on leadership, this one stands out and offers new perspectives on what it takes to compete effectively through enduring excellence and ethics. Read this book for its keen insights and practical wisdom about how to lead with character, grace, and results that make sense. A book of wisdom and practical advice, no matter what race you find yourself in."

—**Barry Z. Posner,** PhD, Accolti Professor of
Leadership, Santa Clara University, and
Co-author of *The Leadership Challenge,*
Credibility, and *The Truth About Leadership*

"*Triple Crown Leadership* is way out in front of the pack of current leadership books. First, because this remarkable father-son author team has combined practical wisdom learned from experience in the toughest business situations to cover the core issues of sustainable leadership—ethics, values, and meaning for the organization, customers, and employees. Second, because this book is simply a good read. Every chapter is chock-full of things you can take away and use for your own work and life. Bravo for a triple crown book!"

—**Bob Aubrey,** Author of *Creating Aspirational Leaders* and Practice Leader for People Development Consulting, Mazars

"This important book offers a unique perspective, represented first by the successful father-son coauthors and second by the many leaders they interviewed. The authors' multigenerational perspective establishes unusual credibility for their daring assertion that excellent organizational results can be achieved by ethical means over an enduring period of time. While their claim may at first appear elusive, the authors back it up with practical advice, drawn from much experience, as to how their 'trifecta' can be won. They have convinced me, more than I have dared to believe before, that high organizational ideals can become a reality! And *that* is a pearl of great price."

—**Dr. Larry Donnithorne,** Author of *The West Point Way of Leadership*

"This book makes a compelling case for the kind of leadership we so desperately need today. Triple crown leaders don't take the easy way, they find the better way. If you want to excel and endure with integrity, join this triple crown quest."

—**Frances Hesselbein,** CEO, The Frances Hesselbein Leadership Institute, Former CEO, Girl Scouts of the U.S.A., and Presidential Medal of Freedom Recipient

"When I saw the chapter on 'Head and Heart,' I knew this book would be significant. Very few leaders are advocating this integration of our intellectual capacities with our emotional sensibilities. The Vanoureks have hit on a powerful model that will change organizational life if leaders are willing to open themselves to it. Some may call it leading-edge thinking, but a man from Galilee taught this long ago."

—**John Horan-Kates,** President, Vail Leadership Institute

"Right now, people are looking everywhere for answers: What's real? What's true? What works? The good news is, the answers are right here in this gem of a book."

—**Alan M. Webber,** Co-founder, *Fast Company* magazine, and Author of *Rules of Thumb: 52 Truths for Winning at Business Without Losing Your Self*

"In the age of Conscious Capitalism, we need leadership that touches people where they live. Here's an inspiring field manual from a passionate father and son team."

—**Patricia Aburdene,** Author of *Megatrends 2010*

"Bob and Gregg Vanourek capture what a coming-of-age generation expect from themselves and their leaders—excellence and character. But their greatest gift may be to show us how to navigate the inevitable challenges on the path to significant impact. This is a powerful and insightful book."

—**Peter Sims,** Author of *Little Bets* and Co-author of *True North*

"Today's leaders must tap into something deeper—in themselves and others. This book takes you into that important and inspiring terrain."

—**Chip Conley,** Author of *Emotional Equations* and Founder, Joie de Vivre Hospitality

"Running an enterprise is often a lonely task. The Vanoureks' diverse experiences and insights make *Triple Crown Leadership* a reassuring and thought-provoking companion."

—**Seth Goldman,** Co-founder and TeaEO, Honest Tea

TRIPLE
CROWN
LEADERSHIP

TRIPLE
CROWN
LEADERSHIP

Building

EXCELLENT, ETHICAL, AND
ENDURING ORGANIZATIONS

BOB VANOUREK

GREGG VANOUREK

New York   Chicago   San Francisco   Lisbon
London   Madrid   Mexico City   Milan   New Delhi
San Juan   Seoul   Singapore   Sydney   Toronto

Copyright © 2012 by Bob Vanourek and Gregg Vanourek. All rights reserved. Printed in the United States of America. Except as permitted under the United States Copyright Act of 1976, no part of this publication may be reproduced or distributed in any form or by any means, or stored in a database or retrieval system, without the prior written permission of the publisher.

1 2 3 4 5 6 7 8 9 10   DOC/DOC   1 8 7 6 5 4 3 2

ISBN   978-0-07-179150-2
MHID   0-07-179150-7

e-ISBN 978-0-07-179151-9
e-MHID   0-07-179151-5

Library of Congress Cataloging-in-Publication Data
Vanourek, Bob.
    Triple crown leadership : building excellent, ethical, and enduring organizations / by Bob Vanourek and Gregg Vanourek.
        p. cm.
    Includes bibliographical references and index.
    ISBN 978-0-07-179150-2 (alk. paper) — ISBN 0-07-179150-7 (alk. paper)
  1. Leadership.   2. Leadership—case studies.   3. Business ethics.   4. Social responsibility of business.   I. Vanourek, Gregg.   II. Title.
    HD57.7.V368   2012
    658.4'092—dc23
                                                                      2012014944

McGraw-Hill books are available at special quantity discounts to use as premiums and sales promotions or for use in corporate training programs. To contact a representative, please e-mail us at bulksales@mcgraw-hill.com.

This book is printed on acid-free paper.

To June, my life partner,
to whom I am eternally grateful

To Kristina, Alexandra, and Anya,
with all my love

CONTENTS

FOREWORD

We're excited to write the Foreword to this book. For decades we—father and son—have worked to advance personal and professional effectiveness by focusing on key dimensions of leadership, including character, competence, and trust. We have sought to identify and articulate universal leadership principles that lead to sustained, superior performance—principles that are able to stand the test of time, cross cultures, and endure.

In *Triple Crown Leadership*, Bob and Gregg Vanourek—another father-son team—make powerful new leadership contributions, supplementing their own illuminating experiences with rich stories from leaders around the world. The result is a rare combination of deep insight and helpful research, and an important book that simultaneously speaks to foundational principles and higher aims while advocating clear and specific practices.

The "triple crown" quest to build excellent, ethical, and enduring organizations is a vital one for all leaders. It is highly consistent with our own message of character (ethical), competence (excellent), and sustained superior performance (enduring). Effective leaders excel today even while looking to the horizons of tomorrow. They create exceptional value for all stakeholders (not just shareholders) through sustainable practices. Indeed, one of our definitions of leadership is *getting results today in a way that, by inspiring trust, increases our ability to get results tomorrow.*

Bob and Gregg not only recognize this; they insightfully point to *how* to make it happen. They show leaders how to achieve compelling results without cutting corners—by unleashing the abundant talent of their colleagues, leading with both head and heart, and flexing between "steel and velvet" as the situation requires. The reality in our lives and organizations is that ends and means are inseparable. *How we do what we do* makes all the difference.

Triple Crown Leadership is relevant and timely. It addresses the important organizational challenges of our age. It cuts through the clutter of complexity and slogans, providing smart and helpful guidance for leaders about today's pressing problems. The book rejects easy, quick-fix answers. Instead, it identifies the principles and illuminates the practices leaders are using to craft high-trust, high-performance organizations and avoid the traps that lead to organizational breakdowns.

Triple Crown Leadership is also actionable—for CEOs, senior executives, board members, managers, supervisors, individual contributors, and even workers without formal authority. It contains practical insights from leaders who have clearly been in the trenches about how to hire great people, create a culture of trust, and align teams for sustainable performance.

Finally, *Triple Crown Leadership* inspires. It calls us to the post of the race of our lives—one worthy of our best efforts and deepest aspirations. It signals hope in a fast-moving world full of big challenges and concentrates our gaze on the exciting track ahead. In effect, it is an offering of trust—and nothing is as inspiring as an offering of trust.

We live in a world that is overmanaged and underled. The greatest need in our global society today is for better leadership—from all of us. The call has been made; now it's time for each of us to take the reins.

—Stephen R. Covey and Stephen M. R. Covey
March 2012

TRIPLE

CROWN

LEADERSHIP

INTRODUCTION

CALL TO
THE POST

Leadership is a quest.

—Max DePree, leadership author

I t was the quest of their lives.

They were gunning for the Triple Crown, needing three big wins in a row: the Kentucky Derby and the Preakness, which they had, and now the Belmont Stakes.

Penny Chenery had saved her father's Meadow Farm, a sprawling 2,600-acre racing stable just north of Richmond, Virginia. After courageously refusing to sell the farm despite family pressure and financial distress, she acquired a special horse by way of a coin toss with a competing stable.

Chenery called him Secretariat. He was a magnificent thoroughbred with a blazing red coat, white "stockings" around three ankles, and a big white star on his forehead. His voracious appetite matched his big, broad frame. When she first saw "Big Red" prancing around in a field, Chenery wrote a single word in her diary: "Wow!"

Growing up in Quebec, Ron Turcotte—too small to be a lumberjack—labored with workhorses in the logging fields. With his passion for horses, he became a hot walker, cooling thoroughbreds after their workouts, and then a jockey. As a jockey, he earned a reputation for an unrivaled work ethic and unimpeachable integrity while winning often.

Trainer Lucien Laurin, a former jockey himself, was on the verge of retirement. As a trainer, he had won more than a thousand races. Having won the Kentucky Derby once before, he declared, "I want another shot at the Triple Crown."

Chenery and her talented team pinned their hopes on Big Red, and he had been taking the racing world by storm.

The first Triple Crown test came at the ninety-ninth running of the Kentucky Derby in 1973, with more than 134,000 people— the biggest crowd ever—at the regal Churchill Downs racetrack in Lexington.

It did not start well.

Secretariat broke last. He was up against archrival Sham and eleven other fearsome contenders. But Big Red ran each quarter mile faster than the one before—precisely the opposite of most horses at such a trying distance—accelerating even through the finish line a mile and a quarter from the start. He won by two and a half lengths in a thrilling late surge with a track record that still stands.

Next up was the Preakness at the Pimlico track in Baltimore, Maryland, with its tight turns. Secretariat broke last again, but then surged forward early in the race, to the surprise of all, picking off the competing horses one by one. Big Red won by two and a half lengths, again with Sham in second.

With two of the three victories needed, they were poised for racing glory. It had been a quarter century since the last Triple Crown champion. Many commentators dismissed the possibility of another one, given how the sport had changed over the years, with foreign buyers taking promising thoroughbreds overseas, as well as advances in technology, medicine, and breeding that equalized the racing field. But the Meadow Farm racing team had captured the nation's attention. In the run-up to the Belmont Stakes in New York, Secretariat had appeared on the cover of *TIME, Newsweek,* and *Sports Illustrated.*

Called "The Test of the Champion," Belmont has the longest dirt track in thoroughbred racing, at one and a half miles. Race day brought stifling ninety-degree heat and humidity, but at post time the crowd was totally focused on the starting gate.

Announcer Chic Anderson called the race:

> And they're off . . . Sham and Secretariat are right together into the first turn . . . Sham getting a head in front as they move around the turn . . . They're on the backstretch. It's almost a match race now . . . Secretariat now taking the lead . . . The lead is increasing. Make it three, three and a half . . . Secretariat is blazing along . . . moving like a tremendous machine . . . Secretariat by twelve . . . Secretariat by fourteen lengths on the turn . . . Secretariat is all alone . . . Secretariat is in a posi-

tion that seems impossible to catch. Secretariat leads this field by eighteen lengths . . . Secretariat has opened a twenty-two-length lead. He hits the finish . . . twenty-five lengths in front . . . An amazing, unbelievable performance by this miracle horse.[1]

But Anderson was wrong.

It was impossible to judge such a wide margin of victory from the announcer's booth. Confirmed after the race stewards studied the video, Secretariat won by a staggering thirty-one lengths—about a hundred yards—cutting an astonishing two and a half seconds off the track record and setting a world record that has stood for almost forty years.[2] The Triple Crown was theirs.

Spectators were awestruck. Kent Hollingsworth, editor of a leading horseracing publication, said, "I don't believe it. Impossible. But I saw it. I can't breathe. He won by a sixteenth of a mile . . . He ran so far beyond known reference points, he left us with no measurable comparison."[3] Award-winning sportswriter Hugh McIlvanney wrote, "None of us can ever expect to see the like of that again."[4]

Author Marvin Drager wrote, "The superlatives were endless . . . One called it the greatest performance by a racehorse in this century." Others compared it to the best feats of Joe Louis (boxing legend), Jesse Owens (track star), and Jack Nicklaus (golf superstar). They dubbed him "Super Horse" and "Horse of the Century."

"When he accelerates," wrote Pete Axthelm in *Newsweek,* "he produces a breathtaking explosion that leaves novices and hardened horsemen alike convinced that, for one of those moments that seldom occur in any sport, they have witnessed genuine greatness."

Secretariat holds the record for the fastest Kentucky Derby and Belmont Stakes ever. He would have set the track record in the Preakness except for a clock malfunction. Jack Krumpe, president of the New York Racing Association, said, "He was a power that transcended racing."

At Belmont, Turcotte and Secretariat rose to a state of peak performance, demolishing the field behind them.

THE TRIPLE CROWN

The story of Meadow Farm and Secretariat, as we shall see, is about more than astonishing athleticism and the will to win. It is also about teamwork, heart, character, stewardship, flow, adversity, and inspired leadership. The Meadow Farm racing team accomplished three significant things: they achieved extraordinary results, they achieved them with honor, and their results have stood the test of time. Their record was excellent, ethical, and enduring (what we call the three Es). They rose to the occasion of their three big races. It was the ultimate triple, and thus an apt metaphor for the focus of this book: building (1) excellent, (2) ethical, and (3) enduring organizations.

Accomplishing such a triple requires a different brand of leadership. We call it *triple crown leadership*. Like its counterpart in thoroughbred horseracing—the "sport of kings"—it is all too rare. Since 1875, there have only been eleven Triple Crown winners, making it "the most elusive championship in all of sports."[5] To achieve it, a horse and its racing stable must win three brutally competitive races in different states over five weeks. The thoroughbreds race at distances from one and a quarter miles (in the Derby) to a punishing one and a half miles (at Belmont) in whatever weather and track conditions exist on race day. For jockeys, it is a complicated challenge of race strategy, strength training, diet, and teamwork with a thousand-pound animal. At speeds approaching forty miles per hour, a fall can be fatal.

Each May, the Kentucky Derby starts the run for the Triple Crown. Some hail the Derby's "Run for the Roses" as "the most exciting two minutes in sports." Others call it the "fastest two minutes," with a dozen or more thoroughbreds hurtling at breakneck speeds, their jockeys perched precariously on their backs, millions watching on television, and tens of thousands of racing fanatics at the track in tailored fashions and exquisite hats drinking mint juleps and cheering for their favored steed.

Triples in any context are difficult and rare. Triples in baseball are rarer than home runs. Triple plays are even rarer. The batting triple crown goes to the player who leads the league in the same year in home runs, batting average, and runs batted in. The last time that happened was 1967. In other sports, scoring a "hat trick" of three goals in a game is rare, as is nailing a triple axel in women's figure skating. Only occasionally does a film win best picture, best director, and best actor or actress at the Academy Awards.

For organizations, achieving excellent results is rare enough— much less doing it with integrity and staying power.

FAILED LEADERSHIP

Unfortunately, in our world today, we see too much of the opposite. Today, we are witnessing failures of organizational leadership at a massive scale. For example, look at:

- The global financial crisis and European debt crisis

- The bankruptcy of Lehman Brothers and the abuses at AIG, Countrywide, and Fannie Mae

- The worldwide "Occupy" protest movements, with the "99 percent" hurling invectives at the corporate malfeasance and government corruption of the "1 percent"

- The Deepwater Horizon oil spill in the Gulf of Mexico and the way BP and other leaders passed the buck

- The recent breakdowns at two paragons: Toyota (massive recalls due to safety and quality problems) and Johnson & Johnson (product recalls, lawsuits, allegations of kickbacks, and more)

- The recent scandals at the International Monetary Fund, FIFA (the international governing body of soccer), and governments in Italy, India, Germany, Russia, Indonesia, China, Brazil, Japan, Nigeria, Austria, and more

- The Penn State sexual abuse scandal, where leaders looked the other way

There are many underlying causes in these debacles, but a common denominator is failed leadership. The sad thing is that we are repeating history. Five years ago, there was a stock options backdating scandal. A decade ago, it was Enron, Arthur Andersen, WorldCom, HealthSouth, and Adelphia. There were scandals in the Olympics, baseball, cycling, the Red Cross, the United Way, the Catholic Church, and, yes, horseracing. Go back also to the savings and loan crisis and junk bond craze.

Is this record acceptable? Can't we do better than this? Are we content to suffer through cycles of crises and scandals every few years, even as the stakes rise with the interconnectedness of financial markets and technology systems? That we have arrived at this unhappy place again, facing these risks, speaks to the depth and intractability of our problems. It is all too clear: we need better leadership.

Despite these challenges, we are optimistic about the prospects for change. We see encouraging signs from many organizations around the world, but we need new approaches applied more aggressively and broadly. It is time to raise our sights and standards, time to change our organizational imperatives, and time to raise our leadership game.

This book addresses big questions: What kind of leadership does it take to build excellent, ethical, and enduring organizations? How can we lead ventures for both high performance and positive impact on all stakeholders? How can we avoid breakdowns in performance, integrity, and sustainability? We know it is possible, because we have seen it in action and been part of it at times.

Most people want to be successful, maintain their integrity, and have a positive impact. These aspirations are powerful, but they are under attack from organizational dysfunction, ethical compromises, and unsustainable practices.

Too many talented people labor in organizations that do not live up to their values and aspirations. Too many leaders sell out, succumb to short-term pressures, and take the easy way out. The rationalizations are legion: "That's just the way the world is." "Everybody's doing it." "It's just this one time." "It's not really hurting anyone."

The central message of this book is that leaders should commit to the overriding aim of building excellent, ethical, and enduring organizations. With the right kind of leadership, these three pillars can be mutually reinforcing and dramatically raise performance, engagement, and impact. Using certain leadership practices, we can address the root causes of our problems and set our organizations on a remarkably higher trajectory.

THE QUEST

Perfection is not attainable, but if we chase perfection, we can catch excellence.

—**Vince Lombardi,** legendary coach of the
champion Green Bay Packers

Along with Coach Lombardi, we propose something radical: that we "chase perfection," embarking upon an epic quest for the triple crown of excellent, ethical, and enduring organizations. Some people view "ethical" and "enduring" as implicit in "excellent," but ethical and enduring are so important, and so often neglected, that we draw them out for special emphasis. Today, there is so much focus on making your short-term numbers that the ethical and enduring dimensions get drowned out.

Those undertaking this quest can expect to encounter daunting obstacles. With the leadership practices in this book, we fill their rucksacks with tools for the trek. Such quests are part of human nature. Through the ages, seekers have pursued truth. Explorers sought to circumnavigate the earth by sea and by air. Adventurers raced to the poles, to the depths of the ocean, and to the heights of Everest. Astronauts sought to demystify the heavens and walk on the moon. Patriots seek freedom for their people.

What is your quest? Are you chasing power or riches, fame or glory, recognition or approval? What is your organization's quest?

Crushing the competition? Enriching the officers? Enriching shareholders? No wonder the 99 percent are shouting.

For decades, the aim of most businesses was singular: to maximize short-term shareholder value. We are now suffering the consequences of that maxim taken to the extreme, ignoring the caveats to do so honorably and over the long term. Instant gratification predominates. Those who focus solely on profit and share price today face a backlash and a barrage of questions: What about ethical boundaries? What about negative externalities and social impact? What about long-term value creation and sustainable practices? Even Jack Welch, famous for driving for shareholder value as GE's former CEO, has said, "Shareholder value is the dumbest idea in the world. Shareholder value is a result, not a strategy."[6]

But there are also problems with the alternatives. "Doing well by doing good" is a noble maxim, but putting blind faith in it is destined to disappoint. The "win-win" is not automatic. In fact, it can be elusive. Choosing to operate ethically and sustainably is only the beginning. Leaders must figure out how to do that while achieving excellent results, maintaining the viability of the enterprise so it can run the next race. There are real tradeoffs and tough decisions here. It requires strong leadership and lots of midcourse corrections.

Today, we do not need more of the same old approaches. We need a quest that raises our sights, summons our passions, unleashes our talents, and calls our better angels to the post. Building an excellent, ethical, and enduring organization is difficult, but it can be done. It requires a commitment from many people over many years and a different brand of leadership.

Notably, that leadership is not what most people think, and it is certainly not just about the person at the top. It is a job for leaders throughout the organization, even those who do not think of themselves as leaders.

This quest is a worthy and inspiring endeavor—perhaps the seminal leadership challenge of our age. It is a quest we must undertake if we are to address our challenges and honor our aspirations.

OUR RESEARCH

This book draws upon our own leadership experiences as well as research and interviews with leaders in more than sixty organizations in eleven countries: Austria, Brazil, Canada, China, France, Germany, India, Japan, Sweden, Taiwan, and the United States. The organizations include global corporations; social enterprises; education, government, and military organizations; turnarounds; and startups. We interviewed leaders from Cisco, eBay, GE, Google, Infosys, KIPP, Mayo Clinic, Princeton University, Share Our Strength, Spotify, the Strategic Air Command, Xerox, Zappos.com, and more, as well as horseracing experts. (For the full list and more detailed information, see the Appendix.)

We went beyond the usual suspects. Ever heard of the company that cleaned up the most dangerous buildings in the United States, turning a toxic plutonium site into a wildlife refuge? How about the dying small town that survived a devastating tornado and transformed itself into a world-leading community?

Of course, none of the organizations we cite is perfect. They have all made mistakes and will surely stumble again. *Triple Crown Leadership* is not a success study designed to list great organizations. Others have attempted that task, only to see how fleeting that mantle can be. *Triple Crown Leadership* is about a quest, not a list. We journey into quest land, not list land, seeking the leadership practices that build excellent, ethical, and enduring organizations. Our focus is not retrospective but prospective—looking forward using the early markers and signposts we see today from pioneering practices. The book is written by and for leadership practitioners, supported by research.

Triple Crown Leadership also builds on the work of esteemed leadership authors, from Peter Drucker and Warren Bennis to Michael Beer, Jim Collins, Bill George, Robert Greenleaf, Ron Heifitz, Rosabeth Moss Kanter, James Kouzes, Marty Linsky, James O'Toole, Barry Posner, and more. We draw upon their findings and build on their insights.

WHAT'S IN IT FOR YOU?

Triple Crown Leadership is for those who seek high performance, integrity, and impact. Senior executives from CEOs to board members will find practical applications here. Managers and aspiring leaders will gain a road map they can use to lead more effectively. Even the everyday worker, not necessarily interested in leading, will find tools to succeed and thrive.

We do not view leadership as the sole prerogative of people with fancy titles, corner offices, and loads of frequent-flier miles. That is one of the fallacies that has held so many enterprises back. We purposefully focus on *leadership*, not the *leader*. Triple crown leadership is a group performance, not a solo act.

We also view leadership as a choice, not a position, a trust, not a right. Leadership is a way of thinking, being, and acting that we—*every single one of us*—can apply in all settings. Triple crown organizations don't just expect leadership from the upper echelons. They encourage and develop leadership from all quarters. They promote a pervasive leadership dynamic and in the process build a culture of character.

Triple Crown Leadership covers a wide array of organizations across sectors, industries, and continents. The book is rich with new concepts you can begin implementing immediately, a framework for how to contend for the crown, and stories of leadership in action, plus an exciting trip to some of the greatest horseraces of all time.

WHY US?

Those embarking upon this quest are wise to scrutinize their guides: who are Bob and Gregg?

We have been CEOs of and officers in a wide range of organizations, from small businesses and social ventures to global corporations traded on the New York Stock Exchange. We have worked in an array of sectors and industries—high and low tech—including universities, a foundation, and a think tank.

Perhaps most importantly, we have worked in some of the most challenging environments of all: startups and turnarounds. We have been at the launch of pioneering new ventures—scaling at blinding speed, unable to hire people quickly enough, and learning the hard way by making every mistake in the book.

We have been called in to lead turnarounds, including some doozies: reversing $100 million per year in negative cash flow and cleaning house after government ethics investigations, attacks by short sellers, and libelous rumors. Our organizations have won awards, and we have been at both ends of terminations. We have worked against dirty competitors, confronted ripping-mad investors, and tried to reenergize burned-out and disenchanted employees. We have seen turnarounds through to successful completion, finally thriving after years on life support.

We have worked with narcissistic leaders and suffered the consequences of myopic strategies and good-old-boy boards. We have seen more rounds of layoffs and "near-death experiences" than we care to remember, with dire consequences for good people.

Fortunately, we have also been blessed with incredible colleagues and wise mentors. We have emerged from our challenges with stronger organizations, successful turnarounds and startups, lessons learned, and experiences that have shaped our character and given us hope.

We have traveled a similar journey, father and son, a generation apart, coming to the same conclusions about leadership, now eager to share those insights with you.

We are fed up with poor leadership, dysfunctional organizations, unethical and unsustainable practices, and recurring scandals that crush dreams and wreak havoc on people's lives.

We have seen great leadership in action. We have been privileged at times to be part of it. It changed our lives. We know it can change yours too.

At certain times, we are all called to the post of leadership. The bugle sounds. It is time to mount our horses for the race ahead. Look down the track and envision the race you want to ride. Much depends on you. We wish you Godspeed on your triple crown leadership quest.

CHAPTER ROAD MAP

Chapter 1. The Triple Crown Quest: Excellent, Ethical, and Enduring

In their quest for excellent results, most organizations fall short. Some cut ethical corners. Meanwhile, leaders today face new expectations about social impact and sustainability. The real question is not just how to achieve the results imperative, the ethics imperative, or the sustainability imperative, but how to achieve all three. Like the famous Triple Crown of horseracing, it is difficult—but not impossible—to achieve. It requires a different brand of leadership, one that builds a culture of character and infuses organizations with a powerful new leadership dynamic.

Part One. Triple Crown Leadership Practices

Chapter 2. Head and Heart

Triple crown leadership starts with new approaches to choosing, developing, and rewarding people. Most organizations focus on knowledge, skills, and experience—"head" issues. Triple crown leaders, by contrast, recruit for all that plus character, emotional intelligence, and "fit" with the organization—people with both "head" and "heart."

Chapter 3. The Colors

Triple crown leaders employ their organization's shared purpose, values, and vision as sacrosanct "colors" to represent their quest. The racing colors worn by the horse and jockey trace their lineage to medieval knights, whose colors represented their honor. In organizations, the colors are standards by which people can judge their options and make decisions. The purpose grounds, the values guide, and the vision inspires.

Chapter 4. Steel and Velvet

Triple crown leaders know when to invoke the hard edge of leadership—the steel bit—that demands excellent results, insists upon ethical practices, and resists the allure of short-term thinking. They also know when to invoke the soft edge of leadership—the velvet stroke—that patiently builds the culture of character. They collaborate and "bite their tongues" to let others lead. They get beyond their natural leadership style. Triple crown leadership requires the judgment to flex between the hard and soft edges of leadership, depending on the situation and the people, without appearing to be inconsistent.

Chapter 5. Stewards

On the racetrack, it takes more than just a great horse to win. It takes effective teamwork from the owner, trainer, jockey, veterinarian, grooms, stable staff, and more. So it is with organizations. Triple crown leadership is a group performance. People are empowered by the organization's colors, not the authorities. Triple crown leaders foster stewardship. In horseracing, stewards are the external officials who regulate the race. Inside triple crown organizations, stewards develop and protect the organization's colors and culture of character. They work on the enterprise, not just in it. Here we define new responsibilities for the board, CEO, officers, and people without formal authority.

Chapter 6. Alignment

Triple crown leadership aligns organizations to achieve extraordinary results, sometimes achieving peak performance. They execute remarkably, yet retain the flexibility to make midcourse corrections. These organizations can achieve a state of "flow," like Secretariat and jockey Turcotte in the Belmont Stakes. Here we provide a step-by-step system for aligning organizations for their triple crown quest.

Part Two. Leadership in Action

Chapter 7. Breakdowns

Why do some organizations fail to achieve their desired results, cross ethical boundaries, or fail to endure? Why do some high-performing organizations fall from grace, sometimes into disgrace? We examine three instructive examples: Toyota's unintended vehicle-acceleration crisis, the raft of problems recently at Johnson & Johnson, and the rise and dramatic fall of a storied horseracing dynasty at Calumet Farm. We address where they broke down and highlight leadership practices that could have kept them in contention for the crown.

Chapter 8. Turnarounds

How do triple crown leadership practices apply in turnarounds? What must leaders do differently to tailor their efforts to the unique challenges of crisis or transformation? We examine several cases— Rocky Flats, Sensormatic, and Cisco Systems—to draw out the keys to leading turnarounds aiming for the three Es.

Chapter 9. Startups

Startups face three unique challenges: extreme uncertainty, time pressure, and resource constraints. Here we examine the leadership adjustments needed to address those challenges and explore what entrepreneurs can do to position their ventures for high performance, integrity, and impact.

Chapter 10. Social Impact

Leaders today must address social impact as well as performance: What impacts are they having on employees, customers, shareholders, suppliers, communities, the environment, and the world? These questions apply to companies, nonprofits, and new hybrid ventures. What leadership practices can help organizations fuse financial performance with social impact so that they are mutually reinforcing? Here we look at several examples across sectors.

Chapter 11. Snapshots

How can we assess progress in building excellent, ethical, and enduring organizations? In this chapter, we take snapshot looks at Infosys, KIPP, and Google to determine how they are faring in their triple crown quest and what kinds of challenges they have encountered along the way.

Conclusion: At the Post

For too long, we have settled for mediocre results and watched leaders pursue short-term financial results at the expense of ethics and sustainability. We have settled for naïve prescriptions about sustainability without figuring out how to reconcile it with the results imperative. For too long, we have given up on the triple crown quest. Here we call aspiring leaders to the starting gate with a new race plan for building excellent, ethical, and enduring organizations.

Appendix: About the Research

Here we provide an overview of our background research and interview process, including a list of the sixty-one organizations we interviewed from eleven countries.

Postscript: Sport of Kings or Business of Knaves?

Like all industries, horseracing has its ethical challenges. In this Postscript, we note the issues—from performance-enhancing drugs and gambling to responsibilities to jockeys and horses—and the efforts to address them.

Note to the Reader: Throughout the book, we quote extensively from the leaders we interviewed. All quotes from those leaders are from our interviews with them, unless otherwise indicated. We use "Triple Crown" when referring to the horseracing championship and "triple crown" when referring to organizational leadership.

CHAPTER ONE

THE TRIPLE CROWN QUEST— EXCELLENT, ETHICAL, AND ENDURING

*What is the use of living, if it be not to strive for noble causes
and to make this muddled world a better place . . . ?*
—Winston Churchill

I t was a quest that crossed generations: *finding a better way.*

It started with a father, William Worrall Mayo, and his small medical practice in Minnesota in the 1860s. Twenty years later, his two sons joined him. They were obsessed with finding better ways to help patients. Humble and curious, they invited outside physicians into their practice, creating what was arguably the first integrated group medical practice in the world.

Practicing medicine with this kind of team-based approach was revolutionary at the time. Individual physicians were supposed to have all the answers. Rejecting that thinking, the Mayos believed that pooling the knowledge and skills of doctors would lead to better results.

"No one is big enough to be independent of others," said the Mayo father, to which his son William J. Mayo added: "The best interest of the patient is the only interest to be considered." Those were the founding precepts that made what was then called "the Mayos' clinic" distinctive.

According to Drs. Kent Seltman and Leonard Berry in *Management Lessons from Mayo Clinic,* "Mayo Clinic is the first integrated, not-for-profit medical group practice in the world and one of the largest."[1] It is a global leader in healthcare delivery, research, and education, with a sterling brand in the healthcare industry. With its four main hospitals and additional affiliated hospitals and clinics in the Mayo Clinic Health System network, it serves more than a million patients annually—a spectrum of patients from the international elite to Medicare recipients. With its reputation for excellence, patients from all corners of the globe come for diagnosis and treatment, and doctors come to learn new techniques. Since many people go there only after exhausting all other options, Mayo physicians face some of the toughest medical cases. In today's age of spiraling healthcare costs, Mayo Clinic has been able to maintain high quality while keeping costs comparatively low, according to independent studies. For over twenty straight years, Mayo hospitals have earned top rankings from *U.S. News & World Report.*

The Mayos' quest for a better way has yielded a stunning record of impacts and innovations, including:

- Influencing the way medicine is practiced throughout the world

- Helping to establish the medical residency education system so prevalent today

- Developing one of the world's first centralized systems of individual medical records for patients (versus previous systems organized by physician)

- Creating a system for numerically grading cancer (still used today), dramatically effective methods to treat rheumatoid arthritis, and innovative tuberculosis cures

- Performing the first federally approved total hip replacement in the United States in 1969, heralding a new era of joint replacement

- Training and employing Nobel Prize–winning physicians and researchers

Mayo's innovations are no accident. Clinic leaders proactively monitor the practices of other medical organizations and study companies like 3M and Xerox that are famous for innovation.

Equally important is Mayo's record of ethical leadership. Its "Spirit of the Clinic" lays out Mayo's ethical commitments: service, not profit; patient first; interest by staff in every other member; willingness to change; excellence; and integrity. According to Dr. Seltman (Mayo's former director of marketing), "Mayo Clinic has built one of the strongest brands in the world . . . by preserving the essential elements of what the organization is."[2] Mayo does not take these values for granted. All new hires (from nurses and janitors to accountants) receive extensive orientation in the "Mayo Way," specifically designed to help them understand and appreciate how their jobs affect patients. Mayo employees go the extra mile because they know that together they are helping people and saving lives.

Mayo's values drive day-to-day decisions. For instance, when a Mayo cardiologist faced a choice between two pacemakers for his patient, he consulted with Dr. Robert Waller (then Mayo's CEO), who agreed that he should use the new and less invasive pacemaker even though it was not yet approved for reimbursement from Medicare. Even though it was a bad deal financially, Waller said it was a "no-brainer" because it was the one that was best for the patient.

Through such collaboration and consultation, physicians and leaders make better decisions. According to Paul Roberts in *Fast Company,* "For all of its prowess in science and technology, the Mayo Clinic owes much of its success to its culture."[3] The clinic has placed on *Fortune*'s prestigious "100 Best Companies to Work For" list for the past nine years in a row.

Perhaps most impressive is how Mayo's record of excellence and ethics has stood the test of time. Mayo Clinic works hard to maintain its reputation as an innovator. In 2010, the clinic invested $790 million in research and education. Its approach is both high tech and high touch—combining the smart use of technology with old-fashioned customer service and attentive care. On the technology side, for example, Mayo makes innovative use of social media, blogs, and Intranet videos; created one of the largest electronic medical record systems in the world; and developed a "Virtual Mayo Clinic" presence on Second Life, an online virtual community. On the touch side, you don't just get a doctor at Mayo Clinic: you get a swarm of physicians consulting with each other about your case (they even call themselves "consultants"), as well as a team of support professionals working to provide you with the highest-quality care and even hospitality and comfort. Meanwhile, Mayo invests generously in more than a hundred community programs, plus energy conservation efforts and sustainability practices.

Of course, Mayo has had problems and made mistakes. Over the years, critics have faulted it for moving too slowly and for being attached to old ways. Experts recently complained that Mayo is spending too much money on costly proton beam treatment facilities due to perverse Medicare funding incentives and competition from other hospitals.[4] Of course, one can also find critiques of doctors, diagnoses, and patient treatment, but Mayo's long-term results, impacts, innovations, and commitment to ethical practices are exceptional.

Mayo Clinic exemplifies the ultimate aim of triple crown leadership: building an excellent, ethical, and enduring organization. See Figure 1.1. We discuss each of these elements in turn below.

Figure 1.1   **Triple Crown Leadership**

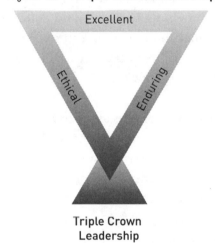

EXCELLENT: THE FIRST LEG OF THE TRIPLE CROWN

Leadership is defined by results not attributes.

—**Peter Drucker,** author and
management consultant

Getting results is one of the preeminent tasks of leadership. Triple crown leadership seeks not just any results, but excellent results—compelling and exceptional outcomes.[5] As at Mayo Clinic, it strives for the pinnacle of performance.

In different fields, there are beacons of excellence: for inspired product design, we look to Apple; for brand management, we look to Procter & Gamble; for financial reporting, the *Wall Street Journal*; for advanced military missions, the Special Forces.

Ensuring clarity about ultimate aims—and measures of success—may sound obvious but is not always straightforward. *Harvard Business Review* editor Julia Kirby cataloged the many different measures used in various business "success studies" over the years.[6] For *Good to Great* and *Great by Choice,* Jim Collins and his colleagues used cumulative stock returns relative to the general stock market and matched pairs. For *In Search of Excellence,* Tom Peters and Robert Waterman looked at compound asset and equity growth; ratio of market to book value; and return on capital, equity, and sales. Ten other success studies used ten other sets of measures, each over different periods. Each organization must set its own standards for excellent results.

One of the problems today is an overly narrow focus on results for shareholders (and with a very short time horizon). When assessing results, it is essential to consider multiple stakeholders, including employees, customers, suppliers, communities, and society, looking at both positive and negative impacts on people as well as natural resources. Triple crown leadership seeks outstanding financial performance and positive social impact.

As we address in chapter ten, measuring social impact can be tricky. Sometimes leaders must develop creative approaches. Shirley Tilghman, president of Princeton University, consistently one of the top-ranked U.S. universities, told us she measures success with metrics like "the distinction of the faculty, their prize-winning books, their Nobel prizes, alumni loyalty and giving," as well as what members of an alumni class have done with their lives by their twenty-fifth reunion.[7]

Aspiring to excellent results and impacts is the first leg of the triple crown quest. But the question arises: *how are they achieved?*

Transforming a University

Shortly after the University of Denver (DU) hockey team made it to the "frozen four" finals of the national championship tournament, an ethical dilemma arose. DU's then-chancellor, Dan Ritchie, told us:

> In the semifinals, our star player scored the goal that won it for us 1–0. Before the finals, however, he broke one of our athletic program rules. It didn't involve a crime, or even breaking the NCAA rules, but it broke *our* rules. The normal course of action would be to sit him out for the following game. Our coach, George Gwozdecky, asked, "What do we do?" I turned it back and said, "George, what do *you* think we should do?" He said, "We should sit him out." So we did.

The chancellor and the coach knew there would be howls of protest from some in the community. Ritchie and Gwozdecky took the heat. Ritchie explained, "It was in the national news that we had benched our star. We never told what rule he broke. He sat there in his street clothes during the game. That's the kind of thing you need to do to demonstrate you're serious about ethics."

The DU Pioneers won the championship anyway, and they won it with honor—a lifelong lesson for the players and a teachable moment for the community.

To make this brave choice under pressure, Ritchie and Gwozdecky relied on DU's values, which Ritchie and his colleagues had formulated in prior years. In the 1980s, DU was in crisis. University trustees asked Ritchie, the former chairman and CEO of Westinghouse Broadcasting, to take over as chancellor. According to fellow trustee Joy Burns, "We were borrowing money to make payroll," and there was "over $60 million in deferred maintenance" on buildings.[8] Ethical issues kept arising in the central office, boardroom, and classrooms. University leaders looked at other institutions for guidance and were disappointed with what they found: weak ethics courses that were taught rarely and not integrated throughout the curriculum. So they initiated a campuswide dialogue.

The students debated whether ethics should be a central focus at the school. They even put it to a vote, and it won handily. Then the students put that challenge to the faculty, who also embraced it. Then they took it to the board. According to Ritchie, "Ethics became the foundation in everything we teach and everything we do."

Ritchie and his team developed a new strategic plan, with ethics at the heart of the university, and circulated drafts widely among faculty, staff, students, and trustees for input. A new university vision emerged ("To be a great private university dedicated to the public good"), backed up by a new set of shared values ("Excellence, Innovation, Engagement, Integrity, and Inclusiveness").

Ritchie enlisted cable television pioneer Bill Daniels, a leading proponent of values-based leadership, for financial support. Daniels donated $11 million as a challenge grant, asking the business school to incorporate business ethics into its core curriculum.

Through these and other efforts, leaders at all levels ensured that ethics pervaded the institution, from classroom to faculty lounge to hockey rink. In 2011, *Bloomberg Businessweek* ranked DU's Daniels College of Business second in the United States in ethics.

Years before the frozen four hockey incident, a previous DU hockey coach was verbally abusing his players. Ritchie told him to stop, but he didn't. Even though the coach had an impressive record of winning, DU fired him and replaced him with George Gwozdecky, who brought a national championship, and then another, with honor. Through this systematic process, with bold leadership along the way, DU achieved excellent results ethically.

ETHICAL: THE SECOND LEG OF THE TRIPLE CROWN

It is one thing to achieve outstanding results; it is another thing to do so ethically, especially when others are cutting corners. Operating ethically is the second imperative of triple crown leadership. To us, "ethical" simply means acting in accordance with accepted principles of right and wrong—acting with integrity. It means paying attention to *how* the results are achieved. Triple crown leaders insist on doing the right thing.

All leaders confront ethical challenges and dilemmas. It is an occupational hazard, no matter the field. Does your organization downplay safety complaints to hit its financial targets? Does it acquiesce to the customs official asking for a "facilitating payment" (bribc)? What if your rival is doing it, or the entire industry? What if your boss asks you to backdate orders to shore up the previous quarter's results?

In our experience, many people take ethical leadership for granted. While they have sophisticated spreadsheets to help them navigate financial tradeoffs and multifaceted strategies to help them achieve competitive advantage, they may oversimplify ethics as merely upholding the law or avoiding lying and cheating. If only it were that simple. As we shall see, it takes proactive leadership to instill and enforce ethical behavior in an organization.

Though they overlap, there is a big and important difference between ethics and law. Some laws are unethical and warrant civil disobedience. Should the citizens of the Arab spring uprising capitulate to government crackdowns on Internet use and public meetings to abide by the laws of authoritarian regimes? Should soldiers comply with commanders' orders to attack peaceful protesters? More often, laws are fuzzy and leave room for interpretation. Sometimes the laws do not keep pace with new technology. Leaders of high-tech companies face complex intellectual property and privacy issues that have ethical as well as legal dimensions.

Most ethical letdowns occur because there is pain or discomfort involved with ethical behavior. People feel pressure or fear, and they rationalize unethical decisions to avoid pain. For example, people can rationalize lying to others to avoid hurting them (and thereby feeling guilty). They can accept, ignore, or pretend not to notice ethical violations—or make only halfhearted objections. That way, they can avoid being mocked or pegged as disloyal, which might threaten their job security.

Often, the ethical path is the harder one; yet we have brains wired to rationalize behavior that protects us from pain and conflict and from standing out from the group. Ethical fortitude relies heavily on courage to face adversity and social pressure.

However, even courage is not enough. Sometimes, ethical dilemmas arise that require not only character but judgment.[9] For example, do we bribe our way into a new market where bribery is a common business practice because we are certain our medical device can save lives there, and we cannot otherwise enter the market? Do we exaggerate our product features in order to win a government contract because we know the community will benefit from our offering, and it may not otherwise gain approval?

We are all flawed. Since we all make mistakes, we are wise to solicit help and input from others as sounding boards and accountability agents. Heated debates occur among reasonable people who can disagree on what is ethical. Such debates can be healthy and help maintain the ethical imperative.

Triple crown leaders make ethical decisions after analysis, reflection, and consultation with colleagues and confidants. It helps to apply simple standards such as "Would this violate any of my core beliefs?," "Can I live with this on my conscience?," "How would I feel if this were on the front page of the newspaper?," and "What would my family say about this decision?" It also helps to analyze the situation from the perspective of all the relevant stakeholders and brainstorm alternative responses—holding out for a good solution and refusing to "satisfice," to quote Nobel laureate Herbert Simon.

People generally consider themselves ethical, but researchers have shown that people overrate their own ethical fortitude and are surprisingly good at rationalizing unethical behavior.[10] The statistics below reflect the grim evidence on ethics:[11]

- The 2010 Global Fraud Study, based on multiyear data from 106 countries, estimates that organizations worldwide lose more than $2.9 trillion to fraud.

- According to a 2011 survey of a thousand Americans, 34 percent of respondents have witnessed or had firsthand knowledge of workplace wrongdoing.

- According to LRN surveys, only 56 percent of U.S. workers define their current company as having an ethical culture, and 36 percent report having left a job because they disagreed with a company's ethical standards.

- According to a Rutgers survey of 24,000 students at seventy U.S. high schools, 95 percent of students said they participated in some form of cheating, whether it was cheating on a test, plagiarizing, or copying homework.

- According to a 2008 survey of nearly 30,000 U.S. teens, 64 percent admitted to cheating on an exam in the past year, and 30 percent said they had stolen items from a store.

- Research shows that 45 percent of Americans feel the current state of morality in the United States is poor (versus 15 percent saying good or excellent), and 76 percent feel that morals are getting worse.

What are leaders to do about such grim statistics? For starters, progress is impossible without an explicit and firm commitment to ethical practices. Thomas McCoy, former executive vice president at Advanced Micro Devices (AMD, the chip manufacturer), told us, "Rule number one is: Do everything with integrity. We cannot compromise integrity."[12] Yancey Hai, vice chairman and CEO of Delta Electronics (an award-winning global leader in clean energy solutions based in Taiwan), told us, "You must have a high degree of integrity; otherwise, you don't belong here."

Commitment is essential, but it is only the first step. Organizations must also create systems and processes for instilling ethics into the enterprise, covering all aspects of the operation, from recruiting and rewarding people to reporting abuses and maintaining transparency. We address these practices in later chapters.

There is also a big difference between ethics on paper and ethical leadership in practice. Enron had a distinguished board, a first-rate code of conduct, extensive employee training on responsible business practices, and even ethics officers. Yet the reality on the trading floor and in the executive office suites made a mockery of the pronouncements, mostly due to a corrupt culture at the top.

Fortunately, there are many positive examples of ethical leadership and practices. Each year the Ethisphere Institute publishes a list of the World's Most Ethical Companies. On the list in 2012 we find Patagonia, Timberland, eBay, Electrolux, Xerox, UPS, Swiss Re, GE, PepsiCo, Singapore Telecom, Starbucks, CH2M Hill, Natura Cosmeticos, Stora Enso, Vestas, Wipro, and many more. In the pages ahead, we dig into many of their stories.

Linking Ethical and Excellent?

A growing body of evidence suggests a possible link between ethics and excellent results. We believe that makes sense, as many stakeholders will reward organizations for ethical behavior, fair treatment, and responsible practices. According to the Ethisphere Institute, firms on its World's Most Ethical Companies list have outperformed the S&P 500 by an average of 7.3 percent since 2007 in terms of shareholder returns. Ethisphere executive director Alex Brigham adds, "In addition to increased financial performance, ethical companies benefit from better brand reputation, consumer loyalty, and higher employee retention rates."[13] See Figure 1.2.

Corpedia, a compliance and ethics consultancy, found that the average five-year return of companies on its Ethics Index was 102 percent, compared with 26 percent for the S&P 500.[14] According to

Figure 1.2   **"Return on Ethics"**

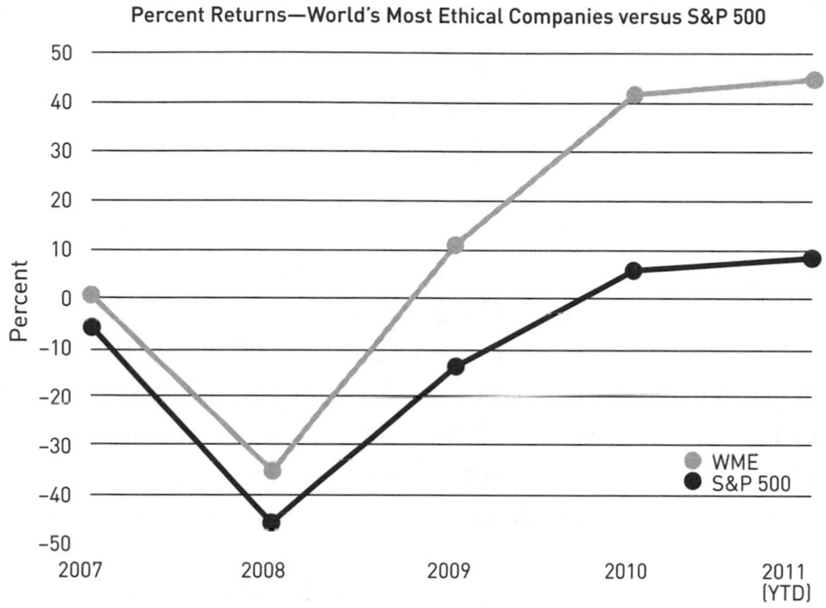

Percent Returns—World's Most Ethical Companies versus S&P 500

Note: This compares shareholder returns from the World's Most Ethical (WME) Companies Index from the Ethisphere Institute to the S&P 500. *Source:* "2011 World's Most Ethical Companies," Ethisphere Institute, 2011. See also Andrew Tonner, "10 Stocks with a Conscience to Crush the Market," *Motley Fool*, July 19, 2011.

a 2011 Corporate Executive Board survey, organizations scoring the highest marks for their level of integrity outperformed those with the lowest by more than 16 percentage points in shareholder returns.[15] Of course, such statistics address correlations, not causation (that ethical behavior directly increases shareholder returns).

When organizations are succeeding, they can enjoy the ride with the wind at their backs, relying in part on momentum for forward progress. When organizations are struggling or in crisis, by contrast, the temptation to cut corners can be immense. Desperate people do desperate things. Organizations need values-based leadership practices and powerful cultural norms to avoid these traps, as we shall see. Ethical behavior is tested most under duress.

ENDURING: THE THIRD LEG
OF THE TRIPLE CROWN

The wagon rests in winter, the sleigh in summer, the horse never.
—**Yiddish proverb**

Some organizations accomplish impressive feats by pulling out all the stops, sacrificing the long term for the short term. They cut corners or abuse some stakeholder group (such as employees or vendors) in order to gain temporary advantage. Eventually, they face a rude awakening and realize that they cannot sustain such manufactured gains because they borrowed from a future quarter or from resources needed elsewhere, or they depleted irreplaceable assets.

One of the great scourges of our age is "short-termism." Former U.S. vice president Al Gore said, "The future whispers while the present shouts." A staggering *78 percent* of the managers surveyed in a large-scale study of CFOs and CEOs admit to sacrificing long-term value to achieve smoother earnings.[16] Before HealthSouth's indictments and multibillion-dollar restatement of financial performance, the firm had met earnings predictions to the penny for forty-seven straight quarters.[17] A coincidence? Unlikely.

In July 2011, former Federal Deposit Insurance Corporation chair Sheila Bair wrote, "The common thread running through all the causes of our economic tumult is a pervasive and persistent insistence on favoring the short term over the long term, impulse over patience."[18] In the wake of the recent global financial crisis, a group of VIPs from different sectors published a manifesto, saying we "have allowed short-term considerations to overwhelm the desirable long-term growth and sustainable profit objectives of the corporation."[19]

It is one thing to achieve excellent results ethically for a while; it is another to sustain them over time. Triple crown leadership focuses not just on achieving excellent results and establishing ethical practices but on making them endure. The endurance imperative has two dimensions:

- *Internal.* Sustaining people (not burning them out or otherwise abusing them) and maintaining the financial health of the organization

- *External.* Ensuring appropriate and sustainable levels of resource consumption, while minimizing harm to others

The Long Game

The race is not always to the swift, but to those who keep on running.
—Unknown

Thankfully, we also have examples of organizations that reject the siren call of short-termism and instead play the "long game." Many of the organizations we interviewed have impressive track records dating back centuries: Princeton (1746), DuPont (1802), Perkins School for the Blind (1829), Mayo Clinic (1864), GE (1878), and Coleman Corporation (1899). The Great Law of the Iroquois Confederacy held that "In our every deliberation, we must consider the impact of our decisions on the next seven generations." Panasonic founder Konosuke Matsushita had a five hundred–year plan for his company. Paul Polman, CEO of British-Dutch consumer goods giant Unilever, said, "If you buy into [Unilever's] long-term value-creation model, which is equitable, which is shared, which is sustainable, then come and invest with us. If you don't buy into this, I respect you as a human being, but don't put your money in our company."[20]

When Amazon.com went public in 1997, its founder and CEO Jeff Bezos issued a manifesto in which he wrote that "It's all about the long term" and that the company is focused on building "something that we can tell our grandchildren about." In interviews, he has argued that by lengthening its time horizon, the company can engage in endeavors that it could never otherwise pursue. In 2011, the *New York Times* reported that Amazon "remains one of the world's leading growth companies and its stock has soared 12,200 percent since its public offering."[21]

We reviewed *Fortune*'s rankings of the World's Most Admired Companies and found that twenty-seven companies made the list six years in a row from 2006 to 2011. Thirteen companies made Ethisphere's list of the World's Most Ethical Companies every single year since the rankings were started in 2007. Sixteen companies made Corporate Knights' list of the World's Most Sustainable Companies every year from 2006 to 2011. In the nonprofit sector, we can look to Charity Navigator's list of Ten Consistently Excellent Charities and rankings of the best colleges, hospitals, and more for examples of enduring excellence.[22]

CONNECTING THE THREE Es

How are the three Es (excellent, ethical, and enduring) related? There are both tensions and synergies among the three. There are tradeoffs in some cases, and how they relate depends on the nature of the leadership and quality of decisions. There is no magic win. Triple crown leadership requires building an organization that makes them work in concert.

Ultimately, an organization cannot be excellent without being ethical. Unethical practices can boost performance temporarily, but over time they carry multiple costs that overwhelm perceived short-term benefits: litigation and other legal expenses, fines, heavier compliance costs, reporting hassles, delays, employee dissatisfaction, and damage to the organization's reputation.

Similarly, unsustainable practices have costs (direct and indirect, short and long term), including loss of customers, supply chain disruption, employee turnover, hiring barriers, resource depletion, reputational damage, increased regulations, and more.

Ethical and enduring practices do not lead to excellent results in and of themselves. They are necessary but not sufficient. Leaders must devise a strategy and plan for all three, taking none for granted.

Finally, leaders should recall the inherent value of ethical and enduring practices. They should not need return-on-investment calculations to insist upon ethical and enduring practices.

TILTS

Some people wonder whether triple crown leadership requires giving equal priority to "excellent," "ethical," and "enduring" considerations.

Our answer is no. There is no such magic formula. Sometimes "tilts" are required.

Sometimes short-term considerations must take precedence in order to save the organization. Heavy criticism may follow, but it will be moot if the organization goes out of business. Other times the reverse is needed: leaders must be willing to dampen short-term results in order to make long-term investments to set the enterprise up for future success given where the market is headed.

There is, however, one hard and fast rule: triple crown leaders do not compromise on the ethical imperative. Once they do so, they have stepped onto a slippery slope. Ethical compromises set a bad precedent, communicate a reverberating message, undermine credibility, and will likely come back to haunt them many times over. Leaders have to draw the line. Better to fail with honor than succeed with disgrace.

Aside from the unwavering ethical imperative, leaders must decide which tilts are necessary and when.

SUSTAINABILITY AND THE TRIPLE CROWN

How do sustainability and corporate social responsibility (CSR) fit with triple crown leadership? Sustainability and CSR are broad terms that mean different things to different people.[23] The sustainability and CSR movements have a big tent under which many approaches can find cover, from the "triple bottom line" of people, profit, and planet to fair trade, human rights, shareholder democracy, transparency, good governance, and more.

When done well, and not used cynically for public relations points, sustainability and CSR support all three legs of the triple crown quest: they can be drivers of excellent results, a grounding force in ethics, and a stabilizing force that helps organizations endure. Sustainability has an ethical foundation: irresponsible use of resources and societal and environmental harm are unethical, as is exploiting people in organizations or their supply chains.

Leaders navigating these waters must make judgment calls. As they assess harm caused by their organization (for example, via pollution from manufacturing), the question arises about how much harm is reasonable versus the product's benefits, and whether they are taking adequate steps to mitigate negative impacts.[24]

As leaders navigate these decisions, researchers are investigating whether there is a positive relationship between corporate social performance and corporate financial performance, and if so, in which direction does it work: does good social performance drive good corporate financial performance or vice versa? Unfortunately, no definitive answers have yet emerged, in part due to data-collection and measurement challenges (measuring financial performance is much more straightforward than measuring social performance) and mediating variables.[25]

Meanwhile, business leaders are marching forward, and their views are changing rapidly. According to a 2011 survey of 2,874 executives and managers from 113 countries, two-thirds indicated that sustainability is critically important to being competitive in today's marketplace, up from 55 percent the year before; and about 31 percent said their companies are currently profiting from sustainable business practices.[26] For others, it takes time to develop and fine-tune. According to a 2008 survey of more than five hundred senior U.S. executives, 74 percent accepted that responsible corporate citizenship can help increase profits.[27] An overwhelming majority of hundreds of finance executives and investment professionals surveyed by McKinsey believe CSR creates shareholder value. According to Matt Kistler, senior vice president of sustainability at Walmart, "If this [their sustainability initiative] was not financially viable, a company such as ours would not be doing it."

The business case for sustainable practices includes the potential for increased sales, cost reduction, risk mitigation, reputation enhancement, operational efficiency, customer loyalty, revenue diversification, pricing premiums, innovation benefits, competitive advantage, and talent attraction, motivation, and retention.

Nowadays, it is common to hear that organizations can "do well by doing good." If only it were that simple. It depends greatly on how they go about it. Many companies shine on CSR metrics but achieve mediocre or poor financial performance. Look at the recent performance of Nokia, Siemens, and Vodafone, to name a few. The job of triple crown leaders is to figure out *how* to do well by doing good. (See chapter ten for more.)

A CULTURE OF CHARACTER

The triple crown quest helps to create a unique culture in an organization: what we call a "culture of character." We think of organizational culture simply as "how we do things here"—how people behave.[28] Culture forms over time and drives what happens when the authorities are not present. It sets the tone for the organization and the norms for what is acceptable to the group. Culture is a powerful force in determining how an organization operates. Lou Gerstner, after his spectacular turnaround of IBM, wrote that "culture isn't just one aspect of the game—it is the game."[29]

Organizations with a deficient culture pay a big price in lost revenue, reputation, lawsuits, and more. Think of all the corporate scandals in recent years and how many of those firms were rife with toxic cultures driven by greed, conflict, gamesmanship, mistrust, backstabbing, and exploitation.

By contrast, organizations with a healthy culture—think of Southwest Airlines, Zappos.com, Patagonia, and DreamWorks—set in motion a self-reinforcing, positive cycle with their stakeholders. Employees identify more with the enterprise and bring more of their talents and efforts to the table. This can positively affect productivity, staff retention, profitability, and relationships with customers and suppliers.

Researchers have found a "strong relationship between constructive organizational cultures and financial performance."[30] According to a 2011 McKinsey report, "Culture matters, enormously. Studies have shown again and again that there may be no more critical source of business success or failure than a company's culture."[31] Author James Heskett estimates that an effective culture can account for 20 to 30 percent of the difference in performance versus "culturally unremarkable" competitors.[32]

A healthy, constructive culture by no means guarantees success, but it provides the foundation for building an excellent, ethical, and enduring organization. In a culture of character, everybody expects excellent, ethical, and enduring performance and impact. Organizations seeking the triple crown build a culture of character through their leadership practices. Culture is the legacy of leadership. A culture of character is the legacy of triple crown leadership.

BENEFITS OF TRIPLE CROWN LEADERSHIP

Excellent, ethical, and enduring practices are worthy in and of themselves but also carry notable benefits:

- Insiders commit to the organization in ways they seldom otherwise would, challenging each other to find solutions, fueling innovation, refusing to roll over, and unleashing breakthrough ideas.

- The organization can avoid the devastating costs of ethical implosions.

- Employees experience more joy at work, with greater satisfaction and fulfillment.

- Stakeholders reward the enterprise with increased business and support.

- Infighting due to lack of trust, disrespectful behavior, and cutthroat competition decreases or disappears.

The case is building for a new brand of leadership. There is a growing cadre of thought leaders pointing the way forward. In *Higher Ambition*, Michael Beer and his colleagues write about a new breed of leaders who "deliver extraordinary economic and social value." Jim Collins based his seminal works on "building enduring companies from the ground up." In *Sustainable Excellence*, Aron Kramer and Zachary Karabell link sustainability with corporate excellence, arguing for lasting solutions to social and environmental challenges with lasting value for investors. In *SuperCorp*, Rosabeth Moss Kanter depicts "how vanguard companies create innovation, profits, growth, and social good."

Still, the triple crown quest is demanding and not for the faint of heart. Ron Turcotte, Secretariat's jockey, told us, "The Triple Crown was not meant to be easy." People make mistakes. Values collide. Markets shift. Technologies advance. Ventures drift. The key to building a triple crown organization is not in the hands of a single "superleader" but rather in the hands, minds, and hearts of ordinary people who become extraordinary leaders and stewards of the culture of character.

It is time to put building an excellent, ethical, and enduring organization at the top of our priority list. The challenges we face demand nothing less.

CHAPTER SUMMARY

One of the primary tasks of leadership is to get results—ideally, exceptional results. However, in the pursuit of results, too many leaders cut ethical corners, focus too much on the short term, or engage in unsustainable behavior. Leaders seeking to build excellent, ethical, and enduring organizations engage people more, gain their loyalty and creativity, and build mutually beneficial relationships with other stakeholders. Organizations should put the triple crown quest at the top of their priority list.

Practical Applications

1. What results does your organization seek?
   a. Does it define them by stakeholder group?
   b. Is it achieving exceptional results?
   c. What more must it do to improve its results?
2. Is your organization ethical?
   a. To what extent is ethics considered a priority, with clear values, training programs, confidential complaint channels, and more?
   b. What more needs to be done?
3. Does your organization do only the bare minimum of legal compliance?
4. How do you resolve ethical issues and dilemmas?
   a. What else could you do to make more ethical decisions?
5. Has your organization had ethical breakdowns?
   a. What should have been done differently?
   b. Is it so bad and beyond fixing that you should find work elsewhere?
6. Does your organization suffer from "short-termism"?
   a. How does it approach tensions between the short and long term?
   b. What can it do differently to strike a better balance between them?
7. To what extent is your organization operating sustainably?
   a. What are the most important ways it can improve in this area?
   b. What more can be done to make sure there is synergy between sustainability and profitability?
8. Is your organization having a positive social impact?
   a. How might you influence it to improve in this area?
9. Does your organization have a culture of character?
   a. To what extent are workers engaged and committed?
   b. What are the three most important ways you can contribute to improving the culture?

PART ONE

TRIPLE CROWN LEADERSHIP PRACTICES

CHAPTER TWO

HEAD AND HEART

A horse gallops with his lungs,
Perseveres with his heart,
And wins with his character.

—Federico Tesio, Italian statesman
and thoroughbred breeder

November 1, 1938, 4:00 p.m. Fans packed the racetrack at Pimlico in Baltimore, Maryland, for the much anticipated match race between the two most exciting horses in the country, War Admiral and Seabiscuit.[1]

With forty thousand people present, the largest in track history, track officials opened the infield to alleviate the crush. Throngs of people blocked the announcer from reaching his clubhouse post, forcing him to call the race from the finish line. Forty million people worldwide tuned in via radio, including President Roosevelt, who kept a roomful of advisors waiting.

The race had captured the world's attention in part because it involved diametrically different horses from dramatically different stables. War Admiral was fiery, fierce, and ferociously fast out of the gate. He beat nineteen other top thoroughbreds in the Kentucky Derby, won the Preakness, and broke the Belmont Stakes record while matching the world-record time, thereby winning the Triple Crown and becoming "Horse of the Year."

His owner was Samuel Riddle, a conservative Eastern sportsman and racing legend, who had also owned the incomparable Man o' War. Riddle looked down on Western racing. With esteemed trainer George Conway and talented jockey Charlie Kurtsinger, they formed a daunting team of racing elites with white-collar respectability.

Seabiscuit, on the other hand, was short and fat, with knobby knees and a crooked leg. He was only famous for how much he could eat and sleep. He was named after a cracker favored by sailors. Early on, he showed little promise, finishing fourth in his first race and often finishing last. Considered lazy, he did not win until seventeen races later.

Eventually, the Biscuit found a new owner in Californian Charles Howard, a self-made business mogul who hung out with celebrities such as Bing Crosby and Fred Astaire.

Howard hired "Silent Tom" Smith, an unconventional loner and reputed horse whisperer, as his trainer. He was a frontiersman who sometimes slept in the stalls, and he had an uncanny knack for restoring broken mustangs and washed-up thoroughbreds.

After studying the Biscuit, Smith saw something others missed and told Howard, "Get me that horse. He has real stuff in him. I can improve him. I'm positive."[2] Howard recalled later that "somehow I knew he had what it takes . . . We had to rebuild him, both mentally and physically, but you don't have to rebuild the heart when it's already there, big as all outdoors."[3]

Howard and Smith teamed the Biscuit with Red Pollard, a pugnacious Canadian jockey who was broke and virtually homeless. They saw raw talent in him, too, and fire in his belly.

Seabiscuit responded to Smith's unconventional training and Pollard's steady hands. In his second year, he won eleven of his fifteen starts. He banked turns at full speed as few horses could. The crowds loved him. It was the Great Depression, and people admired how such an ordinary horse could become so extraordinary. He gave them hope.

After several postponements due to muddy tracks, the match race was finally on, white collar versus blue collar, East against West. After two false starts, the rivals bolted off. Everyone expected War Admiral, the overwhelming favorite, to take the lead, given his explosive starts and Seabiscuit's tendency to hang back. But Smith had secretly been training Seabiscuit at night on lightning-fast starts. Seabiscuit sprinted to the lead. Then War Admiral surged forward, taking the lead, and Seabiscuit responded to even it up. The horses flew around the turns as a mob of people in the infield ran along the rail to get a closer look.

In the home stretch, Seabiscuit found another gear. Announcer Clem McCarthy called it live: "They're head and head, and both jockeys driving . . . Seabiscuit leads by a length. Now Seabiscuit by a length and a half . . . Seabiscuit by three. Seabiscuit is the winner by four lengths! And you never saw such a wild crowd . . . they're roaring around me!"

Though War Admiral ran his best time, Seabiscuit beat him, with a time that was the fastest ever for that distance. Even today, many call it the greatest horse race of all time.

How was it that Howard and Smith came to place their bet on such an unlikely horse? They saw something in the Biscuit's eyes when challenged by rivals. When engaged in a real contest, he poured out his heart.

HEAD AND HEART

A good head and a good heart are always a formidable combination.
—Nelson Mandela

Seabiscuit illustrates a central point about the quest for the triple crown: both head and heart are required.

The way most leaders go about identifying and developing talent is utterly insufficient for what is needed to create a triple crown organization. They focus mostly on the head and neglect the heart. They emphasize hard skills and capabilities like knowledge, skills, and expertise. They assess intelligence, education, pedigree, experience, technical competence, skills, and other conventional indicators.

Of course, those factors are critical, and sometimes raw brainpower is especially important. Princeton's president, Shirley Tilghman, told us, "Brains really matter. You can't be a leader here if you're not smart." Ron Sugar, former CEO and chairman of Northrop-Grumman (a global provider of military and commercial security systems), told us, "A lot of our work is literally rocket science, so we have 45,000 outstanding scientists and engineers."

Even in intellectual and technical environments, the head is only part of the equation. Lynn Easterling, vice president and deputy general counsel at Cisco (the global networking solutions company), told us, "I can teach the hard skills, but I can't teach good character or good relational skills. It's much easier to find people with the hard skills than it is to find the people with both the hard and soft skills."

The term "heart" is rich with meaning. Parker Palmer, a distinguished author and teacher, captured it well: "I'm using the word 'heart' as they did in ancient times . . . It meant that center in the human self where everything comes together—where will and intellect and values and feeling and intuition and vision all converge. It meant the source of one's integrity. It takes courage to lead from the heart."[4]

Heart includes intangibles such as character, will, passion, compassion, courage, and persistence. Heart encompasses what energizes people, what carries them through adversity, what drives them to win.

Palmer observed that people are healthy and whole only when they involve both their head and heart. The Vail Leadership Institute espouses what it calls an "inside-first" leadership philosophy. According to its founder and president, John Horan-Kates, "This whole concept is built around the notion that leadership starts with one's character, which largely resides in the heart, and emanates out from there."[5] Triple crown leadership integrates head and heart.

In his bestselling book, *Authentic Leadership,* Bill George wrote that great companies must "figure out how to tap into people's hearts—their passions and their desires to make a difference through their work."[6] Lorrie Norrington, former president of eBay Marketplaces (the global division of eBay that manages its e-commerce sites), told us, "The heart really matters in leadership. Without heart, it isn't possible to create passion, dedication, and lasting change in your business."

As we saw with Seabiscuit, heart reveals the character within. People with heart show a fierce commitment to their enterprise, demonstrating loyalty to their colleagues and passion for the group's aims. They show a healthy ambition to win and build something enduring and impactful. This fuels their performance and sustains them amid adversity. Football coach Vince Lombardi once said, "Heart power is the strength of your company."

Heart Impact

Those who have impacted Gregg most over the years have been those who led with their hearts. In college, it was a philosophy professor who trembled with intensity sometimes as he spoke about the great questions of life and how we should live it. Years later, in a startup company, it was a committed colleague who, though generally friendly and thoughtful, would get right up in your face if you did anything that would get in the way of building a great company. Gregg saw that when you put your heart into it, you invite others to do so as well, transforming their relationship with the work.

Some leaders say this heart stuff is too soft and fluffy and not sufficiently actionable. We disagree. Triple crown leadership proactively seeks, develops, and rewards people with both head and heart. It fills the enterprise with them, transforming both the people and the place in the process.

We focus below on two key heart components: integrity and cultural fit.

Integrity

I look for three things in hiring people. The first is personal integrity, the second is intelligence, and the third is high energy level. But if you don't have the first, the other two will kill you.

—**Warren Buffett,** CEO of Berkshire Hathaway

Heart begins with one's personal integrity. As covered in chapter one, people with integrity do the right thing even when it is personally painful. The origin of the word "integrity" comes from "integer," which means "one," or "the state of being whole and undivided." People with integrity are authentic and comfortable in their own skin, flaws included.

Triple crown leaders are adamant about hiring people with character. They look for trustworthiness, humility, courage, eagerness to serve, realization there is something bigger than the self, and even a sense of personal purpose, often flowing from a spiritual perspective. Triple crown leaders do not expect perfection, but they do probe for what people learned when they made mistakes.

Heart traits are worthy in and of themselves but also have important benefits. Stephen M. R. Covey, author of the books *Smart Trust* and *The Speed of Trust,* writes, "Trust is a function of two things: character and competence. Character includes your integrity, your motive, your intent with people. [What we call heart.] Competence includes your capabilities, your skills, your results, your track record. [What we call head.] And both are vital."[7] Covey shows how this powerful combination dramatically speeds things up in organizations—accelerating to the "speed of trust"—leading to measurable increases in results.

After Jack Chain's career in the U.S. Air Force as a four-star general, capped as an exceptional Commander in Chief of the Strategic Air Command, he signed a contract to be executive vice president of Burlington Northern Railroad. When approached later to become CEO of a large, prestigious firm where his skill set was a great fit, he declined because he had a five-year contract with Burlington. "A contract is a contract," he explained.

President Tilghman seeks a "strong moral compass" for Princeton's faculty and staff, and the university has long been proud of its honor system, dating back to 1895. Students pledge they will neither give nor receive assistance on assignments and examinations and will report any violations they witness. The faculty takes them at their word and refrains from proctoring exams. It is, in a sense, a century-long integrity lesson that is still in session today.

Triple crown leaders watch for signs of integrity flaws in new recruits and colleagues, including excessive ambition, controlling behavior, hypercompetitiveness, bullying, narcissism, arrogance, or greed. Perhaps the biggest red flag is ego. Our friend Chuck Wachendorfer quips, "My ego is not my amigo." Bob painfully recalls ego trips he was on early in his career:

- *"I want to run something."* (Out of business school—all about Bob being in charge of something—*anything*—as long as he was boss.)

- *"I can beat him."* (Bob thinking to himself about a talented colleague during a meeting.)

- *"Honey, I'm doing it for you and the kids."* (Bob's response when asked by his wife, June, why he was working so hard and traveling so much. Her response: "You're not doing it for us. You're doing it for *you*.")

Triple crown leaders develop integrity through ethical training programs and reward it in performance evaluations. The top criteria Procter & Gamble use to determine promotions for senior executives are "character, values, and integrity."[8]

Cultural Fit

The second key component of heart is cultural fit. Triple crown leaders get to know people at a deeper level to assess whether they are a good fit with the enterprise.

Ursula Burns, CEO of Xerox (the global business process and document management company), focuses on "fit and fitness" for the company culture when interviewing executives. She is personally involved with the hiring decision of every person in the top two levels of the company: "I want to know who they are," she explained to us. "I want to make sure they fit the organization and have fitness for what we want them to do. I want them to fit with our values and culture."

Burns no longer interviews to determine task skills, relying on others to screen such head matters. Instead, she probes for character, humility, empathy, emotional intelligence, self-awareness, authenticity, and fearlessness. In other words, she looks for heart.

As Burns knows, fit with the culture requires emotional intelligence, including the ability to work well with others despite differences and challenges. According to psychologist Daniel Goleman, emotional intelligence entails "managing feelings so that they are expressed appropriately and effectively, enabling people to work together smoothly toward their common goals." Many of the leaders we interviewed placed emotional intelligence at or near the top of the list of their hiring criteria.

Phil Soucy, co-president and CEO of Modern Technology Solutions (a small, employee-owned defense systems contractor), looks for integrity and emotional intelligence: "I've seen people have troubles in those areas," he explains. "They may be very knowledgeable in their discipline, but if they lack emotional intelligence it just does not work."

Alan Lewis is owner and chairman of Grand Circle Corporation, the largest U.S. direct-market tour operator of international vacations for older Americans. He says, "Alignment with my company's culture and values counts far more than do skills or experience. In most cases, if an associate shares our values, we can teach the job skills." He says that adopting a "values-based hiring model" years ago and hiring for cultural fit "contributed to the long-term success of our associates and of our organization."[9]

TRIPLE CROWN WEIRD

- On a scale from one to ten, how weird are you?
- What is your theme song?
- When was the last time you broke the rules/policy to get the job done?
- Tell me about a time you recognized a problem/area to improve that was outside your job duties and solved it without being asked. What was it, how did you do it?

—Interview questions for new recruits
at Zappos.com[10]

At twenty-four, Tony Hsieh sold his first company to Microsoft for a cool $265 million. He dabbled in venture capital and then built up a new startup, a zany online shoe retailer called Zappos.com. A decade later, he sold it to Amazon.com in a stock transaction valued at $1.2

billion. Not a bad run. Both of Hsieh's companies were home runs financially, but in his eyes only the second was a true success.

What made the difference? Some might point to head elements like industry-leading web site loading times and fleets of robots that ship inventory in minutes. But to Hsieh (who has remained with the company as CEO), it is all about the heart—the company's people, values, and culture.

After a while in his first company, Hsieh realized it was not a fun place to work. With Zappos, he wanted to do it differently, filling the company with people he liked and trusted—people he would want to hang out with. According to Hsieh:

> We have interview questions for each of the core values, and we do two sets of interviews. Our hiring team does a standard set of interviews looking for relevant experience, technical ability, and so on. Then our Human Resources department conducts interviews specifically for culture fit, including things like humility, fun, and weirdness. Recruits have to pass both. We've passed on a lot of really talented people who could have made an immediate impact on our bottom line. If they are not a culture fit, we won't hire them.

Given the venture's breakneck growth in its early years, Hsieh was concerned about having so many new managers who were not yet steeped in the culture. He emailed the entire staff asking for input about what made Zappos unique and then distilled their responses into a list of ten core values. He also collects short essays from employees each year about the Zappos culture and publishes them annually (unedited) in a Culture Book. The company bases half of employee performance reviews on whether people are living up to the Zappos values and contributing to the culture.

At Zappos, all new employees receive four weeks of training before starting their jobs. Halfway through the training, they have a standing offer of $3,000 to leave the company—no questions asked.

That amount increases to $4,000 once the training ends. Zappos designed "The Offer," as the company calls it, to ensure that employees are fired up about working there. Only 2 to 3 percent of people take the money and run. By forgoing the money, the rest reveal their commitment. Their heart is in it.

Zappos customer service reps are famous for finding creative and surprising ways to delight customers, from sending flowers to grieving customers to helping them find local pizzerias delivering late and even referring them to competitors when items are not in stock.

With strong head and heart driving its fanatical customer service, Zappos reached $1 billion in sales in ten years and now has eight million customers. In 2009, the company was the highest-ranked newcomer on *Fortune*'s 100 Best Companies to Work For, appearing on that list again in 2010, 2011, and 2012. Zappos has also earned awards for customer service and ethics.

Triple crown leaders looking to follow the company's lead can focus on three key activities: recruiting, developing, and rewarding both head and heart.

RECRUITING HEAD AND HEART

> *Acquiring and keeping good people is*
> *a leader's most important task.*
>
> **—John Maxwell,** leadership author

Triple crown leaders systematically recruit certain kinds of people, investing time and energy to get it right. They are always on the lookout for good people, keeping notes on and staying in touch with candidates. The worst time to start the hiring process is when someone has left a position vacant. At Avery International (a division of the global company that provides adhesives for consumer and office products), Bob recalls that the group vice president (GVP) was always searching for talent, even when there was no opening.

He recruited promising talent into an assistant-to-the-GVP position with the intent that a move to a general management or special assignment would come soon. He jealously guarded that position in budget proposals to ensure a steady flow of new talent.

Some people wonder, "Can you really screen for integrity and cultural fit? Isn't that too mushy to evaluate? Doesn't it mean being judgmental about people?"

Yes, no, and yes. Triple crown leaders screen for this mushy stuff because it is essential and has hard benefits. They are very judgmental—that is, selective—about whom they hire. For them, leadership is a group performance, and so there is no higher priority than getting the right people with head and heart. We recommend panels of interviewers to get different perspectives. (See the Supplement at the end of this chapter for interview questions that address heart qualities.)

Over the years, Bob learned the value of deep reference checks. First you ask a candidate for references (all glowing, undoubtedly). Then you call those references personally, listen closely for signs of character (and other key points), and finally ask, "Who else might be able to tell me about this person?" Then you call those new sources and do it again. By the time you get to the third ring of references, patterns emerge. What was a whisper in the first round ("Bill is a great visionary") becomes a shout ("Bill is poor on details and follow-up; his head is always in the clouds"). Ben Heineman, former senior vice president for law and public affairs at GE and author of *High Performance with High Integrity,* told us, "Every major hire should be accompanied by serious due diligence including reference checks on their character."

Patience is essential when interviewing. Pressure always exists to find someone fast to fill a vacancy, but rushing to hire someone who lacks character or cultural fit becomes a painful and costly mistake. Take the time to get it right. A job offer entails an ethical commitment to a person, just as accepting an offer entails committing to the enterprise. Honor those commitments by doing your homework carefully.

DEVELOPING HEAD AND HEART

The real test of character for a leader is to nurture those people whose stars may shine as brightly as— or even brighter than—the leader's own.

—**Warren Bennis,** leadership author
and professor

The U.S. Special Operations Forces are made up of Army Special Forces (Green Berets), Navy SEALS, and Air Force Special Tactics Units. They represent the top 1 percent of the armed forces. They are trained to conduct high-risk missions and deliver effects vastly disproportionate to their size. They are famous and feared. Why?

After highly selective screening, they employ a grueling training process, including psychological exams, firearms and munitions training, surveillance and espionage skills, and more. After induction, their intense training continues. Before initiating a live raid, a unit may conduct full "dress rehearsals" more than a hundred times.

Setting the bar so high helps the Special Operations Forces achieve extraordinary performance, providing what author Andrew Sobel calls "recruiting gravity," a pulling force that draws new talent.[11]

Talent attracts talent. Once an organization earns a reputation for excellence, it becomes a talent magnet.

General Electric is famous for training and development, spending about $1 billion a year on training, much of it at its acclaimed facility in Crotonville, New York.[12] According to the company, more than nine thousand employees participate in Crotonville leadership programs annually. Its 191 most senior executives spent a minimum of twelve months in training and professional development programs during their first fifteen years with GE.[13]

In *The Talent Masters,* authors Ram Charan and Bill Conaty lament that "the great majority of companies that control their finances masterfully don't have any comparable processes for developing their leaders or even pinpointing which ones to develop." Charan and Conaty find that leaders in organizations with exceptional people practices "invest at least a quarter of their time in spotting and developing other leaders."

According to "The State of Talent Management," a 2008 study by Hewitt Associates of seven hundred senior leaders, most organizations hold their executives and managers accountable for achieving business results, but a mere 10 percent hold executives accountable for developing their direct reports, and a paltry 5 percent indicate that their managers consistently demonstrate the ability to develop employees.[14]

Developing People

In our experience, most development programs spend little time on heart elements. What are some of the ways to develop both head and heart? It starts with recognizing that development is not the job of human resources, nor is it just sending someone off for a few days of training. Development is a critical responsibility of all leaders and must be ongoing. Here are some effective development practices:

- **Leadership assignments.** The best way to develop leadership is to give people actual leadership assignments—challenging projects accompanied by coaching and direct and immediate feedback on how they are doing. Aspiring leaders should seek leadership opportunities proactively—whether at work or in the community—and volunteer for stretch assignments.

- **Personal feedback.** Supervisors should provide regular and constructive feedback, mostly in one-on-one sessions. The process should include patiently getting people to open up and talk about what they are struggling with and why, with mutual discussion of how they might overcome obstacles.

- **360s.** Often, surprising and helpful insights come from 360-degree reviews, in which employees receive feedback from all directions, including subordinates, peers, and supervisors.

- **Mentors.** Mentors can be a tremendous asset for aspiring leaders and "high potentials," providing guidance about long-term issues and career paths.

- **Peer groups.** Leaders can benefit greatly from the dialogue of small peer groups meeting regularly, building trust, sharing hardships and best practices, and delving into heart issues in a safe and confidential environment.[15]

- **Rotation.** Job rotation programs help people learn different sides of the business, develop new relationships, and stretch their skill sets with new roles.
- **Personal development.** Some organizations today go beyond professional development and assist with the personal development of their people, recognizing the importance of aligning professional work with personal values and aspirations.[16]
- **Renewal.** Good development efforts encourage renewal mechanisms such as exercise, reflection, sabbaticals, and even meditation or prayer. Finding sanctuary (perhaps through a walk, hike, or run) allows people to reconnect with their hearts.

REWARDING HEAD AND HEART

There are two things people want more than sex and money—
recognition and praise.

—Mary Kay Ash, founder, Mary Kay Inc.

It is not enough to recruit and develop exceptional people. Triple crown leaders must also recognize and reward them effectively.

GE's Heineman advocates designing compensation systems to include pay for "performance with integrity." He recalls that GE was systematic about measuring and rewarding performance with integrity, anonymously surveying 130,000 people, asking whether the company cut ethical corners to make its numbers. The company assessed leaders against their peers, using a matrix of how many audit issues were open, how many environmental issues leaders had, and more. While by no means perfect in its track record, GE puts significant resources into assessing and rewarding performance with integrity.

Despite good intentions, many compensation systems incentivize the wrong behavior. Michael Critelli, former chairman and CEO of Pitney Bowes (the global mail stream manufacturer and service provider), told us, "Occasionally integrity issues are a problem due to 'bad apples,' but often they are the result of giving people financial targets with compensation incentives that they cannot meet honestly."

At Yum! Brands (the global fast-food company that operates in more than a hundred countries with 2011 revenues of $12.6 billion), all senior leaders have their own personal recognition awards. Pete Bassi, the former chairman of Yum Restaurants International, told us, "Yum is all about a reward and recognition culture. At the meetings of the top three hundred executives, you are required to bring your recognition symbol for display. Yum takes recognition to a whole new level. I've had people break down and cry when they receive their award."

What are some of the ways you can reward people, touching their hearts? In an age of tweets and Facebook updates, personal visits and handwritten thank you notes can go a long way. Recognition can range from awards and praise in front of peers at special meetings to small gifts, such as coffee mugs, spot cash, or a "wall of fame" with pictures. Recognition—ideally coupled with creativity and fun—is an important building block of the culture of character, as long as the praise is legitimately earned and the appreciation is genuine.

HEAD AND HEART AT MAYO CLINIC

As we saw in chapter one, Mayo Clinic has endured as a high-performing organization for more than a century. Its enduring success begins with its people. Mayo has built a culture that prioritizes recruiting, developing, and retaining great people.

Dr. Leonard Berry, professor at Texas A&M University, told us, "Mayo Clinic could not have sustained itself for more than a century and thrived as it has without major mistakes along the way had it not been so conscientious in hiring well," including hiring for values, work ethic, and commitment to the clinic's culture.

In their book *Management Lessons from Mayo Clinic,* Dr. Berry and his associate Dr. Kent Seltman observe that Mayo seeks "not stars, but a constellation."[17] Those who want personal accolades will not fit in at Mayo, but those who thrive on teamwork will excel. Mayo is not looking for homogeneous candidates. Embracing diversity and innovation, Mayo values what it calls "jarring individuals," employees who question the status quo and shake things up, as long as they uphold Mayo's shared values.

Mayo's recruiting is deliberate. Drs. Berry and Seltman use the analogy of casting a Broadway show to describe the clinic's hiring process. If candidates pass the initial screenings, Mayo convenes a panel of four to eight people to interview candidates for up to ninety minutes to probe their underlying values and beliefs.

Annual turnover among Mayo's nurses is 4 percent, versus an industry average of 20 percent, and it maintains high overall staff retention rates.[18] Mayo's approach attracts people of the highest caliber who seek affiliation with a world-class enterprise. For example, it recently attracted nearly seven thousand applicants for 360 positions in its residency and fellowship programs.[19]

The recruitment process is only the beginning. Meeting the clinic's exacting standards requires continuing interest by every member of the staff in the professional development of all the others. At Mayo, professional development is woven into surgeries, consultations, staff meetings, and career paths—just about everything employees do.

Since most physicians are either not interested in leadership positions or not necessarily cut out to run a multibillion-dollar enterprise, Mayo's leaders are constantly looking for doctors with leadership potential. They put aspiring physician-leaders on a comprehensive development track with committee leadership assignments and extensive training. Those who thrive obtain greater responsibility, eventually leading significant parts of the enterprise. Mayo overwhelmingly promotes from within, in part because the values and behaviors of existing employees are known, shaped by the "Mayo Way."

Mayo also develops leaders by rotating them to different assignments, giving them valuable new experiences. Rotation makes job change common and unremarkable, making it easier for leaders to move people who are not performing adequately.

One final key is Mayo's reward system. In many hospitals, the financial incentives are perverse, with quality and cost considerations undermined by rigid rules and doctors competing against each other for referrals, bonuses, and promotions. At Mayo, physicians and staff are well paid and compensated through an all-salary system. They are not paid by the number of tests conducted, patients seen, or surgeries performed. They can focus on quality, not quantity.

According to Dr. Seltman, "Most people at Mayo Clinic feel they are a better employee there than other places they have worked. They don't want to be the one who lets Mayo Clinic down. Mayo inspires people to do their best."

CHAPTER SUMMARY

The first step in triple crown leadership is putting together a triple crown team. Triple crown leaders devote rigorous attention to recruiting for, developing, and rewarding both head and heart. Head involves the knowledge, skills, and experience necessary for the work. Heart involves integrity, emotional intelligence, and fit with the desired culture of character. People deficient in either do not make the cut.

Practical Applications
1. To what extent do people in your organization have good head and heart qualities?
2. How have leaders in your organization shown heart?
3. What do you do to assess a job candidate's heart qualities?
   a. What else could you do?
4. What does your organization do to develop both head and heart in people?
   a. What else should it do?
5. How do you develop people you work with?

   a. What else could you do?
6. Does your organization recognize and reward people appropriately, including both head and heart and both results and integrity?
   a. What more should it do?

CHAPTER SUPPLEMENT: INTERVIEWING FOR HEART

In addition to the normal questions about educational background, work experience, knowledge, and skills, here are some examples of questions that can help assess a person's character and cultural fit:[20]

1. What do you know about the culture of our organization?
2. How do you fit with our culture? *(If the interviewees are not familiar with the culture, describe it in detail. Then ask again how they think they fit.)*
3. What were two of your most important formative experiences? How did they affect you?
4. Who are the people who have influenced you the most, and how?
5. Describe two humbling experiences you have had. What did you learn from them?
6. What mistakes have you made, and what did you learn from them?
7. What personal characteristics do you struggle with? How do you address them?
8. What are your personal values (your core beliefs or guiding principles)?
9. Have you ever fought for an ethical belief or principle? Explain.

10. What leadership experience have you had? Tell us about one good example and one bad example. What did you learn from them?
11. How do you approach leadership?
12. Why do you want to lead?
13. Why do you want to work here? *(Probe for the real reasons. See if they get beyond talking points and platitudes.)*
14. What are the most important things in your life and why?
15. What is the single most important thing I should remember about you after you leave?

(Note if you are getting canned responses or seeing any red flags, especially any hints of ego—such as focusing too much on "I" in work stories, as opposed to "we.")

CHAPTER THREE

THE COLORS

*If you want to build a ship, don't drum up people together
to collect wood, and don't assign them tasks and work,
but rather teach them to long for the endless immensity of the sea.*

—**Antoine de Saint-Exupery,** French author
and pilot

At 9:25 p.m. on May 4, 2007, the tornado siren in Greensburg, Kansas, sounded.

The tornado that followed was 1.7 miles wide—wider than the entire town—with winds over two hundred miles per hour.[1] The storm leveled more than 90 percent of the town. Nine of the 1,500 townspeople died, and most survivors lost nearly all their possessions.[2] According to former mayor John Janssen, "We had fire hydrants pulled out of the ground along with their pipes. The water tower was gone. We had no power . . . We had six feet of rubble everywhere."

Before the tornado, the community had a dwindling population and depressed labor market. Now this. With so much devastation, many people wondered, "Should we even rebuild the town at all?"

Then something remarkable happened. In the days following the tornado, several community leaders gathered in a tent on the lawn of the city administrator and began exploring their options. At the first community meeting held in a large FEMA tent a week after the tornado, then-mayor Lonnie McCollum announced that Greensburg would build back in an environmentally friendly manner. Perhaps they could do something really big and make it the most energy-efficient town in the nation.

Given the complexity and cost, there was considerable skepticism among the residents. Some just wanted a return to normality as soon as possible. Others were intrigued by the bold vision.

After extensive community dialogue in the months following, the town rallied to the vision of becoming "Stronger, Better, Greener." The city council decided to power Greensburg with 100 percent renewable energy and create a model for the world. All new city buildings would meet the very highest environmental standard, Leadership in Energy and Environmental Design (LEED) platinum, which few buildings nationwide met at the time. No U.S. city had ever made such a commitment.[3]

Today, Greensburg uses solar, wind, and geothermal energy; natural light; improved insulation; and state-of-the-art windows.

Through partners, carbon-offset purchases provide funding for the town's wind farm, with ten turbines designed to produce enough electricity to power four thousand homes.

Just two years after the crisis, Michelle Moore of the U.S. Green Building Council reported that Greensburg represented "the greatest commitment to green building anywhere in the U.S . . . pound for pound, Greensburg is the greenest city in America."[4] In 2011, there was one LEED-certified building for every eighty-six people in Greensburg, more than in any other city on the planet.[5]

One of the leaders of the green-building initiative, Daniel Wallach, formed a nonprofit organization, Greensburg GreenTown, to promote the effort and share its lessons with the world. With other community leaders, including the mayor, city administrator, and city council members, Wallach helped the townsfolk develop a transformational vision. "We just kept painting pictures for people that got them in touch with their heart," he told us. "The community decided this was our common vision, and everybody was going to work together to achieve this greatest good for the community."

Of course, vision alone was not enough. The enormous undertaking required commitment and resources, as well as effective management and coordination with government agencies, community groups, and volunteers. According to Wallach:

> It's phenomenal to be part of a community where about thirty different leaders at all levels—the county, the city, the hospital, the school, on and on—came together and took their piece. That took every one of these leaders getting on board in their own way and putting aside their egos in order to do this as a team.

Naturally, no visionary undertaking like GreenTown is without critics. Some have raised concerns about the pace of the cleanup and the wisdom of rebuilding green in an area prone to tornados; some have questioned whether green buildings are affordable for the community and why the town purchased wind turbines manufactured overseas. Triple crown leaders need thick skins for their soft hearts.

Despite the concerns, most of the people in town embraced the vision. The color green symbolized that vision and even found its way into the name of the enterprise that helped the community rise again. A color signified the vision, and the vision was essential in the town's extraordinary resurrection.

THE COLORS

In horseracing, each stable registers a unique set of colors worn by its horses and jockeys, a tradition dating to 1762 in England. These colors trace their origin back even further to medieval knights jousting on horseback, whose colors represented their chivalry and honor and to which they dedicated their lives and fortunes.[6]

Today, in order to race at famed New York tracks such as Aqueduct, Belmont Park, and Saratoga, thoroughbred owners must register their distinctive colors with the Jockey Club in New York. The owners furnish distinctive colors and shapes such as rings, diamonds, crosses, and stars in unique combinations for the jockeys' silk or nylon jackets and caps. Watch any race, and you will see how important the colors are in grasping which horse is which in the fast-moving scrum.

Triple crown organizations also have their metaphorical colors: their purpose, values, and vision. These organizational colors bind the people together in common cause, as they did at Greensburg, providing meaning and serving as a rallying call. The colors provide the standards by which people behave and make decisions. They reveal the heart and soul of the organization. Triple crown leadership is about an ongoing quest to uphold the organization's colors, where:

- The purpose grounds.

- The values guide.

- The vision inspires.

Even nations have metaphorical colors—their distinctive and defining foundations and aspirations. Think of the Magna Carta, the great English charter of 1215, limiting the power of the king and establishing laws and rights. Think of the U.S. Declaration of Independence, which decreed, "All men are created equal" and endowed with unalienable rights, including "Life, Liberty, and the pursuit of Happiness." Think of the multicolored South African flag, symbolizing unity in a new nation that emerged from postapartheid, multiracial elections following Nelson Mandela's release from prison after twenty-seven years. Most great endeavors have metaphorical rallying colors, aspirations that summon people to new heights.

Many organizations adopt a mission, values, or vision statement, but too often the statements are weak, or leaders do a poor job of pursuing and upholding them. In some cases, they become a joke, fueling cynicism. Triple crown organizations take these declarations much further. They carefully formulate and doggedly abide by their colors, building their organizational character on the foundation of the colors. They ensure that the colors are a call to the quest for an excellent, ethical, and enduring organization.

Below we examine the three components of our metaphorical colors—purpose, values, and vision—including how triple crown leaders elicit and infuse them into the DNA of their organizations.

PURPOSE

Five a.m. in the Cafeteria

Bob: It was five a.m. in the company cafeteria, the third such session I had conducted since the previous day, and I was confident it would go well.

I had recently taken over as president of Monarch Marking Systems, a company of two thousand employees in Dayton, Ohio. Monarch was an autonomous subsidiary of Pitney Bowes and the industry leader in price-marking systems. We were going through challenging times. The technology had shifted in our industry with the widespread adoption of bar codes in the early 1980s, and we had to reinvent ourselves quickly or risk going out of business.

I was pumped up about the new purpose statement we had crafted. I had written the first draft, and the senior team had edited it. We were pleased.

In yesterday's town hall meetings at three p.m. and seven p.m., no one had said much. They just sat listening, arms folded. Most people were uncomfortable speaking publicly in a room with hundreds of people. The third shift was smaller and usually less reserved.

For the five a.m. crew, I reviewed the quarterly results, talked about the upcoming company picnic, and then said I wanted to read our draft purpose statement. It began: "Our purpose is to maximize our shareholders' return on their invested capital." It droned on from there with more MBA-speak.

I paused and asked, "Well, any comments?"

Silence. They all just sat there, looking at their shoes.

Then a hand in the back of the room rose slowly.

"Yes," I said, "Your thoughts?"

"Well," came the response, "I'm not sure what 'maximize shareholders' return on whatever' means, but, anyway, that's not why I work here."

Everyone turned around to see who had spoken. You could hear the early-morning traffic on the street outside. At that moment, I realized I had a decision to make: explain our fiduciary obligation to shareholders and defend why we needed profits to exist, or open a dialogue, risking a verbal mutiny.

I realize now that momentary decision was monumental for me. I decided to ask the brave soul in the back of the room why he worked at Monarch. Then we got a spirited dialogue going, with many others chiming in. People talked about their pride in the products, what they were learning, and how they were able to help customers. Most of all, they talked about their colleagues and about feeling part of a good team and giving back to the community through our service days and charitable contributions.

We continued this dialogue companywide over several months, led by a small group of volunteers with my encouragement and active involvement. Ultimately, we synthesized a new purpose, values, and vision for Monarch. Making profits was still there, but only as a result of "creating value for people" (our new purpose), as well as other more aspirational values and visions.

An organization's purpose (or "mission," as it is often termed) addresses *why* the enterprise exists. (We much prefer "purpose" to "mission," because the latter often denotes a particular task or goal, whereas purpose gets at the ultimate aims of an organization. We shall use "purpose" in lieu of "mission." The concepts we outline are the important points.)

People hunger to know that their organization has a worthwhile purpose and that their work is meaningful and significant. Are they building something excellent, ethical, and enduring? Will they have a positive impact? According to a British study, 70 percent of respondents indicated they want their working lives to be more meaningful. Among twenty- to thirty-year-olds, it was 82 percent. "In the workplace," wrote the authors, "meaning appears to link to a sense of community, to having a higher sense of purpose . . . to consistency of behavior and congruence between personal and organizational values. People want to work for ethical organizations . . . When people experience greater meaning, they appear to be 'in flow,' able to give their best."[7]

John Bogle, founder and former CEO of the Vanguard Group (an investment management company), told us, "People want to be part of something bigger than they are and commit themselves to it."

Authors Linda Hill and Kent Lineback note, "A clear and compelling purpose is the glue that binds together a group of individuals . . . It is the source of the meaning and significance people seek in what they do . . . When workers were asked how important it was that their lives be meaningful, 83 percent said 'very important' and another 15 percent said 'fairly important' (98 percent in total)."[8]

The ideal purpose statement is short enough to fit on a T-shirt and is jargon free. It should be memorable and inspiring.

Table 3.1 provides some good examples.

While the aim of maximizing shareholder value may get some people's juices flowing, it falls flat as a clarion call for employees and can lead to problems with the three Es—causing some to disregard the ethical imperative and longer-term considerations beyond the next quarter.

Some organizations confuse a purpose statement with a company description (for example, "XYZ Corporation publishes research-

Table 3.1 **Purpose Statements**

Bright Horizons Family Solutions (provider of employer-sponsored childcare)	"Make a difference in the lives of children and families."
Walt Disney Company (media conglomerate)	"Make people happy."
Mary Kay Inc. (privately held provider of personal care products)	"Give unlimited opportunity to women."
Merck (global pharmaceutical company)	"Preserve and improve human life."
3M (diversified technology company)	"Solve unsolved problems innovatively."

based science textbooks for high schools"). Such a statement indicates what an organization does but not *why*.

Skeptics dismiss purpose statements as platitudes. Often they are right. Many purpose statements are unoriginal, uninspiring, or disconnected from what people actually feel and experience at work. In too many cases, leaders—if they craft a purpose statement at all—ignore it when immersed in the pressures of day-to-day operations. Triple crown leadership places purpose front and center. For example, Medtronic (a leading medical technology company) employs a Mission Medallion Ceremony, which all new employees attend. The medallions are bronze and show a person rising from an operating table. On the back is the company mission about restoring people to full life and health.[9]

VALUES

The second part of the metaphorical colors—the values—articulates the norms that guide behavior in the enterprise. Values set the ethical compass of the organization (the second leg of the triple crown). They are the principles and standards for how people should behave, reflecting their collective judgment about what is important. Values can be explicit or implicit, but triple crown leaders make them explicit.

Author Rosabeth Moss Kanter calls values a "strategic guidance system" that provides significant advantages to companies in many areas, including competitive differentiation, public accountability, rationale for long-term thinking (rejecting short-termism), guidance for consistent decisions, talent magnets and motivation, and control systems.[10]

We heard about the importance of values repeatedly in our interviews. At Tyco (the global manufacturing company), John Krol, the former lead outside director, told us, "The number one thing in the turnaround of Tyco was a culture of basic values." At eBay (the pioneering online auction company), Lorrie Norrington, former president of eBay Marketplaces, told us, "What everyone at eBay has built in the last sixteen years is a very strong set of values, the most important of which is acting with uncompromising integrity."[11]

See Table 3.2 for examples of values statements.

Ron Sugar, former CEO of Northrop Grumman, told us, "This business is all about trust. If we are providing a B-2 bomber, a nuclear aircraft carrier, or a ballistic missile for our armed forces, their lives depend on us. Our products must have integrity, and we must act with integrity."

In our work with scores of commercial and nonprofit organizations to develop values, we encourage people to identify four to six words that capture the essence of their desired behaviors, with an explanatory phrase or sentence for each value. Sometimes they can combine the values into an acronym, as MidCountry did (CHIEF), making the values much more memorable.

At Sensormatic (an electronic security systems company where Bob served as CEO during its turnaround), the senior staff chose leadership, integrity, teamwork, and excellence as their values, with the acronym LITE. They then added a series of sentences and explanations under each single word. "Leadership" had insights that described how people should act (for example, "be a personal role model"), identified personal characteristics to model (such as "unselfish"), stipulated how to treat others ("with respect"), and specified how they would, it was hoped, be viewed ("with the highest integrity"). LITE was memorable, and the values became an integral part of Sensormatic's turnaround, discussed often as executives wrestled with tough decisions.

Table 3.2 **Values Statements**

DuPont (chemical products and services firm)	Safety
	Concern and care for people
	Protection of the environment
	Personal and corporate integrity
MidCountry Financial Services (financial services holding company)	Compassion
	Honesty
	Integrity
	Excellence
	Fairness
Neusoft (largest information technology solutions and services provider in China)	Simplicity
	Respect
	Accountability
	Collaboration
	Integrity
North Castle Partners (private equity investment firm)	Integrity
	Partnership
	Respect
	Development
	Excellence
	Balance
Northrop Grumman (global provider of military and commercial security systems)	Quality
	Customer satisfaction
	Leadership
	Integrity
	People
	Suppliers as team members

Ideally, values serve as a decision-making tool for people throughout the organization every day. Values give people license to act, avoiding the paternalism of a leader dispensing empowerment from on high. (We address this concept further in chapter five.)

Shared Values

Values are most powerful when they are *shared* values. This only happens when leaders elicit values from the group via a collaborative process.

Who should be involved in that process? Everyone. Even a sprawling organization like IBM rose to this standard when it held its "Values Jam," a three-day web rave that invited more than three hundred thousand IBMers worldwide to weigh in using the company's technology.

While many organizations have values statements, the key is upholding them and weaving them into the fabric of the organization. This requires proactive efforts and constant vigilance from leaders (and others). Lynn Easterling at Cisco (the global networking solutions company) told us, "Integrity is in every single message I've heard our CEO deliver for the past ten years." According to Princeton president Shirley Tilghman, "My most important job is to articulate clearly and consistently what the values of the institution are."

DaVita (a leading kidney care provider) holds "Nights of Honor," recognizing individuals who are exceptional in upholding the company's core values. During the ceremonies, leaders talk about what the honorees did and award a core value pin. COO emeritus Joe Mello told us:

> Now we have a history of doing that at multiple levels within the organization. After we did it with the vice presidents, we did it with our directors. Then our directors did it with our facility administrators. Then we decided we could do this with every teammate [employee]. Any teammate can nominate a

colleague for a core value award. All of a sudden, those values became more than a bunch of words on a poster.[12]

VISION

I have a dream that my four little children will one day live in a nation where they will not be judged by the color of their skin but by the content of their character. I have a dream today . . .
—Dr. Martin Luther King, Jr.

Dr. King's "I Have a Dream" speech in 1963 is a great vision statement. It paints a bold and vivid picture of a better future. It helped move a nation to action after years of moral abuses. Dr. King drew us into his vision by appealing to our moral principles (like justice and fairness) and to our senses. He talked about sitting "down together at the table of brotherhood," "the red hills of Georgia," joining hands, and singing the old spiritual *Free at Last*.

An ideal vision statement provides a clear and compelling picture of what success looks like. The vision should touch all major stakeholders, appealing to their emotions, senses, principles, and dreams. Joseph Jaworski, author of *Synchronicity,* says, "There is extraordinary power in a group connected to a common vision." In his book, *Visionary Leadership,* author Burt Nanus says, "There is no more powerful engine driving an organization toward excellence and long-range success than an attractive, worthwhile, and achievable vision of the future, widely shared." Edward Mueller, former chairman and CEO of Qwest, the telecommunications company that merged with CenturyLink in 2011, told us, "One of the best questions you can ask is, 'What does success look like if we achieve it?'"

In our view, a vision statement should be more detailed and descriptive than a purpose statement. We share some examples in Table 3.3.

While leaders should craft purpose and values for the long haul—ideally, lasting several decades or indefinitely—a vision may need to change more frequently. The average tenure of a Fortune 500 CEO

Table 3.3   **Vision Statements**

City of Charlotte, North Carolina	"The City of Charlotte will be a model of excellence that puts its citizens first. Skilled, motivated employees will be known for providing quality and value in all areas of service. We will be a platform for vital economic activity that gives Charlotte a competitive edge in the marketplace. We will partner with citizens and businesses to make Charlotte a community of choice for living, working, and leisure activities."
PepsiCo (global food and beverage company)	"PepsiCo's responsibility is to continually improve all aspects of the world in which we operate—environment, social, economic—creating a better tomorrow than today. Our vision is put into action through programs and a focus on environmental stewardship, activities to benefit society, and a commitment to build shareholder value by making PepsiCo a truly sustainable company."
Pfizer (global pharmaceutical company)	"We will become the world's most valued company to patients, customers, colleagues, investors, business partners, and the communities where we work and live."
Votorantim (global industrial conglomerate based in Brazil)	"To ensure continuous growth and presence as a major family-owned company that is respected and recognized in the communities where it operates with a focus on creating economic, environmental, and social value through: • Ethical values that guide responsible corporate conduct • Highly competitive businesses • The search for creative and innovative solutions for its portfolio • People motivated to perform at high levels"

is about five years.[13] Should each new chief executive push for a new vision? Not necessarily.

Whose Vision?

As with the purpose and values statements, leaders should elicit a shared vision from people, not impose it from above. There are great expectations these days for leaders to be visionary. While a sense of vision is certainly desirable in leaders, we believe this expectation places too much focus on the leader and a leader-centric model, thereby diminishing the leadership that can and must emerge from the group. According to bestselling leadership authors Jim Kouzes and Barry Posner:

> What people really want to hear is not the leader's vision. They want to hear about *their own* aspirations. They want to hear how their dreams will come true and their hopes will be fulfilled. They want to see themselves in the picture of the future that the leader is painting. The very best leaders understand that their key task is inspiring a *shared* vision, not selling their own idiosyncratic view of the world . . . most adults don't like being told where to go and what to do. They want to feel part of the process.[14]

Warren Bennis, esteemed leadership author and professor at the University of Southern California, sagely wrote, "Effective leaders put words to the formless longings and deeply felt needs of others."

A COLLABORATIVE, SYNTHESIZING PROCESS

Triple crown organizations develop their metaphorical colors in remarkably similar ways. Senior leaders do not impose them. They co-create the colors over time, unearthing them from the deep desires and principles of the people. Triple crown leaders have a sincere belief in the capabilities of people. They view leadership as a group performance in which anybody and everybody can lead, no matter where they currently are in the organizational hierarchy.

A small team of volunteers, a guiding coalition, should in most cases lead the synthesizing process. The process requires deep listening, eliciting views from a wide cross section of internal and external stakeholders. Seeking common themes, the guiding coalition drafts, discusses, listens, debates, and redrafts in an unfolding process.

This process is critical. The result is not a foregone conclusion leading magically to the CEO's preferred terms. The guiding coalition must be respectful of the insights of people, willing to frame and reframe statements, and open to influence. The process must not be manipulative or condescending. Though messy and sometimes frustrating, the process builds buy-in and trust.

In the final versions of the purpose, values, and vision statements, leaders must synthesize the disparate elements. A synthesis creatively fuses two or more elements into something new. It is not a summary. Synthesis takes A plus B plus C and derives D, where D encapsulates the essence of A, B, and C but also adds something new. That synthesis may come from the CEO, the guiding coalition, or the senior leadership team. Patterns form, and a consensus emerges. After all the iterations, a sense emerges of "Yes, that's our reason for being, how we want to behave, and where we want to go." People then buy in and commit.

Collaborative synthesis is a triple crown leadership practice that anyone can learn. It just takes practice. During this synthesizing process, leaders must ensure there is congruence in the colors:

- Congruence between an organization's purpose, values, and vision

- Congruence across divisions, departments, and geographies

- Congruence between the organization's purpose, values, and vision and those of its people

Former Medtronic CEO Bill George, who is currently a professor at Harvard Business School, recalls, "I spent a lot of time encouraging people to think about how their personal values aligned with the company's values, and how their personal mission of leadership aligned with the company's mission. And if they couldn't do that, it was best that they leave."

In startups that have not yet hired any employees, the founders may have to draft the purpose, values, and vision initially. They should seek colleagues who resonate deeply with the purpose, values, and vision, and then revisit them as a team to ensure widespread input and ownership. (We address the special circumstances for startups in chapter nine.)

Conflicting Priorities in a Crisis

Gregg: Going into the meeting, I knew there would be a fight. The financial pressures on K12 (an online education company where I served as senior vice president for school development) in those startup years were acute.

We had landed some major deals in recent months, but one of them faced a sudden crisis. A state agency cut the funding in half for a virtual school that we were about to launch and manage. It was a blatant political maneuver, with painful financial implications for us.

The choice was stark: walk away from the deal to protect our fragile finances, or stick it out and make it work. The financial case for walking away was strong. Going forward at the reduced rate was risky financially, since our cash was tight. K12 had already had some near-death experiences as it burned through cash for product development and hiring growth, and altering the school's operating model to reduce expenses would make it roughly a breakeven deal for us. In addition, it could put downward pressure on our prices, setting a dangerous precedent. Meanwhile, investors were becoming impatient and tightening the screws.

On the other hand, there was an ethical case for making it work. We had signed a contract with a local partner, announced the approval of the new online school, and started enrolling students. It was not just our cash balance at stake; it was also the beginning of the school year for hundreds of students. If we walked away, their parents would have to scramble to find them another school.

The ultimate decision to walk away was a mistake in my view. I had made the best case I could, but the process was disappointing. We hadn't decided which came first: shareholders or customers. Purpose, values, and vision were not part of the discussion.

THE IMPORTANCE OF COLORS

Chip Baird, founder and CEO of North Castle Partners, a private equity firm, told us, "The most fundamental responsibility of leadership is to make sure that people understand down to their bones the values and purpose of the organization." Triple crown leaders understand that mandate.

Sometimes strong organizational colors pay off in unexpected ways. MidCountry Financial Corp. is a financial services holding company started by Robert Hatcher (also CEO) and a group of colleagues. MidCountry was pursuing Pioneer Services, a financial institution serving the military market. Pioneer's owners had decided to sell the firm and invited potential buyers in to listen to Pioneer's pitch. Most companies came in, listened, and then proceeded to negotiate, but Hatcher and his team took a different approach: they came in and said, "Could we just tell you about us first?" They then launched into MidCountry's mission, values, vision, norms, and culture. It totally changed the nature of the conversation. "When we walked out of there," Hatcher told us, "we were soul mates." Pioneer's great team joined MidCountry and continues to set financial records while being socially responsible and active in the community.

Triple crown leaders must act on the colors, constantly reinforcing them in meetings, blogs, newsletters, emails, tweets, videocasts, speeches, annual reports, and, most important of all, daily decisions. People want to see what leaders do when the chips are down. Are they "walking the talk"? What do they do when under pressure to make the quarterly numbers or when feeling the heat from funders? That is the decisive moment when organizations reveal their actual commitment to the colors and demonstrate to all involved that the triple crown quest is genuine.

Organizational colors—the purpose, values, and vision—are essential in building excellent, ethical, and enduring organizations because they:

- Provide meaning

- Guide behaviors

- Inspire people to higher levels of performance

- Influence decisions

- Empower people to act without asking permission

- Attract people with integrity and talent

- Develop trust and commitment

- Build organizational character

James O'Toole, author and professor of business ethics at the Daniels College of Business, succinctly and artfully captured these dynamics with values-based leadership as his anchor:

> Values-Based Leadership → Robust Corporate Cultures → Productive, Innovative, and Ethical Behavior → Sustainable Growth = Good Business[15]

To O'Toole, a certain kind of leadership (values based, which we endorse) leads to a healthy culture (our culture of character), leading to productivity and innovation (our excellent) and ethical behavior (our ethical), leading to sustainable growth (our enduring), resulting in good business (our triple crown organization).

To illustrate these benefits, let's look at an extraordinary social venture that has put its organizational colors to good use.

SHARE OUR STRENGTH: THE COLORS IN ACTION

"Goodness, you must love spaghetti," I said to seven-year-old Keshan as he came up for his third helping of spaghetti during our after-school meet.

"Yes," he said. "We never get this at home."

"You never get spaghetti at home?" I replied.

"No," he said. "I mean we never get dinner at my house."[16]

Today, about a quarter of children in developing countries are underweight or stunted. As we write, there is mass famine in Somalia. Even in the United States, fifty million people, including more than seventeen million children, lack the means to get enough nutritious food on a regular basis.[17]

Bill Shore and Debbie Shore, a dynamic brother and sister team, have worked on hunger and poverty relief for decades. In 1984, they started a nonprofit called Share Our Strength (SOS) in a Washington, D.C., basement with little more than a mission and a $2,000 credit card advance.

The colors of their organization are clear, driving everything they do. The purpose of SOS is to "end childhood hunger."[18] Its values are:

- Preserving the innovation spirit

- Upholding quality and integrity

- Mobilizing new people to join our network

- Encouraging creative freedom and fun

SOS's vision, which it set in 2006, is to increase participation in nutrition programs (such as school breakfasts, summer meals, and food stamps) so dramatically that childhood hunger in the United States will be a thing of the past by 2015.

The process of setting these organizational colors took about nine months, starting with a small group and then branching out to other key stakeholders. According to Bill Shore, staying true to the colors has required a disciplined focus on the long-term dynamics entailed with poverty:

> The really bold, ambitious things that you want to accomplish are going to take a long time. All the incentives in any organi-

zation always run to the short term, the immediate gratification to make the quarter's numbers and make the budget. It's really important for somebody to keep their eye on the prize, even if it's ten or fifteen years out, and ensure that you're organizing and allocating the resources to achieve that.

At SOS, the values are sacrosanct. "A lot of things change," says Shore, "but your core values don't change. You must fill the organization with people of high integrity. We focus on creating an environment where people can make a career, where people are the guardians of the values because they've been here a long time and they care about them."

Shore also focuses on modeling the shared values. He once terminated a talented CFO who was abusive. He explains, "We weren't willing to have those kinds of skills at that organizational cost." Trustee Noel Cunningham once told a fellow board member who had used an SOS event for personal publicity purposes, "Maybe it's time for you to go." (Shortly thereafter, the board member resigned.)

Of course, there is more to SOS than its colors. It also fosters a culture of entrepreneurship and employs an innovative business model. For example, Community Wealth Ventures, a commercial subsidiary of SOS, helps other nonprofits become financially sustainable by generating revenue through innovative business ventures and partnerships. Its approach goes beyond "giving a man a fish," and even beyond "teaching him how to fish," to "teaching him how to build a fishery."

According to Shore, "Some organizations fight hunger by showing pictures of children with bloated bellies. We fight hunger by signing contracts with large corporations who are going to get marketing advantages by working with us. It's a very different model . . . We see a nonprofit and think differently—not just about redistributing wealth but actually creating wealth."

Like all the organizations we interviewed, SOS is not perfect. A similar organization, Feeding America, is larger and has grown faster than SOS in recent years after rebranding itself from America's Second Harvest. Poverty and hunger remain problematic, fueled by the global financial crisis. While SOS still has a lot of work to do in realizing its ultimate aims, its story is rich with leadership lessons.

For example, SOS started Taste of the Nation in which some of the nation's best chefs donate their time and talent to raise funds for hunger relief. The event spans fifty-five cities across North America involving over ten thousand chefs and restaurateurs. Through these efforts, SOS has raised over $300 million and provided support to more than a thousand nonprofit organizations around the world, facilitating more than forty million meals for children through grants. It is a powerful example of an organization that honors its colors.

CHAPTER SUMMARY

People can commit to an organization wholeheartedly if it has a compelling purpose, values, and vision—its colors. Leaders must engage all in developing the colors through a collaborative process, thereby increasing ownership and buy-in. The colors should be a call to the triple crown quest for an excellent, ethical, and enduring organization. The colors should be memorable and reinforced by leaders often through their words and deeds.

Practical Applications

1. Does your organization have a written purpose statement?
   a. Is it clear, compelling, short, memorable, and inspiring? In which of those areas could it improve?
   b. Does it address why the organization exists instead of simply describing what it does? What improvements may be needed?
   c. To what extent does your organization work toward the purpose?
2. Does your organization have written values?
   a. Do the values set clear standards for how people in the organization should behave?

      b. Is there an explanatory phrase or sentence for each value?

      c. Are the values memorable, preferably with an acronym?

      d. What changes are needed to improve them in these or other areas?

      e. To what extent do people in your organization uphold the values?

3. Does your organization have a written vision?

      a. Does it paint a bold, vivid, clear, and compelling picture of what success looks like?

      b. Does it touch all major stakeholders?

      c. What changes are needed to improve it in these or other areas?

      d. To what extent do people in your organization work to realize the vision?

4. Can you recall the purpose and the values without looking them up?

5. Were they set collaboratively or imposed by edict?

6. Are they widely shared by people throughout the organization?

7. To what extent are they reinforced through frequent messages and actions from leaders?

8. To what extent does the organization adhere to the colors when the pressure is on? What do you do?

9. Are your own personal purpose and values congruent with the organization's purpose and values?

      a. If there are significant conflicts, can you influence the organization to change?

10. Are all the departments and sections of the organization working coherently toward the purpose, values, and vision? How can this be improved?

11. Do the colors point to the quest for an excellent, ethical, and enduring organization? What changes might you make to integrate any missing elements?

12. Would your team benefit from having its own purpose, values, and a vision (that coheres with the organization's colors)?

      a. Could you practice facilitating the collaborative synthesizing process, enhancing your leadership capabilities? What first steps will you take to initiate this?

CHAPTER FOUR

STEEL AND VELVET

Not often in the story of mankind does a man arrive on earth who is both steel and velvet, who is as hard as rock and soft as drifting fog, who holds in his heart and mind the paradox of terrible storm and peace unspeakable and perfect.

—**Carl Sandburg,** poet and author,
writing about Abraham Lincoln

n July 1862, President Abraham Lincoln made the most momentous decision of his presidency.

It was a wrenching time. The Civil War had been going badly for the Union, and Lincoln's eleven-year-old son, Willie, had died recently, devastating the president.

Lincoln abhorred slavery, but he knew that the Constitution implicitly protected it, greatly limiting his presidential options. He believed slavery would die out over time. His paramount objective was to save the Union, but more and more that was looking like a lost cause. The Confederate Army benefited militarily from slaves, who served as staff support and manual laborers so others could fight. Lincoln judged that the trajectory of the war might shift if the Rebels lost their slaves, who would be free to join Union forces. He decided that ending slavery in the Confederate states was a legitimate use of his constitutional war powers as president, bridging a military necessity with a moral one.

In his July 22 cabinet meeting, Lincoln read a draft of the Emancipation Proclamation he had privately composed, welcoming suggestions but emphasizing that he "had resolved upon this step." Most cabinet members were stunned. Secretary of State William Seward suggested Lincoln wait until a Union battlefield victory before announcing the proclamation to avoid the appearance of desperation. Lincoln agreed and pocketed the draft.

On September 17, the Union had a bloody victory at the Battle of Antietam in Maryland. Five days later, Lincoln reconvened his cabinet and reread the draft proclamation, again welcoming suggestions, but reiterating that his decision was final.

On September 23, 1862, Lincoln issued the Emancipation Proclamation, declaring that on January 1 all slaves in the Confederate states would be "henceforward, and forever free." That act changed the course of a war, a people, and a nation.

Lincoln often invoked steel resolve. He was the first U.S. president to order the draft. He declared martial law. Fearing sabotage and treason, he suspended the writ of habeas corpus, thereby allowing detention without trial. Yet, through it all, the integrity of "Honest Abe" was well known and unshakable.

But Lincoln also led with a velvet touch. He persuaded people by personal visits, even on the battlefields. He listened deeply and engaged in warm conversation and mischievous storytelling. He sought input from others, even his rivals, asking for guidance and learning from their advice. He prayed and read often, retreating to solitude amid the crushing pressure of the Civil War. He patiently and methodically built alliances, much as he did with the members of his cabinet, forming them into what historian Doris Kearns Goodwin called a "team of rivals."[1]

Abraham Lincoln was a "steel and velvet" leader. He was able, as Sandburg said, to embrace the paradox of the terrible storm and the perfect peace.

And so it is with triple crown leadership. Triple crown leaders know when to invoke the:

1. Hard edge—the steel bit—of leadership, demanding excellent results, insisting upon ethical practices, and resisting the allure of short-term thinking that borrows irresponsibly from the future
2. Soft edge—the velvet stroke—of leadership that patiently builds the organizational character in which a unique and powerful leadership dynamic can thrive

Triple crown leadership requires flexing between steel and velvet. We address each in turn below.

STEEL

In steel mode, triple crown leaders decisively exercise authority and power—within ethical boundaries—to get results. Steel requires confidence, discipline, and toughness.

Ursula Burns, now CEO of Xerox, told us about her time in 2001 as president under then-CEO Anne Mulcahy, with the company on the verge of bankruptcy: "When we were in the bunker, we were losing money, had no cash, and had just changed from bad leadership. We had customers, shareholders—everyone you could imagine—pissed off at us. When we were in the bunker, Anne led a certain way. Her beacon was survival. It was 90 percent her power to be the shining light by which the organization, customers, and shareholders believed." Mulcahy effectively invoked steel leadership during the Xerox turnaround.

Steel is the hard edge of leadership. It involves getting results, executing through the hierarchy, and committing to tough decisions and forceful actions.

In steel mode, leaders expect team members to execute plans on schedule and within budget. They make difficult, sometimes controversial, decisions, knowing when to invoke the "terrible storm." They must be willing to go against the tide and risk popular support.

Leaders acknowledge reality, no matter how dire, while still offering hope. They must make decisions, often unilaterally, to ensure survival. They use expertise, power, and position authority. Through clear direction and regular follow-up, they hold people accountable for their commitments. When invoking steel, the leader is the lonely chief *execution* officer.

When flexing to steel mode, leaders bring order, even in the fog of ambiguity. They have the guts to admit when they make mistakes, knowing not every move will be right, and quickly alter course.

All three elements of the triple crown quest require steel:

1. Failure to get results is unacceptable.
2. Failure to act ethically is unacceptable.
3. Failure to maintain those commitments over time is unacceptable.

Through all three imperatives, steel leadership sets and reinforces the character of the organization.

Steel leadership must not be taken too far. It is not bullying, intimidating, or manipulative. It does not use fear as a motivator to maintain power. It is not the iron fist within the velvet glove. It is not autocratic rule cloaked within a false, soft exterior.

Steel leadership should be "rigorous, not ruthless," as Jim Collins has noted.[2] Triple crown leaders deeply value their associates, even when they must invoke steel. What differentiates triple crown steel from intimidation and bullying is the purpose, the intent, of the leadership. Triple crown leadership flexes to the steel edge in service of building an excellent, ethical, and enduring organization. It deploys steel sparingly while staying within ethical bounds.

The Limits of Steel

Ursula Burns told us that the bunker days, when Ann Mulcahy was the sole face of the Xerox turnaround, could not be sustained: "An organization doesn't live by any individual. There's danger in that happening." Leadership that is only steel corrodes.

There are two risks here: using too much force or using force too often. When either happens, it can break the culture of character and shut down the leadership in others. As people wait for direction, they abdicate their initiative and creativity.

When there is an excess of steel, people filter their input and flatter the leader.[3] When this happens, the leader's ego can get out of control, resulting in self-destructive behavior. Steel-only leadership is unhealthy and unsustainable.

Sharon Oster, a popular economics professor tapped to serve as interim dean of the Yale School of Management, learned about the limits of steel in a faculty meeting she described to us. After she forcefully drove the meeting toward her preferred approach, a colleague took her aside and counseled, "You got the right policy, but you must live to play another day. That's just not the way you want to run this railroad."

Steel-only leadership fails.

VELVET

Velvet is the soft edge of leadership, encompassing collaboration, relationships, and stewardship, using persuasion, not position power. By using velvet, leaders empower colleagues to become fellow leaders and co-creators.

When flexing to the velvet edge, the leader shows humility, even vulnerability at times, not pretending to have all the answers. She shows confidence in the team, trusting that *together they can solve any problem*. She reinforces the concept that triple crown leadership is a group performance in which anyone and everyone can lead at times.

Velvet leadership involves listening patiently and connecting with people. It celebrates diversity in people and thought. Operating at the velvety edge puts an organization into a "leadership-centric" mode.

Velvet leadership trusts, thereby building trust. It facilitates creativity. It seeks consensus, not majority rule, asking, "Even if you disagree, can you live with this decision?" If objectors can live with the decision, the group moves on. If not, the dialogue continues.

Velvet leadership entails asking questions, nurturing, praising, and often saying "thank you." It encourages fun and relieves stress. Velvet leaders let others lead, building their capabilities. They tolerate mistakes to let people learn, so long as those mistakes do not jeopardize the organization's survival. This leadership-sharing approach develops others. In velvet mode, the leader is the chief *character* officer.

Jim Unruh, the turnaround CEO at Unisys (the global information technology company), told us, "Long term, I don't think you get where you want to go if you're just on the hard side. It takes listening, rewarding, encouraging, and being open to changing direction. Are people truly participating, or is it a charade where I'm letting them talk and not really listening?"

Mayo Clinic leaders, in their own creative twist on velvet leadership, use a "timeout" for some people who violate the organization's norms. They send violators home for a few days with full pay and their duties covered by others, asking them to think about the transgression and decide whether they still want to work at Mayo. The policy is remarkably effective.

The Limits of Velvet

Drs. Berry and Seltman told us about the head of Mayo's orthopedics practice, who learned the practice was losing money. He observed that each physician was using his or her own preferred implant, of varying quality and cost, for joint replacements. He sought to convince these accomplished physicians to choose from only a few options to boost quality and contain costs.

Many physicians told him they could not concern themselves with the price of the implant, because at Mayo "the needs of the patient come first." (A natural reaction based on Mayo's values.) They would continue to choose the implant they thought best.

The leader commissioned a study, and the data disproved the physicians' justifications. But the doctors didn't buy it, insisting the data were wrong. He invited them to check the data for errors (a velvet offer) but insisted on moving forward based on the evidence until it was proved wrong (a steel decision).

Eventually, the physicians agreed. In two years, the practice went from losing $2 million a year to making $6 million. Dr. Berry told us, "He had to use both hard and soft leadership to get the physicians to make the change. Otherwise it would have blown up in his face."

Leadership only at the soft edge has major drawbacks and risks. It can fail to get results, appearing wishy-washy. It invites inaction, frustration, confusion, "analysis paralysis," and groupthink. Hugs around the campfire are nice, but sometimes an organization needs to blow things up.

Velvet-only leadership fails.

GETTING BEYOND YOUR NATURAL LEADERSHIP STYLE

In 1967, Penny Chenery took over her family's 2,800-acre Meadow Farm in Kentucky when her father became ill. She had spent the previous eighteen years in Denver raising her four children.

Because the farm was just holding its own financially, Chenery's leadership began with tests of steel interspersed with touches of velvet. Chenery terminated her father's twenty-year trainer, who was condescending. She cut the number of horses stabled from 130 to 68 to get costs under control. She read everything she could about thoroughbreds and relied heavily on patient counsel from longtime Meadow Farm secretary Elizabeth Ham and family friend A. B. ("Bull") Hancock, owner of nearby Claiborne Farm. She refused to sell Meadow Farm, despite intense family pressure to do so, feeling a moral obligation to her father and his dreams, resolving to make it profitable again.[4]

Chenery bred mares to the stallion, Bold Ruler, producing a foal she called Secretariat. When her father died and the family faced a staggering estate tax bill, she engaged Seth Hancock, Bull's son, to syndicate two-year-old Secretariat for stud at the unheard of price of $190,000 per share, raising a record $6 million.[5]

Though most owners were aloof and inaccessible in public, Chenery cheerfully signed autographs for fans and was quick to laugh, a warm and gracious woman with a naturally velvet disposition.

Chenery became the first female president of the Thoroughbred Breeders and Owners Association and president of the Grayson–Jockey Club Foundation for Equine Research. She won the Eclipse Award of Merit for a lifetime of outstanding achievement in thoroughbred racing, becoming known unofficially as "the first lady of racing."[6]

Penny Chenery was able to move beyond her natural velvet style and summon steel leadership when needed, flexing as circumstances required.

It seems paradoxical that triple crown leadership is both steel and velvet. After all, people have their natural personalities. People enter leadership roles with a disposition that drives them to be either commanding or collaborative, introverted or extroverted, cautious or decisive, relationship oriented or task oriented.

We cannot change our DNA, and we should be authentic, as former Medtronic CEO Bill George has written, avoiding the trap of trying to lead like someone else.[7] But we can change our behavior.

For decades, managers have relied on a battery of tools, such as the Myers-Briggs Type Indicator and the Insights Discovery System, to understand their natural personality profiles and obtain insights about their preferred leadership style.[8] These are useful starting points, but only a beginning.

Triple crown leadership requires getting beyond our natural leadership styles. Just knowing yourself well and following your personality instincts is insufficient.

Chip Baird, CEO of North Castle Partners (a private equity firm), told us, "Leaders have dominant genetics. They can lead with people skills, technical skills, or formal authority—sometimes ordering, sometimes inspiring, sometimes cajoling, sometimes placating. I think an effective leader has to be able to use all those skills, regardless of what their core leadership genetic is."

Mike Critelli, former CEO of Pitney Bowes, told us about how hard it was for him to get beyond his natural leadership style. By nature, he was fast moving and aggressive:

> I was very comfortable blowing up existing systems, but I realized that only a small percentage of the population could function that way. There were many decisions that I consciously did not make. Before I arrived, there was clearly a preference from employees for the CEO to make decisions. But building organizational capability requires a CEO to bite his or her tongue. That was a hard change for me.

Joe Mello, COO emeritus at DaVita (a Fortune 500 provider of kidney care), told us, "People have very different styles, many different Myers-Briggs profiles. But the managers in our organization who have done best know which decisions should be collaborative and which need to be more directive. They know when to stop the conversation and decide."

Triple crown leadership requires stepping out of your natural behavioral box:

- The shy foreman must speak up in front of large groups.

- The quiet administrator must be a courageous "voice of one" in a staff meeting, even when others resent her for making waves.

- The reflective thinker must make a quick decision when circumstances demand it.

- The dominating vice president has to learn to shut up and listen.

Cheryl Dorsey, president of Echoing Green (a nonprofit funder of social entrepreneurs), phrased it this way: "I'm a natural mover, not a bystander. If nobody talks, I talk. I'll jump in if there's a pause: that's my natural behavior. I need to rewire myself, but people have to help me. Sometimes entrepreneurs need to be coached out of their instinctual behaviors."

Some people object, saying people "are who they are" and cannot change. We disagree. People can change their behavior.

FLEXING BETWEEN STEEL AND VELVET

In the quest for the triple crown, the key is not just steel, or just velvet, or some murky middle ground between them. The key is to understand the context and people, judging each time whether to move toward the hard or soft edge. There is continual movement back and forth.[9] We call it leadership "flex."

Four-star general Jack Chain oversaw much of the U.S. nuclear arsenal as Commander in Chief of the U.S. Strategic Air Command (SAC). When he learned about a minor security violation at an air base, he had the officers in charge of security on every SAC base flown into the Omaha headquarters. He stood them all at attention and "chewed their asses." Even though a single sergeant in the field blew it, Chain reminded them that they were in charge of all the sergeants. He said they were part of a larger team, the team had failed, and they had brought great discredit on SAC. Then he walked out. "When you have a nuclear weapons mission," he explained to us, "there is no tolerance for error."

More often, though, Chain relied on velvet leadership. He also told us:

> You can't just stay at the hard edge. You will not earn any support. You have to take care of your people and care about them from your heart and soul. You've got to love them. If they are screwing up, you have to discipline them, but you still have to love them. You have to know about their spouse and children, how they are doing at home. You have to worry about all your direct reports and whether they are taking care of the next level, and the next level, all the way down.

Chain was able to flex between ramrod steel and soft velvet, in the process earning the respect and best efforts of his air corps.

Similarly, Dr. Andres Alonso, CEO of Baltimore City Schools, learned to flex across this spectrum artfully. When he took over in 2007, the district was in trouble. Enrollment was down from 190,000 students in the 1960s to 81,500, decimating the district's budget and morale. Many parents, teachers, and experts viewed it as a failing system. Amid all those challenges, Alonso had to flex often:

> It's necessary to veer between hard and soft because we are constantly dealing with different situations and different

people. I have been incredibly hard. We terminated almost five hundred positions in the central office in two years. But the daily work requires far more of the soft, because most people want to do what's right. There has to be versatility. It can mean being tremendously hard in conversations with the city council, and twenty minutes later being in a parent meeting, listening for an hour, acknowledging everything that is being said.

Triple crown leadership is not about a steel leader with a velvet colleague, or the reverse. Such a pairing can be schizophrenic for an organization, creating confusion and slowing it down. Bill George, former CEO of Medtronic, told us, "You have to have the leadership to do both. The top person can't be the soft side and then have someone else, the number two person, lean the hard way. You've got to do both yourself."

Bob learned this lesson when he and a colleague took over Recognition Equipment as co-CEOs. The company was in a tailspin due to an ethical crisis caused by allegations of bribery, with customers, employees, and shareholders bailing fast. Bob and his partner divided the CEO responsibilities. Despite their best efforts to coordinate, they were inadvertently sending mixed messages. Ultimately, Bob's partner departed.[10]

Can leaders really be decisive and resolute while at other times being light in their touch, deferring to others, and letting others lead?

Elizabeth Crossman, chair of the board for Habit for Humanity International (the Christian nonprofit organization that builds affordable housing for people in need), told us, "As a board, we have confidence that our CEO has a balance between the soft and hard edges of leadership. If leadership is too far on the hard edge, you're going to stifle creativity; too much on the soft side, you can flounder. Balancing between directing and empowering is an art."

How do leaders determine when to flex their leadership approach?

STEEL AND VELVET JUDGMENT

With good judgment, little else matters;
without good judgment, nothing else matters.

—Noel Tichy and Warren Bennis,
leadership authors[11]

There are two primary considerations for when to flex to steel or velvet: the nature of the situation and the types of people involved.

1. ***Situation.*** Does the organization need more discipline and controls on its cash burn rate? (More steel.) Is it a nonprofit with good programs but a creeping complacency and broken business model? (More steel.) Is it a government program demoralized by budget cuts and a need to reengage its workers? (More velvet.) Is it the ordinary course of business with meetings, assessments, and feedback loops? (Judicious blend, but mostly velvet.) Each situation has different leadership demands.

   Philip Soucy, CEO of Modern Technology Solutions (a privately held, engineering-services defense contractor), told us, "For me, 90 percent of the time is mentoring, coaching, understanding what's stopping people from being successful. Ten percent is 'No, don't do it that way; do it this way.'" Generally, leaders should use velvet more than steel.

   Lorrie Norrington, the former president of eBay Marketplaces, told us, "Leading in wartime is different than leading in peacetime. Peacetime leadership is about nurturing people and co-creating with them, gently pushing them along at times, while difficult circumstances call for a more directive style. Leadership is very situational."

2. ***People.*** The second consideration for flexing between steel and velvet is the type of people involved. Are we dealing with software coders, tenured university faculty, politi-

cal campaign volunteers, investment bankers, or migrant workers? Is there homogeneity and physical proximity among workers, or are they dispersed globally?

According to Norrington, "Understanding where people are—who needs to be creatively challenged, and who needs to be more directed—is an art."

Dan Ritchie had to adjust his style dramatically when he went from corporate CEO to chancellor of the University of Denver (DU). He quickly saw how academia differed markedly from business. Ritchie faced a challenge when DU needed a new dean for its Daniels College of Business. That job required someone who could effectively manage both the academic and the business side. When the search committee narrowed its list to two candidates, Ritchie was not impressed: "I thought they were way off base," he recalls, "acceptable academically but not otherwise." Time to invoke a mixture of steel and velvet: he chose another candidate (steel) and requested an up-or-down secret ballot by the faculty (velvet). They confirmed Ritchie's choice, and the new dean had a long and successful tenure.

Anchoring in the Colors

As leaders flex, how can they avoid being viewed as inconsistent and damaging their credibility? The key is to always operate in accordance with the organization's colors: the purpose, values, and vision. Such anchoring to defend the colors builds organizational character. Author James O'Toole says, "Leaders must . . . adapt the unnatural behavior of *always* leading by the pull of inspiring values."[12]

To avoid confusion, leaders should take the time to explain, especially when they are invoking steel, why they are taking those actions and how the decision remains consistent with the colors.

At Pitney Bowes, Mike Critelli told us, "There was a lot of pressure from investors and analysts to set public earnings targets when the stock price was declining. I refused to do it. I wanted achievable targets that did not strain the ethics of the organization. The message we sent to our people was to avoid doing whatever they had to do to make the numbers when they couldn't be achieved through good customer care."

One quarter, Pitney Bowes missed its earnings target by two cents. The head of U.S. sales and marketing told Critelli that he could have put programs in place to hit the target, but they would have been wrong for the customer. Critelli publicly commended him. "Our miss hurt the stock price," he recalls, "but I learned the stock would recover. Our reputation and credibility are very fragile, and they can't recover if we act unethically or do things that hurt customers." In this case, Critelli employed both steel (refusing to set earnings targets despite pressure) and velvet (public recognition of ethical leadership) in service of the organization's colors.

Even though leaders anchor their flexing in the colors, sometimes conflicts in values arise. Classic values conflicts are truth versus loyalty, justice versus mercy, individual versus community, and short term versus long term. Debates about these conflicts have been ongoing for millennia. So triple crown leaders encourage spirited dialogues about the shared values and their different interpretations. They recognize that the quality of decisions improves when there is active debate. Just raising the issue about how a proposed action stacks up against the triple crown standard leads the group to examine the decision creatively, often finding a better way that is more consistent with the values and strategies.

Enhancing Your Flexing Capabilities

Flexing between steel and velvet is hard. Most leaders develop this capacity gradually over time, sometimes unconsciously reverting to their natural style. Triple crown leaders work to enhance their flex capabilities through a variety of methods. For example, they:

- Understand and communicate their own natural leadership style

- Understand the leadership styles of their colleagues

- Take time to reflect on how to handle situations and people

- Ask for help from colleagues, coaches, mentors, friends, and family, soliciting honest and direct feedback on how they handled circumstances and what they might have done better

- Explain their decisions and behavior in terms of the organization's colors

Protecting the Mavericks

One special case in making flexing decisions concerns "mavericks." On the open range, mavericks are the unbranded animals free to roam. In an organization, a maverick is an independent innovator or performer, often exceptional and quirky, who does not run easily with others.

Whirlaway was a wild and unmanageable racehorse. He invariably ran to the outside rail, causing him to lose. Hall of Fame trainer Ben Jones, recognizing that the steel bit bothered Whirlaway's sensitive mouth, figured he needed a jockey more adept at managing the horse. He turned to Eddie Arcaro, known as a "good-hands" jockey because he maintained a velvety-light touch with the reins even with his incredible strength. Arcaro was also a consummate racing strategist and tactician, known for impressive maneuvers on the track. With Arcaro in the saddle, Whirlaway went on to win the 1941 Triple Crown and race an incredible sixty times, finishing in the money in fifty-six of them.[13] Many hail Arcaro—the only jockey with two U.S. Triple Crowns—as the greatest jockey of all time.

Many breakthrough ideas come from mavericks. The job of the triple crown leader is to protect and coach the mavericks, *as long as they support the colors of the organization.* We are not talking about tolerating "star" performers who violate the organization's colors. Those people have to go (see below). Too many leaders look the other way at star performers who disregard the values, holding those performers to a different standard—a failure to invoke steel.

On the other hand, mavericks who support the colors are worth protecting. Joe Mello of DaVita told us, "You need mavericks. You should embrace them. They test the assumptions that you're managing with. Our CEO does a remarkable job of seeking out dissenting opinions, recognizing, respecting, and honoring them, particularly in group settings. People see that it's okay to have a dissenting opinion."

Norrington, formerly at eBay, told us, "Mavericks tend to be very passionate about their ideas. The question is how to nurture and cultivate those ideas while ensuring they are living the values. If that doesn't work, then eBay is not the place for them."

Leaders must invoke steel to protect the mavericks and velvet to get the best from them.

Taking Casualties

One of the hardest aspects of triple crown leadership is taking "casualties" in the organization, deciding when people must depart.

In 2002, Tyco (the diversified global manufacturing company and service provider) was a mess. CEO Dennis Kozlowski and CFO Mark Swartz were accused of stealing more than $150 million from the company. They were convicted and sentenced to eight to twenty-five years in prison. The company agreed to pay $2.92 billion in a shareholder class-action settlement.

After the scandal, John Krol joined the board as lead director, and Ed Breen took over as CEO. Most organizations might have switched one or two board members, but Krol and Breen replaced the entire Tyco board, an unprecedented move for such a large public company. They sensed the need for drastic changes, including a board not associated with the previous management.

During the shake-up, 290 of the top executives left Tyco within six weeks. Some of the old managers were "playing to an $8 million a year bonus," recalled Breen, "and doing things that weren't in the long-term interests of the company. You have to get the rotten apples out."

In our experience, there are two main reasons leaders must take casualties. *First*, leaders must remove poor performers or reposition them in jobs better suited to their skills. This entails a judgment call about whether people have been given ample time, resources, and training—and a second chance in most cases—to prove their abilities and work ethic. By not removing or repositioning poor performers, leaders invite poor results and damage the culture. The hope is that these people can be successful elsewhere.

Second, leaders must also remove people who do not fit with or who detract from the organization's culture of character, *even if they are high performers*. See Figure 4.1 for some of the cultural "misfits" we have encountered.

Figure 4.1 **Cultural Misfits Who Must Become Casualties**

- *Ball hogs*, who do not play well with others
- *Bad apples*, who rationalize unethical behavior
- *Bullies*, who intimidate others
- *Unguided missiles*, who attack people
- *Naysayers*, whose negativity infects others
- *Malicious compliers*, who acquiesce to a request knowing negative consequences will result
- *Saboteurs*, who sabotage equipment, projects, and colleagues
- *Destructive achievers*, who hurt others while accomplishing things
- *Toxic personalities*, who poison the culture

Joe Mello of DaVita told us:

> We moved many people out of the organization despite the fact
> they were driving good business, because they didn't have a
> good mission and values score on our assessment matrix. The
> first time, it was a public execution: we had a vice president
> who was excellent on business results but did not live by the
> core values. He thought they were a joke. We terminated him.
> We made it known the reason he was gone was that he didn't
> manage by the mission and values. Once you do that, the mes-
> sage gets around.

Phil Soucy of Modern Technology Solutions told us, "We had
someone heading our contracting activity who was perfect. She
knew her stuff and had tremendous experience, but it was 'her way
or the highway.' She couldn't work with others. I had to let her go."

When Medtronic CEO Bill George learned about illegal behavior by the company's independent distributors in four countries, he
decided to fire them and the Medtronic business chief overseeing
them. "In the old days," he explained, "no one wanted to ask what
the overseas distributors did. Their independence was a shield for
unethical behavior, as long as they signed a statement indicating they
would be ethical. But he knew what they were doing to get the business." When certain colleagues protested, saying those were good
people, hard to replace, and perhaps unaware of the activities, George
didn't buy it. "We'll start over," he said. "We don't tolerate jerks."

When asked about people who commit ethical violations at
Xerox, Ursula Burns puts it simply: "We fire them. It's the clearest
decision we ever have to make."

A few days before we interviewed Yancey Hai, CEO of Delta
Electronics (a leading Taiwan-based manufacturer of power supply,
electronics components, and video display), a purchasing manager
was fired for using his father's factory as a supplier without going
through the proper qualification process.

Too many leaders fail to take the necessary casualties or do it soon enough. They turn a blind eye to inappropriate behavior, often because the individual is a star performer or because the leaders have an aversion to conflict. When they fail to take decisive action, they damage the organization's culture of character and their own moral authority. They reveal a lack of commitment to building an excellent, ethical, and enduring organization.

Leaders must also make judgment calls about when second chances and creative interventions are appropriate. When he was co-captain of his college soccer team, Gregg caught a freshman goalkeeper cheating on a mandatory fitness test and confronted him. After discussions between the player, coach, and co-captains, the player agreed to retake the fitness test, sit on the bench during the first game of the season, and run extra wind sprints and laps for a week. He admitted his mistake and accepted the consequences to stay on the team, and hopefully learned a lesson.

Triple crown leaders recognize that we all make mistakes. The challenge is determining a course of action that is reasonable, fair, and worthy of the triple crown quest.

CHAPTER SUMMARY

Staying stuck in your natural style is insufficient for triple crown leaders. They recognize that there are hard and soft edges to leadership and that one must flex between those edges based on the situation and the people involved but always anchored by the shared values. Velvet empowers other to lead. Steel holds people accountable for results while acting ethically and sustainably. Steel protects mavericks and terminates poor performers and toxic culture-killers.

Practical Applications

1. What steps have you taken to understand your personality profile?
   a. What is it?
   b. Have you communicated it to your colleagues?
2. Do you know the personality profiles of your colleagues?
   a. What are they?
3. To what extent are you getting beyond your natural leadership style when the situation requires it?
4. To what extent are you flexing between steel and velvet?
5. How might you further develop your ability to flex your leadership?
6. When facing an important decision, do you check with colleagues to learn if there is a perceived values conflict? Explain.
7. When you make a tough decision, do you explain how it fits with the organizational colors? What are some examples?
8. Who are the mavericks in your organization?
   a. What can you do to coach, protect, and defend them more?
9. Do you have any poor performers who are being tolerated in the organization?
   a. How might you help them be better performers?
   b. If they cannot improve or be repositioned, how can you help them be successful elsewhere?
10. Do you have any cultural misfits?
    a. How will you approach the situation? Do they warrant a warning or dismissal?

CHAPTER FIVE

STEWARDS

Leadership is your choice, not your title.

—**Stephen R. Covey,** bestselling author
and professor

"I'm getting out. I've had enough."

And so widely respected veterinary surgeon Dr. Gregory Ferraro walked away from his lucrative practice treating racehorses.[1] Outraged about the abuse of steroids, painkillers, and other drugs on the track, he wrote:

> Treatments designed to repair a horse's injuries and to alleviate its suffering are now often used to get the animal out onto the track to compete—to force the animal, like some punch-drunk fighter, to make just one more round. Equine veterinary medicine has been misdirected from the art of healing to the craft of portfolio management, and the business of horse racing is in the process of killing its goose with the golden eggs.[2]

In his 1993 interview with veteran sportswriter William Nack for *Sports Illustrated*, Ferraro said: "This isn't going to make me very popular, but racing should be held accountable for this. I had the biggest practice and the best stables. I could see what was happening and where it was going . . . There's a lot of pressure involved."

As Nack followed racing from the 1950s to the 1990s, he noticed an increasing incidence of breakdowns in which horses suffered injuries during a race, sometimes breaking a leg and falling—at great risk to all the horses and jockeys. Like any good investigative journalist, he pursued the story.

The more Nack talked to people, the more frustrated he became. "I could not get any answers from veterinarians," he told us. "Some of them weren't looking me in the eye when I was talking to them."

Then Nack met Ferraro, who blew the lid on the shady practices in a multibillion-dollar industry. Ferraro's confession was courageous because it came at great personal and professional cost.

Horseracing is not alone in this challenge. (Industry leaders in thoroughbred racing have since made much progress. See the Postscript at the end of this book.) No industry or sector is immune from ethical challenges. We see such issues in business, government, nonprofits, sports, education, the arts, and religions. In many cases, laws and regulations can help, but only so much. Regulations alone are not sufficient. Regulations should be the floor for an organization's conduct, identifying only the minimum required but not the standard sought by leaders. Triple crown leaders accept their fiduciary obligation to place the interests of other stakeholders above their own personal interests. Regulations cannot anticipate all the possible creative workarounds and loopholes, and regulators cannot monitor all the actors. There will always be people who fudge or break the rules when they think they can get away with it, the pressures are great, or the rewards are large enough to risk the chance. Others like to skate close to the edge, seeing how far they can push a legal interpretation or if they can avoid scrutiny from watchdogs.

For decades, racing stewards have monitored thoroughbred races. Serving as onsite regulators, they are essential to race integrity. Using high-speed video cameras to watch and review races, stewards can post an inquiry or objection, and they determine the official results.

Stewards verify the identity of horses (so owners do not swap in "ringers"), validate the pari-mutuel betting machines (which pool bets and then calculate payoff odds after deducting the house's take), inspect race facilities and equipment, watch for obstruction violations during races, and resolve disputes. Stewards levy reprimands, fines, and other penalties. They commission blood samples to screen for banned substances. They are the external regulators of the sport.

As Nack and Ferraro showed in their exposé, external stewards alone cannot monitor everything. It also takes a phalanx of internal stewards who guard the organization's culture of character.

Triple crown organizations distinguish their leadership by:

1. Empowering many leaders throughout the organization
2. Encouraging those leaders to serve as stewards

Below we examine both facets in turn.

THE STABLE

The top leader's job is to get others to lead.
—**Bill George,** former CEO, Medtronic

In thoroughbred racing, some people believe it's all about the horse. But in reality, though the horse is critical, it takes a whole stable to win the Triple Crown.

The jockey can help a horse recover from a starting gate stumble and can pick his way through openings in the field, deciding whether to hug the inside rail amid the scrum of horses or run on the longer, open outside. The jockey makes split-second, life-or-death decisions, signaling the horse with the reins, his legs, and soft entreaties or sharp commands. *Los Angeles Times* sportswriter Jim Murray once remarked, "Bill (the Shoe) Shoemaker didn't ride a horse, he joined them . . . Most riders beat their horses as if they were guards in slave-labor camps. Shoe treated them as if he were asking them to dance."

Trainers must prepare a half-ton animal to run at near full speed for more than a mile within the stress and noise of the track. They must build speed, strength, and endurance, all without being able to talk to their athlete about which muscle is sore. Trainers help owners select the right jockey and decide which races to run, avoid, or scratch at the last minute.

Stable owners decide which horses to buy and breed, which trainers and jockeys to hire, which races to enter, and more. The exercise riders, grooms, farriers (specializing in hoof care), and stable hands play a part in ensuring that the horse and jockey perform their best on race day.

Leonard Lusky, president of Secretariat.com (the official web site of Secretariat), told us, "It took the whole Meadow Farm Stable—Penny's father, Penny, a great trainer, all the exercise riders, the groom who makes the horse comfortable, and the jockey—in addition to the horse's bloodline. It takes all these parts together to win the Triple Crown."

Triple crown leadership is a group performance, enlisting anyone and everyone to lead at times, regardless of the organizational hierarchy.

Most people think about leadership from the top down, conflating leadership with authority. But triple crown leadership works up, down, and sideways. Where would Shakespeare's Henry V be without his "band of brothers"? Where would Lincoln be without his "team of rivals"? Where would the Hobbit Frodo Baggins be without Samwise Gamgee, Merry, Pippin, Gandalf, Aragorn, and others in Tolkien's ring quest?

Triple crown leadership unleashes the extraordinary potential latent in people that languishes in far too many organizations. David Barger, president and CEO of JetBlue Airways (a low-cost U.S. airline), advises, "Be mindful that there is incredible leadership all around you. Go find it. Go tap it. Go mine it." Once activated, such leadership can be transformative for the organization and life-changing for the people involved. Unfortunately, this leadership dynamic is all too rare.

For decades, leadership observers have known that the quest for a brilliant or heroic leader to save our organizations is a false search destined to disappoint. Yet we continue to await such saviors. We focus too much on the traits and skills of the people at the top and their leadership style, whether it be directive, empowering, authentic, transformational, or whatever.

This way of thinking is profoundly limiting and has damaging consequences. Too many workers forgo their own initiative and leadership potential as they defer to their leaders, awaiting direction. Too many leaders step on the initiative and leadership potential of their workers, assuming that, as leaders, they must always have the answers and provide direction.

Many people are reluctant to seize the reins of leadership. Jim Unruh, the turnaround CEO at Unisys, told us, "I was shocked at how very senior executives in the organization wanted me to tell them what to do." Leaders must sometimes go out of their way *not* to lead, thereby enticing others to step up.

Without unleashing the leadership latent in people, organizations underperform. Most organizations tether leadership responsibility to authority positions. Most leadership models focus on CEOs or departmental heads. They treat leadership as if it were an individual sport or an executive aristocracy. They genuflect to the leader's vision. In other words, they focus only on the horse. Triple crown leaders focus on the whole stable, not just the horse. See Figure 5.1 for comments from our interviews.

Figure 5.1 **Leadership from the Whole Stable**

Bob Hatcher, MidCountry Financial Corp.: "If you have to lead everything, you're just aggrandizing yourself. The real world needs empowered project teams, individual leaders, all kinds of folks, to have success in their professions and their lives."

Bill Drayton, Ashoka (a global network of and catalyst for leading social entrepreneurs): "The old organizational model where a few people decide things, and then 'manage' everyone else, just can't function in today's environment . . . A team is characterized by the fact that every single person takes the initiative and is a 'changemaker.'"

Liu Jiren, Neusoft: "Leadership at Neusoft is not single people, not the CEO, COO, or the CFO. We need all the leaders from the bottom up."

Empowering Leaders

Traditional empowerment initiatives meant to counteract the heroic leader fallacy often fall short. In collaboration mode, in which everyone is carefully consulted, the process sometimes gets bogged down as everyone chimes in, with no one driving the process forward. The consensus that emerges is often a pale shadow of what the situation requires, or it is a torturously slow exercise that accomplishes too little too late. Examples of the disastrous "groupthink" that can result are legion, from the Bay of Pigs debacle to space shuttle disasters and recent postwar military occupations.

In another common form of empowerment, leaders delegate some authority and responsibility to their subordinates. But this approach can also backfire, making employees dependent upon dispensations from the leader. Such authority can be revoked under pressure, whipsawing back to directive mode, generating frustration or cynicism.

Triple crown leadership employs a different approach: proactive development of leaders *automatically empowered by the organization's colors and culture of character.* With this approach, the shared values and vision guide the leaders. They operate in a more developed state of empowerment, in which the freedom to act is not granted by a higher authority but is instead expected in the culture and enabled by the colors. People in the organization, regardless of title, have a license to act and lead, as long as they do so in accordance with the organization's colors and culture of character. Armed with such triple crown empowerment—backed with the resources, training, and support they need—they can achieve exceptional results. They feel a visceral connection with the organization, wanting to give it their all.[3]

Triple crown leadership ebbs and flows dynamically from person to person—up, down, and around—depending on the person's knowledge, skills, passion, and the nature and urgency of the challenge at hand. Figure 5.2 captures commentary from our interviews.

Figure 5.2   **License to Lead**

Tony Hsieh, Zappos.com: "As long as they understand our long-term vision and values, it makes more sense for them to be the ones who come up with the ideas."

John Janssen, Greensburg, Kansas: "You need individuals who thrive on the dissemination of the leadership and who buy into the vision and values."

Steven Rothstein, Perkins School for the Blind: "I view my job as not to make the decision myself if I can avoid it, so I'll ask them, 'How does this fit in with our values, our mission, and our plan?'"

Ron Sugar, Northrop Grumman: "Because I have the right people, all smart and capable, with the right values, they usually have better ideas on how to solve problems than I do."

Triple crown leadership requires empowering multiple leaders throughout the organization, using the shared values to guide them. Then they take leadership an even bigger step forward.

STEWARDS[4]

Leadership is all about trusteeship.

—**Dr. Manu Kulkarni,** Siddaganga Institute
of Technology

Triple crown organizations *self-regulate* by fostering stewards in the ranks. These stewards serve as trustees for the organization's quest to be excellent, ethical, and enduring, providing the active checks and balances the enterprise needs to be its best. They may or may not have formal authority, but they do have an irrevocable license to act by the organizational colors and culture of character. They have a responsibility to guard the organization's values and monitor its ethics, evaluating both short- and long-term considerations.

Stewards model the desired behavior of the enterprise. They work *on* the business, not just *in* it. Stewards actively step outside their functional positions to influence how others behave, and they reinforce the colors and culture. In so doing, they give the organization its soul.

A Steward Emerges

Bob recalls a defining moment in the turnaround of Sensormatic (a $1 billion producer of electronic security equipment). As we described in chapter three, the senior staff had carefully formulated new shared values—leadership, integrity, teamwork, and excellence (LITE)—to rebuild a healthy culture. They also articulated their leadership commitments, including how they should act (such as "be a role model" and "treat people with respect").

During the senior staff meetings held every Saturday morning while the company was in crisis, each executive reported progress on critical milestones. One vice president, let's call him Phil, failed to deliver on an important assignment week after week. After a while, Bob had enough and grilled him, shouting that his excuses were unacceptable.

Everybody looked down at the table. It was a short meeting.

Afterward, Bob asked Jerry, another vice president, for input on the meeting. Jerry paused for a while and said, "Well, you sure didn't treat Phil according to our shared values."

While he had to hold Phil accountable, Bob realized that public humiliation had been a poor choice. He reconvened the meeting, apologized to Phil, and asked the team for forgiveness for violating their shared commitments.

That Saturday meeting became a defining moment in the turnaround. It is when the team came together, committing to live by the shared values. In fewer than four years, Sensormatic got back on track, regaining its financial health while operating ethically.

Jerry served as a steward that day. He "spoke truth to power," and his courage emboldened others: *We will protect our new character-based culture. We will operate by the shared values. We will hold each other to a new standard.*

Phil delivered his assignment the next week and became a valued team member.

The self-regulation by internal stewards, buttressed by external rules and regulations, contributes to building an excellent, ethical, and enduring organization. With triple crown leadership, stewardship pervades the organization, defining dramatically new responsibilities for:

1. The board
2. The CEO
3. Managers
4. People without formal authority

We outline those new responsibilities briefly below.

1. New Responsibilities for the Board

Boards are vital stewards, responsible for ensuring the long-term viability and health of companies under their charge for the benefit of current and future owners.

—**Simon Wong,** writing in *McKinsey Quarterly*[5]

Should board members serve as triple crown stewards? Isn't that the purview of the CEO and management team? Surely boards are consumed with the important duties of corporate governance, strategy, risk management, compliance, executive compensation, and succession. Can we realistically expect boards to take on stewardship?

Yes, we must. Boards cannot rely solely on the management team to build an excellent, ethical, and enduring organization. Boards cannot discharge their fiduciary duties without attention to the organization's colors and culture of character. Having a good "tone at the top" is not enough. Boards must set a tone that travels from the top all the way down and around.

Gregg saw this as a young leader when helping to launch the Thomas B. Fordham Foundation (an education reform organization) as vice president for programs. He and his colleagues were gung-ho about many projects and possibilities for the new foundation but soon faced constructive and humbling scrutiny from the board. The board's feedback focused rightly on the implications of program decisions over decades, not just the startup phase (the endurance imperative). The long-term perspective they brought, with wise and firm judgment, was invaluable in building an impactful foundation with a clear and compelling long-term purpose. More than fifteen years later, the foundation is now harvesting the yield of those seeds planted by trustees in the early startup days.

At Tyco, John Krol (outside lead director) and Ed Breen (CEO) replaced the entire board in the wake of epic scandals to regain credibility. "The fall of Tyco," Krol told us, "was brought about by lack of governance and board responsibility."

Krol and Breen involved the new board in reviewing and approving the new values, board principles, and company code of conduct. At first, board members did not understand why they were involved in those matters. "We reviewed one or two of these at every board meeting," Krol says, "until everybody had their say. Then the board owned them."

In the process, they developed four core values for Tyco (integrity, excellence, teamwork, and accountability), along with nine behaviors that support them and twenty-five specific descriptors of those behaviors. Twice a year, all Tyco employees receive a grade based on their performance within this framework. Those grades result in a promotion, bonus, or dismissal. Breen personally reviews the top 200 to 250 people and reviews the appraisals of the top fifty or so with the entire board. Every year, the Tyco board also conducts a self-assessment using these values and behaviors. "The board has to live by these values and principles too," says Krol. "It starts with the board."

Decades ago, the vast majority of an organization's assets were tangible, such as cash, equipment, and buildings. Today, intangible assets, including corporate brand and reputation, often predominate.[6] Boards have a fiduciary obligation to protect these intangibles.

Some boards feel they have fulfilled their duty by complying with Sarbanes–Oxley, Dodd–Frank, and other laws and regulations. Boards should go beyond this check-the-box, compliance mentality to ensure that the organization has a culture of character, evaluating its ethics, sustainability, and impacts.

The board should not manage the culture; that is the responsibility of management. The board should work collaboratively with management to define the desired culture and then monitor how management maintains, protects, and enhances that culture. See Figure 5.3.

A recent forum of the *Harvard Business Review* suggested that boards and CEOs develop a written pact for how their company should be managed, encompassing items such as:

- The way long-term shareholder value will be created

- The role of social responsibility in the firm

- Pay practices that foster long-term value creation

- The circumstances under which public expectations should be lowered to avoid jeopardizing long-term priorities

Figure 5.3   **How Boards Become Triple Crown Stewards**

- Make building an excellent, ethical, and enduring organization the board's top priority.

- Ensure board members are truly independent, primarily outsiders, and not cronies of management.

- Consider triple crown leadership principles in their selection, support, and coaching of the CEO as well as officer selection, appraisals, compensation, and promotions.

- Collaborate on the development and dissemination of the purpose, values, and vision.

- Personally model behavior consistent with the culture of character.

- Monitor the organization's hiring and promotion criteria that the leadership is using to ensure a focus on both head and heart.

- Focus on long-term value creation for all stakeholders while holding officers accountable for their short-term performance commitments.

- Regularly discuss ethics and compliance reports at board meetings with the appropriate management representatives present.

- Make site visits to the organization's facilities to gauge how things are really going.

- Ensure the existence of confidential channels for employees to raise ethics and sustainability concerns, including staff, resources, and mechanisms for addressing them.

- Engage independent monitors to conduct periodic surveys of stakeholders on ethics and sustainability and review the results with the management team.

- Require ethics and culture-of-character training for everyone, including the board.

- Ensure that compensation plans do not have unreasonable goals or outlandish rewards. (Good plans include "clawbacks" for improper behavior, requiring the offending person to pay back the funds.)

For example, a pharmaceutical firm could stipulate that leaders will not address an expected shortfall in earnings growth via cuts in research expenditures, since those investments drive long-term value creation for such firms. The forum recommended communicating such a pact to all stakeholders to inform them about the organization's leadership approach.[7] Sounds like a good start to us.

Some claim it is unrealistic to expect the board to play a meaningful role in fostering stewardship while attending four to eight meetings a year that last less than a day. Maybe that is part of the problem: Is too little time spent on fiduciary oversight and too much passing the buck to management? What might the board take off its agenda to address these issues? Might boards devote more time (perhaps with additional compensation) to address these responsibilities? Such an investment might be well worth the expense given the costs of unethical and unsustainable practices.

The job of building an excellent, ethical, and enduring organization is too important for the board to delegate or ignore. The board must embrace triple crown stewardship.

2. New Responsibilities for the CEO

The best leaders turn their followers into leaders,
realizing that the journey ahead requires many guides.

—James Kouzes and Barry Posner,
leadership authors[8]

CEOs clearly have tremendous influence in their organizations. Triple crown CEOs go beyond the narrow mandate of just getting results. They become the prime stewards of the quest for excellent, ethical, and enduring results and impact. That means working with the board and management team to build the organization's colors and culture of character.

The CEO is the principal leadership steward in an organization. She must have the confidence, trust, and grace to foster triple crown leadership. She must be comfortable enough to give her power away at times and wise enough to know when to retain it. Of course, the CEO and the board must align their stewardship via open communication and proactive conflict resolution.

After First Liberty Bank (the firm CEO Bob Hatcher ran before he started MidCountry Financial) acquired a new firm for its portfolio, Hatcher attended the next staff meeting of the acquired company. "Listening to you," he said after hearing their macho banter, "I think that you're having a contest to see who can use the foulest language. I don't talk like that, and I don't want to hear it. You're going to embarrass yourself and customers and offend women." Dead silence followed. During the break, one of the executives shrugged his shoulders and told Hatcher, "We just want to know what the rules are." CEOs set the tone for an organization on a daily basis.

How can CEOs become triple crown stewards? See Figure 5.4.

3. New Responsibilities for Managers

Leaders don't create followers, they create more leaders.

—**Tom Peters**, leadership author

Officers and managers should also be triple crown stewards. Most employees get their leadership signals from their immediate supervisors, not the CEO or the board. Managers must transcend the boundaries of their job descriptions and embrace the organizational colors and character. In doing so, they amplify the efforts of the board and CEO.

The head of marketing should take responsibility, not just for creating the pricing and promotion strategy, but also for building an excellent, ethical, and enduring organization. The head of information technology must build firewalls around the character-based culture as well as the data networks.

Figure 5.4   **How CEOs Become Triple Crown Stewards**

- Make building an excellent, ethical, and enduring organization the top priority.

- Personally practice and develop triple crown leadership.

- Hire and promote only those officers who embrace their roles as triple crown stewards.

- Elevate ethics officers to high positions and consult with them often.

- Require ethics and culture-of-character training for everyone and participate personally to set an example.

- Develop processes to monitor behavior consistent with the colors, such as ethics refreshers, incident reports, and vendor and partner programs.

- Communicate the linkage between the organization's strategy and its triple crown quest to all stakeholders.

- Ensure a focus on the creation of long-term value for all stakeholders while holding officers accountable for their short-term performance commitments.

- Lead the board and senior management in the development and dissemination of shared purpose, values, and vision (the colors).

- Personally model behavior consistent with the desired culture of character.

- Verify that the confidential channels for employees to raise ethics and sustainability concerns are operational and robust.

- Review the periodic surveys of employees, customers, and vendors on ethics and sustainability, presenting the results to the board, with action plans for improvements.

- Get rid of toxic employees who threaten a culture of character, even if they are star performers.

- Ensure that compensation plans contain reasonable goals and rewards.

- Avoid common traps such as excessive ego and ambition.

North Castle Partners operates in the highly competitive industry of private equity investing. Rejecting the single-minded profit obsession of many of its competitors, North Castle has two bottom lines: first, creating value for its investors and, second, upholding the values of its investment team and of the executives running its portfolio companies. North Castle even enshrined that dual focus into its mission statement: "Value and Values."

CEO Chip Baird told us, "We have a culture in which people are constantly calling others on any breakdowns in our values or operating principles. If you don't have a culture where people are able to call each other, including me, on a breakdown, you quickly devolve to hypocritical values on the wall."

Baird once learned a lesson about this from an unlikely source: someone he fired. The man had sold his company to North Castle in part because he was impressed with the firm's values. On his way out, the man told Baird that it may or may not have been a good business decision to fire him, but it certainly was not handled in a way that was consistent with North Castle's values.

"I realized he was right," Baird told us. He discussed it with his senior management team. "A big part of values leadership," he says, "is being able to talk about your own mistakes" so that everybody can learn from them and avoid making them in the future. In this case, a terminated executive helped him become a better steward.

Sometimes it helps to institutionalize stewardship, ensuring that people and processes reinforce it daily. For example, DaVita has a chief *wisdom* officer who serves as a sounding board for people in the organization, helping them solve the ethical dilemmas that invariably arise. Pitney Bowes has long used an ombudsman to investigate and address complaints, as have many companies and governments worldwide.

Bob recalls his early months as co-CEO of Recognition Equipment, then a $250 million New York Stock Exchange company that produced optical character recognition hardware and software. The company was in a tailspin after accusations about the prior CEO bribing officials for a contract. It was time for the first earnings release under the new management. Bob drafted the press release with a positive a spin on the numbers.

Tom, the general counsel, objected in a meeting, "We can't say that." His concern was about perception, not a legal issue: "I don't care if I'm a voice of one in this room," he declared. "We're in an ethical mess. We have to be squeaky clean."

He was right. As a "voice of one," Tom served as a steward, actively stepping outside his position to influence his boss. Bob toned down the press release.

See Figure 5.5 for ways that managers can become triple crown stewards.

Figure 5.5   How Managers Become Triple Crown Stewards

- Focus the efforts of the management team on building an excellent, ethical, and enduring organization.
- Personally practice and develop triple crown leadership.
- Participate actively in drafting the organization's colors.
- Reinforce the culture of character through daily actions and communications.
- Give staff members a license to act in accordance with the colors, thereby building the organization's leadership dynamic.
- Participate in ethics training and mandate it for their staff.
- Coach employees on ethical and sustainable practices.
- Publicly celebrate ethical and sustainable practices from employees and vendors.
- Speak up and object when they have concerns about proposed policies or actions.
- Blow the whistle outside the chain of command when things have gone too far.

4. New Responsibilities for People Without Authority

*Once the game is over, the king and the pawn
go back into the same box.*

—Italian expression

Anyone can lead, regardless of whether they have formal authority. No matter their title, people can influence others through their behavior, and in triple crown leadership they have a license to act. People without authority become stewards when they go beyond their area of expertise to advance the triple crown quest and protect the culture of character.

Over the years, we have witnessed amazing contributions from many people without authority—including young, aspiring leaders without much experience. They bring fresh energy and perspectives to meetings, challenging assumptions and pushing back when leaders operate unethically or unsustainably. Sometimes they have great instincts and insights but lack the confidence to promote them. When one person speaks up, it empowers these others to do so as well. After a few times, it creates powerful momentum. Over time, it changes the culture.

"At Google," Judy Gilbert, the company's former director of talent and now director of people operations at YouTube (a Google subsidiary), told us, "we encourage everyone to take ownership of something, to make things happen, to pull small groups together, to live out the values." As an example, she cited the Google shuttle program, started by someone without any formal leadership role who just wanted to get as many cars as possible off the road to reduce the company's carbon footprint. Google implemented her program throughout the San Francisco Bay Area.

Triple crown stewards ensure people do the right thing even when the authorities are not looking. Unfortunately, that is not always standard practice in most organizations. According to a recent Corporate Executive Board poll, "nearly half of executive teams fail to receive negative news that is material to firm performance in a timely manner because employees are afraid of being tainted by the bad news," and "only 19 percent of executive teams are always promptly informed of bad news that is material to firm performance."[9] Shocking.

David Novak, CEO of Yum! (the PepsiCo spinout operating fast-food businesses in 117 countries and with over 1.4 million employees), says, "It's a leader's job to create a safe haven that allows people to raise issues without fear of losing their jobs."[10]

Bob once had an exceptional administrative assistant who was a leader among her peers and worked assiduously to help the company in its turnaround. One day, Bob drove to a nearby city and back for a meeting. He noted the mileage and gave her the travel receipts. After a while, she came into his office and said, "I can't submit this." She reminded him that he received a monthly car allowance covering trips like that. "How will it look if you submit this expense?" she asked. "It's just not right."

Without her courage to speak up on an ethical issue, an oversight by the CEO could have sent a troubling message to others. She was a steward who made Bob a better one too.

How can employees become triple crown stewards? See Figure 5.6.

Figure 5.6 **How People Without Authority Become Triple Crown Stewards**

- Focus their efforts on building an excellent, ethical, and enduring organization.
- Participate actively in drafting and defending the organization's colors.
- Model exemplary behavior, reinforcing the culture of character through actions and communications.
- Recognize leadership as a choice and an opportunity.
- Recognize they have an automatic license to act in accordance with the colors—and put it to use.
- Speak up when they see someone violating the values.
- Blow the whistle on ethical breaches when things have gone too far.

CHAPTER SUMMARY

It takes a whole stable, not just the horse, to win. Leadership is a group performance, not a solo act. Triple crown leaders move beyond top-down empowerment dispensations or collaborative groupthink to provide an automatic license to act in accordance with the organizational colors and culture of character. They fill the stable with stewards to develop and defend that culture. Triple crown stewards reduce the risk of dependence on a heroic leader. They make better decisions faster because they are closer to the action, bringing the diversity of multiple perspectives. They boost creativity and innovation, generating a feeling of pride in the organization that reverberates throughout the community, attracting other high performers and customers. Triple crown stewards help the organization run its best race—with honor—reaching heights few thought possible.

Practical Applications

1. To what extent are people in your organization waiting for instructions about what to do?

2. To what extent do people in your organization, regardless of their title, have a license to act as long as they uphold the shared purpose, values, and vision?
   a. How do you contribute to this form of triple crown empowerment?

3. To what extent are you practicing triple crown stewardship, developing and protecting a culture of character?
   a. What more should you do?
   b. Have you gone beyond your formal job description to develop or defend a culture of character? How did it work out?

4. To what extent is your board practicing triple crown stewardship?
   a. What more could it do, and how can you help?

5. To what extent is your CEO a triple crown steward?
   a. What more could he or she do, and how can you help?

6. To what extent is your management team practicing triple crown stewardship?
   a. What more could it do, and how can you help?

7. To what extent are people without formal authority in your organization practicing triple crown stewardship?
   a. How can you help promote a stronger organizational leadership dynamic?

CHAPTER SIX

ALIGNMENT

*When most oarsmen talked about their perfect moments in a boat,
they referred not so much to winning a race, as to the feel of the boat,
all eight oars in the water together, the synchronization almost perfect.
In moments like these, the boat seemed to lift right out of the water.
Oarsmen called that the moment of swing.*

—David Halberstam, journalist and author,
writing in *The Amateurs*

"**Y**ou said you wanted to help the war effort, right?" the general asked.

"That's right, General," Sheldon Coleman replied.

Sheldon Coleman was the elder son of W. C. Coleman, founder of the Coleman Corporation, an outdoor equipment manufacturer. He had gone to Washington seeking the general in charge of procurement for World War II.

"We need a compact field stove," said the general. They were meeting on a train while the general was in transit.

"A field stove?" Coleman asked.

"Yes, a portable unit soldiers can carry in the field. It has to be small and light—no bigger than a milk bottle and less than six pounds. And it has to burn fuels found on the battlefield."

"I see," said Coleman, who was scribbling notes furiously.

"And another thing," the general added.

"More?" Coleman thought.

"It needs to operate in a temperature range of minus-60 to plus-125 degrees Fahrenheit."

"Good Lord!" Coleman thought.

"Do you think you can help us?" the general asked. Coleman said he would see what he and his company could do.

When Coleman returned, his engineers went to work straightaway and drafted some rough designs they thought might work. Coleman called the general and, overreaching some, said they had a product.

"Great," said the general. "We need five thousand in sixty days."

(Gulp.)

Coleman formed cross-functional teams to work around the clock, overlapping by thirty minutes so they could brief the incoming group on progress and issues. In sixty days, the company delivered five thousand G.I. (government issue) Pocket Stoves to the front lines in Africa. All told, Coleman produced more than a million for war use.

Tim Daniel, the former vice president of special markets at Coleman Corporation, shared this story with us (which we have dramatized). He told us:

The G.I. Pocket Stove went on to become one of the most trea-
sured items of the American soldier. It provided power to cook
meals, heat in foxholes, and boiled water to drink and shave. It
was top stakes in poker games. On long hikes, soldiers would
discard heavy gear, but never a Pocket Stove. Ernie Pyle, the
celebrated journalist, said that the two most important non-
combat items of World War II were the Jeep and the G.I. Pocket
Stove. To me, this was flow in its greatest sense: committing to
an almost-impossible task, redesigning your business structure
to meet a deadline, and then executing.

Postscript: Remember the tornado that hit Greensburg, Kansas,
described in chapter three? In response, Coleman Corporation
shipped a truckload of lanterns, shelters, coolers, and sleeping bags to
town residents pro bono. Tim Daniel coordinated the effort.

FLOW

What delight to back the flying steed . . . I sit him now!
He takes away my breath! He makes me reel!
I touch not earth—I see not—hear not.
All is ecstasy of motion!

—**James Sheridan Knowles,** Irish playwright,
from *The Love-Chase*

During World War II, the Coleman Corporation worked in "flow."
As we said at the outset of this book, Ron Turcotte and Secretariat
raced in flow at the Belmont Stakes in 1973, demolishing the field by
thirty-one lengths to claim the Triple Crown.

These moments of peak performance occur across domains, from
sports and the arts to programming and chess. Improvisational jazz
musicians get lost "in the groove." Athletes describe it as being "in
the zone." We know that organizations can also achieve flow. How
do we know? We have experienced it.

Flow changes everything. Once you experience flow, you are changed forever, hooked for life on a different way of working. After jockey Red Pollard's come-back ride aboard Seabiscuit at the famous "hundred grander" at Santa Anita, a spectator said Pollard looked like "a man who temporarily had visited Olympus and still was no longer for this world."[1]

Mihaly Csikszentmihalyi, a psychology professor at Claremont Graduate University, has dedicated much of his life to studying flow. The term comes from his interviews with people who have moved into a state of "optimal experience." He called it flow because many of them described it as if a rushing current of water carried them along. In flow, he says, we feel "a sense of exhilaration, a deep sense of enjoyment that is long cherished and that becomes a landmark in memory for what life should be like. This is what we mean by *optimal experience*."[2]

Flow is a state of almost effortless attention and peak performance. Studies have shown that, in flow, heart rate and blood pressure actually decrease, and facial muscles relax.[3] On top of a charging thoroughbred, wrote English jockey Steve Donoghue, "I am so completely in the race that I forget the crowds. My horse and I talk together. We don't hear anyone else."[4]

According to Csikszentmihalyi, a number of factors contribute to flow: deep concentration, focus on the present, loss of ego, clear goals, direct and immediate feedback, a sense of personal control over the task, and a balance between the challenge of the task and one's skills. Flow entails so much absorption in the activity that it alters one's sense of time: hours can pass but feel like minutes.

Flow can occur in individuals and groups, but it is rare and fleeting. No organization can sustain flow continuously. Like ocean tides, flow waxes and wanes. With triple crown leadership, when leaders are employing all five practices described in this book, flow occurs more often and lasts longer.

Wild Horses

Unfortunately, most organizations never experience flow. In our experience, far too many organizations are dysfunctional—some only moderately, others pathologically. They are like a pack of wild horses with stallions, fillies, mavericks, old war horses, and strays charging off, milling around, grazing for a while, and then suddenly racing off again in another direction for no apparent reason.

In many organizations, though people work hard, they accomplish little because they are disconnected and disjointed in their efforts, unclear about how their work fits into the bigger picture. People are stymied by lack of clarity, conflicting priorities, and poor follow-up. This condition leads to frustration, cynicism, and lower performance. Sound familiar?

Unfortunately, dysfunction is both widespread and costly. According to a 2010 Booz and Company survey of more than 1,800 executives, 64 percent say their biggest frustration factor is "having too many conflicting priorities." They report that their biggest challenges are "ensuring that day-to-day decisions are in line with the strategy" and "allocating resources in a way that really supports the strategy." Such organizations pay an "incoherence penalty," with only 13 percent of organizations sampled meeting the researchers' standard of coherence. Companies with more coherence perform better.[5]

According to Gallup's Employee Engagement Index, only 29 percent of employees are actively engaged in the organization's work, 54 percent are neutral, and 17 percent are actively disengaged.[6] Many employees "check out" mentally. The work avoidance schemes they employ are legion, including procrastinating, complaining, muttering, wallowing, and scapegoating. They use "happy talk," avoid reality, and recycle old excuses (for example, "If we only had more resources," or "We tried that before, and it didn't work"). Yet these same people go home and successfully manage a major home remodeling, raise large sums for charity, or serve effectively on a community board.

Author Patrick Lencioni describes what he calls "the five dysfunctions of a team": absence of trust, fear of conflict, lack of commitment, avoidance of accountability, and inattention to results.[7] The consequences can be dire, including lack of follow-up, constantly changing priorities, lack of innovation, departments in silos, lack of teamwork, destructive internal competition, poor results, and unethical practices, all the bane of the triple crown quest. It is sad that so many people work in dysfunctional organizations. Fortunately, there is a remedy.

ALIGNMENT

> *Every bird can fly faster in formation than they can alone.*
> —**Diane Sawyer,** television journalist

The final practice in building a triple crown organization is alignment. If goals are not clear, different people will bring different expectations and unintentionally work at cross-purposes. If people do not see how their work fits into the organizational context, they may inadvertently do things that are disruptive or that do not help the enterprise advance its real aims. If they do not receive feedback on their efforts, they will continue to do the wrong things.

Alignment builds trust between people, and trust helps organizations speed up dramatically, according to author Stephen M. R. Covey in his book *The Speed of Trust*: "When trust is high," he writes, "the dividend you receive is like a performance multiplier, elevating and improving every dimension of your organization and your life . . . In a company, high trust materially improves communication, collaboration, execution, innovation, strategy, engagement, partnering, and relationships with all stakeholders."[8]

The benefits of alignment are numerous. Alignment:

- Clarifies the elements for success

- Focuses people

- Eliminates unessential work

- Connects people and departments

- Builds trust

- Provides continual feedback

- Motivates people

- Fosters teamwork

- Instills discipline

- Builds buy-in and commitment

- Unleashes talent

- Reinforces the organizational colors and culture of character

- Facilitates stewardship

- Creates the conditions for flow

Triple crown leaders align their enterprise for excellent, ethical, and enduring results. As Bill George said in *Authentic Leadership,* "An organization can be both values-centered and performance-driven. The key is aligning the organization's values and performance objectives." Tony Hsieh, CEO of Zappos.com, told us, "My role is to try to get everyone in the organization aligned."

Let's look at another example and then specific steps for how to align an enterprise.

The Pathfinder

Bob first witnessed the power of alignment and flow with the Pathfinder team at Monarch Marking Systems in the 1980s. Retailers had just adopted bar codes—a strategic threat to Monarch's price-marking equipment. In response, Monarch decided to reinvent itself and became a bar code printer company.

Monarch had just introduced a large, rather clunky, bar code printer, the size of a small desk, and the next logical step was to develop a smaller, tabletop version. Monarch's vice president of research and design, Bud Klein, suggested the company outsource the development of the tabletop version and leapfrog the competition by developing the world's first handheld bar code printer. Such an endeavor was risky and unheard of. The company would need new ceramic material and electronics, along with miniaturized computer processors. Many of the technologies were only available experimentally in Japan.

At the time, the development cycle for a product of such complexity was three to four years. Bud proposed a "skunk works" in which the company would radically empower a cross-functional team of committed volunteers to launch this breakthrough product in eighteen months to set the industry standard.[9] If the team botched it, Monarch risked losing its industry leadership in price-marking machines.

Monarch's management relieved the volunteer team members of all other work and administrative tasks, promised them their old jobs back regardless of the results, located them in special quarters, and gave them clear goals in this priority order:

1. Operate by the company's newly defined shared values (remember the five a.m. meeting in the cafeteria described in chapter three?)
2. Launch in eighteen months
3. With certain defined functionality
4. For a targeted unit cost
5. At a specified total program cost

Bob delegated to the team *all* his CEO authority to spend, sign contracts, and hire and fire. The members of the team only had to meet the goals while operating by the shared values. It was the biggest challenge of their careers, a real moon shot, and the buzz on the team was electric. The team members were totally aligned and focused, and they threw themselves into their work.

Soon operating in flow under a young engineering manager, Jim Vanderpool, they launched the Pathfinder on schedule and within budget. It became one of the most successful products in the company's history, still sold in updated versions today and foreshadowing today's wave of computerized mobile devices.

At the end of the project, none of the members of the Pathfinder team wanted to return to their old job or ways of working. Back to business as usual? No way. They had experienced flow. So Bob and his staff reinvented Monarch, deploying such empowered skunk works teams whenever possible.

At other companies Bob subsequently led, many of the successes came from committed people working in alignment, accomplishing incredible results quickly, often achieving flow: Sensormatic's Puerto Rico manufacturing plant moved from chaos to the Shingo Prize for Excellence in Manufacturing in four years; Pitney Bowes reduced defect rates from 20 percent to 2 percent in four years, winning the Malcolm Baldrige Award for Quality in Connecticut.

Below we examine the specific steps in the "Alignment Model," a framework we developed that we have employed successfully with numerous companies and nonprofit organizations.

THE ALIGNMENT MODEL

The Alignment Model contains ten steps in three phases. See Figure 6.1.

Figure 6.1 **The Alignment Model**

Purpose	Aspirational (long term)
Values	
Vision	
Goals	Strategic (medium term)
Strategy	
People	
Structure	
Processes	Execution (short term)
Action Plans	
Communication Loops	

We briefly describe each step below. Again, let's not get hung up on the semantics of the words. What some people call "mission," we call "purpose." It is the concepts that count, not the terms.

  I. *Aspirational alignment.* Addresses the three *long-term* elements of purpose, values, and vision (the colors), which we covered in chapter three. This process should be highly visible among all key stakeholders, internal and external.

    1. *Purpose.* Purpose addresses why an organization exists, its raison d'être. People hunger to know that their efforts are worthwhile, that they are working on something significant. The purpose statement should be short, memorable, and inspiring.

    2. *Values.* Values are the norms that guide behavior in the organization, the standards for how people should behave. Everyone in the organization should know them and be responsible for upholding them.

    3. *Vision.* The vision provides a clear and compelling picture of what an organization aspires to achieve over a decade or so. The vision should describe what success looks and feels like.

  II. *Strategic alignment.* Addresses the *medium-term* issues of goals, strategy, people, and structure. They are focused primarily on internal stakeholders or are shared only with deep-relationship external stakeholders.

    4. *Goals.* Goals are the few critical aims sought by the whole enterprise—the key objectives or targets. They are expressed as results (ends), not how to achieve them (means): for example, achieve a 35 percent market share with product X by the end of 2015. They should cover a medium-term timeframe—no more than three years. Leaders should ensure that goals are clear, measurable, prioritized, and challenging but achievable.[10] While some goals may be organizationwide (for example,

zero ethical violations), it is useful to set goals for major
stakeholder groups, such as one to two each for customers, employees, shareholders, and the community.

5. **Strategy.** In essence, strategy addresses *how* to achieve
the desired goals in light of opposing pressures and
existing resources. It is the master plan that binds the
diverse activities of a group together in the fray of
countless tactical decisions. The strategy should include
the several prioritized, major initiatives on how to
achieve the goals in ways that are different from or
executed better than those of competitors. It should be
based on financial projections, a risk assessment, and a
sensitivity analysis, including a sober assessment of the
likelihood of achieving the specified goals. The strategic planning process can incorporate a range of existing
tools and methodologies, from "blue ocean strategy"
and Michael Porter's "five forces" to critical success
factors, gap analysis, competitive benchmarking, and
more.

In our view, everybody in the organization should
receive a strategy summary.[11] How can employees be
aligned if they do not know the high-level plan to
achieve the goals? If they do not know the plan, they
are relegated to guesswork.

6. **People.** This step specifies who should be involved
in the enterprise and what types of people should be
sought for key positions. It should include the hard
skills, knowledge, and capabilities required, as well as
the personal characteristics, fit with the organization's
culture, and emotional intelligence desired. (See chapter two for more details.)

7. **Structure.** The structure of the organization must
be appropriate to achieve the purpose, vision, goals,
and strategy. Structure involves choosing the proper

organizational form for the enterprise: centralized or decentralized; business units, functional departments (marketing, manufacturing, and the like), geographical, or a matrix organization (pooling people with similar skills for work assignments); board committees; and more. How many layers should there be in the organization? How many levels of management between first-line workers and the CEO? What spans of control should leaders have, and what is the ideal number of direct reports for a manager? What are the respective roles and responsibilities of the board versus the CEO and management, and in what areas must they collaborate or seek approval? Structure also specifies what the venture does internally versus contracting externally. Optimally, it should involve the use of temporary rapid–action teams (such as skunk works) for targeted opportunities.

III. *Execution alignment.* Covers the *short-term* elements to move beyond plans and determine how to get things done.

   8. *Processes.* These are the necessary processes to guide the work, including standards, systems, and policies. They might include processes for people (for example, recruitment, development, evaluation, and succession); accounting and financial controls; product development (such as prototyping and usability testing); manufacturing (for example, statistical process controls); ethics monitoring and sustainability reporting; and even the board (such as board governance guidelines and committee charters). These processes—when handled well and without red tape—keep actions within critical boundaries, promoting efficiency, transparency, and coordination.

   9. *Action plans.* These are the several major, prioritized, short-term actions that must be taken at each level to

accomplish important, nonroutine tasks. They document *who will do what by when,* laying down accountability markers. They are traceable to a schedule, ideally with a budget estimate, and they are unique for each person or unit. "Mary will update the product X promotional campaign by September 30, keeping campaign costs to a budget of $Y." As actions are accomplished or become obsolete, new ones replace them.

10. ***Communication loops.*** Alignment requires tracking and reporting metrics on a regular schedule. Key metrics reported at specified intervals will bring problems to the surface. The metrics should be clear, simple, and accessible and be under the control or substantial influence of the relevant department or person. Using these communication loops, leaders should make adjustments based on market feedback and data, modifying approaches and pivoting business models until they find what works best. Leaders should connect these metrics to performance appraisals, incentive pay, recognition, discipline, and promotions. Such reinforcement is essential for alignment. These metrics and feedback loops give the alignment process teeth. Without accountability, alignment fizzles.

Metrics in Action

Marks and Spencer, the United Kingdom–based global retailer, has a notable approach for communicating its alignment metrics. Company leaders placed a giant electronic ticker in their headquarters' lobby that provides real-time updates on the company's sustainability progress (for example, combating climate change, reducing waste, using sustainable raw materials, trading ethically, and promoting healthier lifestyles).[12] Launched in 2007, Marks and Spencer's "Plan A" currently entails 180 targets for 2015. (There is no "Plan B"—now that's commitment.) The company's overarching goal is to become the world's most sustainable major retailer.

Each alignment step should link with the other steps. The steps should cohere and give organizations what Tyco's Ed Breen calls "operating rhythm," a drumbeat, a cadence of execution that drives the flywheel effect that Jim Collins described in *Good to Great*.

Other existing models and frameworks, such as the McKinsey 7S Framework and the Balanced Scorecard, can help with alignment.[13] Some organizations have created their own versions.

Creating Alignment in a Turnaround

In 2004, the board of Quovadx (a thousand-employee software company, now part of Lawson, a provider of enterprise resource planning solutions) recruited Harvey Wagner as interim CEO to turn the company around. Accused of fraud and running out of cash, the company was in a tailspin. Wagner was committed to an ethical transformation of Quovadx. He told us, "I will go to the board and tell them we had no sales this month rather than have one sale go out that is not right."

Wagner and his team placed their own alignment system on the company Intranet. They called it "VOGI" for vision, objectives, goals, and initiatives. Everyone in the company could see what the individual initiatives were, how they fit together, who was on schedule, and who was not. When new employees arrived, they received a VOGI packet explaining it all.

Quovadx also developed "Rights and Obligations" for all employees as a way to infuse the VOGI responsibilities into its culture. See the following table.

Sample Quovadx Rights and Obligations

Your Rights	Your Obligations
Raise issues and concerns	Offer solutions
Participate in the debate	Support team decision
Make mistakes	Use good judgment
Ask for help	Provide help
Be respected	Show respect

Before long, employees were asking each other "How's your VOGI?" "Everybody was involved in a VOGI," says Wagner. "We were able to bend the focus to what was important all the way up the line within the company and not have people running around doing things that were not specifically agreed to." Quovadx became aligned.

Before its 2007 sale to a private equity firm, Wagner and his team had completely revitalized Quovadx, with $84 million in revenue and $50 million in cash.

HOW TO ALIGN AN ORGANIZATION

Building a visionary company requires 1 percent vision and 99 percent alignment . . . Creating alignment may be your most important work.
—**Jim Collins and Jerry Porras**[14]

In our experience, many leaders do not know how to create an aligned organization. They do parts of alignment, but not all the steps; or they do them top-down without the collaboration necessary to refine and inculcate them into the organization's DNA.

There is a big difference between completing an alignment exercise at a one-shot retreat and actually creating an aligned organization, between having a purpose statement and being purpose driven, between having values and upholding them when the pressure is on, between saying you are vying for the triple crown and actually aligning the enterprise to achieve it.

Alignment is easy to understand, but hard to create and maintain. Lencioni says it is a matter of "embracing common sense with uncommon levels of discipline and persistence."[15] In our experience, many leaders try it only episodically, moving in fits and starts. The vision or values gather dust. Leaders do not share the strategy summary with employees. The goals do not cohere across departments. There are no consequences for missed deadlines. There is no effective follow-up system or operating rhythm.

There are many causes of alignment breakdowns: lack of commitment, focus on wordsmithing documents instead of generating action, abandonment of the process midstream (usually to put out fires, a symptom of misalignment), and lack of discipline and accountability.

How do triple crown leaders shepherd the alignment process? Below are three keys.

Alignment Must Be Collaborative

Alignment requires extensive, multidirectional communication, with deep listening and dialogue, not edicts from the top. Alignment is a back-and-forth, up, down, and sideways leadership process that should touch everyone in the organization, even some outside stakeholders on some steps. A coalition of enthusiastic volunteers representing a cross section of the organization can shepherd the process with support from top leaders and assistance from outside facilitators, if desired.

The leaders must ensure that the process taps into the tremendous capabilities of the people in the enterprise. Alignment is a "we" process, not an "I" process. Triple crown leadership is a group performance. An autocratic leader may get faster action but will not tap into the creativity and commitment of the people. Alignment takes time and patience. It can be messy and frustrating, requiring many midcourse corrections.

The first time, it can take three to twelve months to move through all the alignment steps, depending on the organization and the severity of its issues. It takes time for ideas to simmer, for feedback to percolate from all parts of the organization, and for consensus and buy-in to develop. Recognize that alignment is an ongoing process, not a one-shot fix.

Caution: Nowadays, many people are overloaded with meetings, and the alignment process requires even more meetings. Our experience is that with smart planning, effective meeting facilitation, and focused work between meetings, these sessions can move briskly. Handled well, the time spent aligning the enterprise will pay big dividends.

Alignment Starts Where You Are and Cascades

Where to start alignment depends on where the organization is at the time. Organizations in crisis cannot afford three-day retreats to ponder long-term issues. First, they must stop the bleeding.

If the organization is stable but needs to get reenergized or bring disparate elements together, then starting with a reexamination of purpose, values, and vision is logical, beginning with the board and senior management team, with drafts cascading out and around for input. A vice president should not be asked to draft goals for next year without knowing what the CEO's goals are. Aligned goals require coordination and transparency, not guesswork. This simple cascading step changes the dynamic between the boss and employee, because the employee can also see whether the boss is meeting the goals. Such openness promotes teamwork and trust.

Cascading occurs at retreats and meetings, both in person and virtual. Leaders should use social media and other technologies to facilitate and scale the ongoing conversation, especially in large enterprises.

Alignment should occur at multiple levels: enterprisewide, departmental, team, and individual. Each group can benefit from its own alignment process, even with its own departmental purpose, values, and vision, as long as the purpose, values, and vision cohere with the enterprisewide statements. Each individual's goals, strategies, and action plans should map to those of the relevant team, and from the team to the department, all the way up to the enterprise. See Figure 6.2.

Alignment Must Be Flexible

Leaders must strike a reasonable balance with the Alignment Model. Taken too far, the process can squelch innovation and entrepreneurship, chasing away the organization's mavericks, from whom breakthrough ideas often emerge. Leaders should build leeway and innovation mechanisms into the process to help the venture stay nimble and responsive to changing circumstances.

Figure 6.2   **The Alignment Cascade**

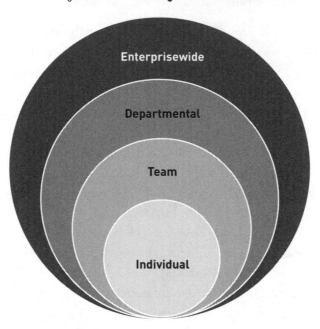

For example, 3M (the global conglomerate known for its long track record of innovation) has used several powerful "intrapreneurial" mechanisms to great effect. 3M requires that each division generate 30 percent of its sales from products introduced in the past five years, ensuring the company will continually refresh its product line and avoid complacency. In the 1930s, it pioneered the "15 percent rule," allowing employees to work on projects of their own choosing, resulting in breakthroughs like Scotch tape and Post-it notes. Others, including Google, have adopted this approach, boosting it to 20 percent. 3M also deploys "Genesis Grants," a competitive internal venture capital fund for innovators. Many such mechanisms can be used to encourage flexibility.

Bear in mind that alignment in and of itself does not work magic. With a flawed strategy or poor execution, even an aligned organization will falter. Also, organizations can align toward the wrong things. For example, a company totally aligned on meeting earnings targets each quarter to prop up its share price may very well achieve that, but perhaps by cutting corners, destroying long-term share-holder value, and utilizing unsustainable practices. Aligning to the three Es is essential.

Alignment Inside and Out

Alignment is not solely an internal endeavor. The alignment process should include external stakeholders such as customers, vendors, partners, shareholders, and the community. External alignment requires open communication, transparency, integrity, trust, and mutual accountability.

Bob recalls working years ago at the Olga Corporation, a women's apparel company. Senior management scheduled annual meetings with their senior counterparts at major retailer clients like Saks Fifth Avenue. Together, they would review progress on the mutual plans and commitments they had set the prior year. For example, the customer might have committed to carry certain products and hold a certain number of promotions. Olga might have committed to introduce some exclusive products for the client and generate a targeted gross profit per square foot of store space. After discussing the results and identifying issues, brainstorming along the way, they then agreed to new annual goals, resulting in powerful customer-vendor collaboration and alignment.

ALIGNMENT IN ACTION AT PERKINS SCHOOL FOR THE BLIND

Steven Rothstein, president of Perkins School for the Blind, told us how alignment helped to modernize and reenergize that historic institution. Perkins was founded in 1829 as the first school for the blind in the United States and once served Helen Keller.

When Rothstein arrived in 2002, some people had worked there for decades without such basics as a performance review. The top twenty managers had never seen their budgets.

Rothstein and his team launched an alignment process, involving hundreds of people. They sent a questionnaire to every employee, student, parent, trustee, and donor. They sent out drafts of their works in progress and held meetings to discuss them, revising drafts based on feedback. They updated their mission statement and strategic plan. Rothstein told us: "It used to be that people would ask a question and not follow up. We now have a system of reporting back and deadlines. I believe that at least half of management is measurement. Now they get monthly numbers. They know the numbers."

The leaders at Perkins now footnote every board meeting agenda item to the relevant part of the strategic plan. All slides in employee town hall meetings indicate where they fit in the strategic plan.

Asked about the keys to the process, Rothstein says, "It's about having a clear vision, finding ways to bring out the talents in those around you around a common set of goals, having a clear strategic plan, seeing how tactical decisions fit in, having the right tools, and getting information on a monthly basis in a form you understand."

Marty Linsky, who teaches leadership at Harvard's Kennedy School of Government, described Perkins to us: "Rothstein took an organization that had barely left the nineteenth century and turned it into the signature organization in the world in services to the blind. He is in my managerial hall of fame. He has completely changed the internal culture, moved the organization into services and places it had never even imagined, and increased the budget and fund-raising exponentially."

Today, Perkins operates in more than sixty countries, serving about two hundred thousand people annually, with revenue of $70 million and a staff of 750. Perkins offers free audio, Braille and large-print books, and hundreds of newspapers by phone. The operations are complex, including a school, early intervention program, library, teacher-training initiatives, publishing house, manufacturing division, technology division, and special services for the elderly. Rothstein told us:

> It takes a tireless focus on excellence. For us, that means if five
> million children didn't go to school today because they are

blind, then our work isn't done. That is inexcusable, morally unforgivable. We change children's lives, one at a time and country by country. I try not to think too much about what people are going to say next week, but instead how will this fit in over the long term. There will be people at the 200th and the 250th anniversary of Perkins looking back on our decisions.

Rothstein described his alignment work to us: "It was so exciting, so energizing, so inspiring, and rewarding." Perkins, while still a work in progress, is advancing on its quest to build an excellent, ethical, and enduring organization.

CHAPTER SUMMARY

With triple crown leadership, organizations can race in flow, achieving peak performance. To get there, they run on an alignment track. They doggedly pursue alignment in their quest for the triple crown.

Alignment is a collaborative leadership process, moving from the long term of why the organization exists to the short term of who will do what by when. Alignment is not a one-shot fix; it is a way of coalescing the people in an organization to work together in a powerful way. While there are several alignment mechanisms, we recommend an approach that involves purpose, values, vision, goals, strategy, people, structure, processes, action plans, and communication loops. Alignment should be collaborative, cascaded, and flexible.

Alignment is our fifth leadership practice for building excellent, ethical, and enduring organizations. All five practices are interrelated: people with character and emotional intelligence embrace the organization's colors, defend them with steel, and use velvet to empower leadership and foster stewardship, all the while aligning themselves for the triple crown quest.

Practical Applications

1. To what extent is your organization aligned?
2. Your department?
3. Your team?
4. To what extent is there coherence between the organization's short-term activities and long-term aims?
5. What are the few key goals your organization has set for the entire enterprise and for each major stakeholder?
6. Has the organization distributed a strategy summary without revealing confidential information?
7. Do you know your boss's goals for this year?
8. Do you and your colleagues have clear plans for who will do what by when?
   a. What more can you do?
9. To what extent does your organization track and report metrics on a regular schedule?
   a. What more can you do?
10. Does your organization have effective communication loops that result in needed changes?
    a. What more can you do?
11. What are the most important things you should do today to align your organization?
12. Your team?

PART TWO

LEADERSHIP IN ACTION

CHAPTER SEVEN

BREAKDOWNS

*The world breaks everyone and afterward
many are strong at the broken places.*

—**Ernest Hemingway,** American novelist,
in *A Farewell to Arms*

ntil that day, she was perfect.

Regal and poised, with a presence people could sense, she was a stunner. Mouths dropped when she appeared. She was tall and graceful, her body sculpted, and her eyes twinkled with curiosity and mischief. Her owners, Stuart and Barbara Janney, and her trainer, the terse Frank Whiteley, loved her deeply and cared for her every need.

Ruffian had run ten races and won them all. Once out of the gate, she *always led* the field. She set or equaled eight records in her first ten races. She had taken the racing world by storm.[1]

Though many consider Secretariat the greatest thoroughbred ever, even his trainer, Lucien Laurin, was enamored with Ruffian: "As God is my judge," he said, "she's better than Secretariat was when he was a two-year-old." Ruffian had swept the Filly Triple Crown.[2] Her time at the Spinaway Stakes was the fastest in history for any two-year-old, colt or filly, including Man o' War and Secretariat.

But the public wanted more. It was 1975, shortly after the infamous Bobby Riggs versus Billy Jean King "battle of the sexes" in tennis. Three different horses had won the Kentucky Derby, Preakness, and Belmont Stakes. When promoters wanted to run all three against each other, the public clamored to add the filly Ruffian against the three colts.

But it was not to be. Avatar, the Belmont Stakes winner, had been shipped to California to race. Then the owner of Master Derby, the Preakness winner, was paid $50,000 to withdraw so there would be a one-on-one match race between Ruffian and Foolish Pleasure, the Kentucky Derby winner. It was girl against boy, head to head.

The July 6 race offered what was then the largest purse for any single event in the history of thoroughbred racing. Analysts expected sixteen to twenty million television viewers.

Jockey Jacinto Vasquez had ridden Foolish Pleasure to victory in the Derby and to second place in the Preakness and Belmont Stakes. But he thought Ruffian was the better horse, and so he chose to ride her in the match race.

Fifty thousand fans crowded Belmont Park. The track was hard and fast. When the starting bell clanged, Ruffian wasn't ready and crashed into the side of the starting gate. Within a few steps, though, she had taken the lead, pounding the track with her trademark powerful lunges that ate up the turf.

But forty-five seconds into the race, the jockeys heard a "loud snap," recounted sports journalist William Nack, "like a dead stick cracking in two."

"Ruffian has broken down!" the announcer shouted. Vasquez tried to pull her up but couldn't. She kept running, trying to finish the race. She ran another fifty yards on a broken ankle, severely compounding the injury. Vasquez leaped from the mount and held Ruffian's leg while the ambulance raced to the scene.

Veterinarians placed a temporary cast on her leg and rushed her into emergency surgery, where she twice flat-lined on the monitor, was revived, and then thrashed around in so much pain and confusion that she further damaged her legs. Mercifully, after hours spent trying desperately to save her, and with the heartbroken owners' and trainer's permission to prevent further pain, the veterinarians euthanized her.

Ruffian was buried the next day in a solemn ceremony near the flagpole at Belmont Park, where she had lived and trained during her tragically short but glorious career, her nose pointed toward the finish line, once again in the lead.[3]

PERSONAL BREAKDOWNS

Take rest; a field that has rested gives a bountiful crop.
—**Ovid,** Roman poet

Just as thoroughbreds can break down from a punishing racing schedule, so too can leaders—even the heartiest. Some leaders have frenetic schedules of meetings and travel or face constant stress and pressure, sometimes aggravated by crisis. As the effects accumulate over time, exhaustion sets in. Though many leaders prefer to just "suck it up" and ignore the risks, those who want to thrive and endure recognize the potential for damaging consequences to their leadership, including losing their moorings, making rash decisions, and prejudging situations. Our interviews confirmed the importance of protecting physical, mental, and emotional health in triple crown leadership. Many of the organizations in our interview set make robust investments in their employees' health and personal development.

As Steven Rothstein at the Perkins School for the Blind told us, "If the leader doesn't take care of himself or herself, it's very difficult to lead other people." Dr. M. N. Channabasappa, director of the Siddaganga Institute of Technology (a leading engineering college in India), told us, "Most of our leaders routinely go through yoga and meditation exercises and participate in social service every week."

Leaders need sufficient sleep, regular exercise, a healthy diet, and places of physical and mental sanctuary. For years, Bob returned from his morning runs feeling physically refreshed and teeming with creative ideas.

Triple crown leadership begins with leading ourselves. Failure to do so leads to problems with all three legs of the triple crown: excellent, in terms of performance problems; ethical, with lapses in judgment and impulsive compromises; and enduring, with an unsustainable pace that wreaks havoc on our health, judgment, and relationships. We agree with author Patricia Aburdene, who said, "The cornerstone of effective leadership is self-mastery." Leaders seeking to avoid organizational breakdowns should start by leading themselves.

ORGANIZATIONAL BREAKDOWNS

Personal leadership is necessary but not sufficient in avoiding organizational breakdowns. In today's volatile global environment, such organizational breakdowns are fairly common. Sometimes a breakdown is a quiet affair with an orderly dissolution of assets. Other times it is a seismic crash with embarrassing headlines, prison sentences, and painful ripple effects. Sometimes an organization rises to the top of its industry and then slowly falls back in the field.

In any list of great organizations, some are likely to descend from great to grim. Witness the success studies cited over the years, with Atari and Wang on the *In Search of Excellence* list and with Fannie Mae and Circuit City on the *Good to Great* list—all since humbled or bankrupted. Witness the demise of financial stars like MF Global (where did that billion dollars of customer funds go?), Galleon Group (the hedge fund whose CEO, Raj Rajaratnam, was convicted of insider trading), AIG, and Lehman Brothers. Even the vaunted Goldman Sachs has attracted recent criticism, as has its former director Raj Gupta, who was linked to the Galleon scandal.

General Electric, founded in 1892, has long been an exemplar company, admired for its financial performance, its leadership development, and its large and influential "Ecomagination" sustainability initiatives. Yet over the past ten years, GE's stock performance has been lagging, trading at half its 2002 level in 2011; and its return on assets has lagged far behind that of its peer group. A large, diverse company operating in competitive fields in many challenging countries, GE has focused on excellence and ethics, as Ben Heineman, Jr., relates in *High Performance with High Integrity*. But in recent years, GE has not achieved excellent financial results.

Of course, breakdowns are not limited to the commercial sector. According to Princeton University president Shirley Tilghman:

> In the early 1980s, Princeton had arguably the best biochemistry department in the world, just stunningly good. But within five years, 90 percent of the faculty in the department had left the university. Excellence is fragile. We should never take it for granted. We should be constantly vigilant in making sure that something that is really good doesn't lose its edge . . . It required a $35 million investment to re-create that department. Luckily, it succeeded, but it is an example of how quickly something can get lost.

Even as we aim high, we cannot achieve perfection. Over the course of their racing careers, the Triple Crown–winning thoroughbreds won less than two-thirds of the time. Many were scratched from races when they were not 100 percent healthy or the track conditions were not favorable to their style.[4]

Like Ruffian, the filly Zenyatta had long limbs and sculpted muscles. She won a record-breaking nineteen consecutive starts. Between 2008 and 2010, her purses exceeded $7 million, making her the all-time North American female money earner. In 2009, she was runner-up to Serena Williams for the Associated Press Female Athlete of the Year. In 2010, she was American Horse of the Year. Yet in her final race, she had an off day and fell almost eight lengths behind. She surged in the final stretch but lost by a nose.[5] Peak performance is impossible to sustain permanently. All organizations stumble. The question is how they respond.

By examining the breakdowns at three heralded organizations, Calumet Farm, Johnson & Johnson, and Toyota, we can extract lessons about how to avoid breakdowns and how to respond if they occur.

Calumet Farm

Calumet Farm was at the pinnacle of thoroughbred horseracing for six decades. With over seven hundred pastoral, bluegrass acres in Lexington, Kentucky, the stable had a track record that was astonishing: nine Calumet steeds ranked among the top hundred racehorses of the twentieth century. Calumet owned eight Kentucky Derby winners and seven Preakness winners, and it won six Eclipse (horse of the year) Awards, the most of any stable. Two Calumet thoroughbreds, Whirlaway and Citation, won the Triple Crown. Citation was the third-ranked horse of the century.

Calumet had eleven hall of fame horses and was the number one money-earning stable for twelve years, boasting renowned trainers and jockeys. In 1978, Calumet's star thoroughbred, Alydar, capped a stellar career with twenty-four finishes in the money (first, second, or third) out of twenty-six starts. In 1982, the stable had $93 million in assets and earned $1.8 million in profits with no debt. Calumet Farm was the epitome of racing excellence. No other stable came close.

Then everything collapsed. Ann Hagedorn Auerbach documents Calumet's problems in her riveting book, *Wild Ride.*[6] Under new leadership, the stable made dramatic changes. After deaths in the family that owned Calumet Farm, a bank held a majority of the voting stock in a trust, but the new leaders arranged to control the board's executive committee. The bank requested a "hold harmless agreement" to avoid liability for future losses. It was among many documents that family members say they signed without full understanding.

The new CEO terminated most of the longtime staff, including exceptional managers and trainers, and the CEO-controlled executive committee authorized him to borrow $10 million on Calumet's behalf. Not long after, the farm had a corporate jet and swimming pools for injured horses on site. Calumet paid $25 million for half the ownership rights in a racehorse named Secreto. When the value of these investments tanked in the "bluegrass bubble" (a rush by investors to own a piece of a thoroughbred horse), the CEO borrowed even more aggressively through a cozy relationship with another bank, whose officer was later convicted of criminal charges.

Soon Calumet's debt had soared to $44 million, and the farm was under tremendous financial strain. Mysteriously, its star horse, Alydar, suffered a leg fracture in his stall and was euthanized. Suspicions swirled around the horse's injury, with allegations that Calumet officials killed the horse to cash in on his $36.5 million insurance policy.[7]

Finally, with debt exceeding $162 million, the legendary stable filed for bankruptcy in 1991, auctioning off the remaining thoroughbreds and real estate. In 2000, the former CEO and CFO were convicted of fraud and bribery. The dynasty that reigned supreme with incredible accomplishments and an impeccable reputation for integrity was in tatters. Ironically, Calumet's leading horse at its demise was Criminal Type.

The fall of Calumet Farm is a modern-day Greek tragedy with numerous culprits, from the CEO and CFO to the board and bank, all seemingly derelict in or oblivious to their fiduciary responsibilities.

The rise to the top can take decades, but without a commitment to build an excellent, ethical, and enduring organization, the fall can be precipitous.

Calumet's new owners were clueless about the triple crown quest. The family owners failed to set up the plans and safeguards to protect and sustain what they had built. Consequently, a greedy executive and his associates wrested control of Calumet and bamboozled the owners into abdicating their fiduciary obligations. Calumet's owners were snoozing at the board table and did not act in the face of increasingly egregious abuses. Most puzzling is the behavior of officials at the bank that held the family trust. How could they let a cabal of insiders wrest control of the enterprise and run it into the ground?

Calumet's demise contains an important lesson: triple crown status can be fleeting. The quest requires courage and vigilance. Leaders must not outsource or farm out the triple crown quest to unqualified people, and they cannot always trust third parties like banks or law firms to do what is right. The board that delegates the triple crown quest abdicates it. Triple crown leadership requires stewardship at all levels.

Johnson & Johnson

In 1982, Johnson & Johnson set the gold standard for crisis management. Someone had laced Tylenol bottles in the Chicago area with poison, causing the death of seven people. The company, under the leadership of then–CEO Jim Burke, quickly instituted a recall, not just in the greater Chicago area or even the Midwest, but nationwide, encompassing all thirty-one million Tylenol bottles in the marketplace. The recall cost $100 million but established J&J as a trustworthy and ethical business.

J&J's actions were based on its 1943 Credo—written by Chairman Robert Wood Johnson, a member of the company's founding family. The Credo outlines J&J's responsibilities in order of importance: first to customers (doctors, nurses, patients, mothers, and fathers), next to employees, then to the communities in which they live and work (including the world community), and finally to their stockholders.

Fast-forward to today: J&J appeared on the cover of *Bloomberg Businessweek* in 2011, with two Band-Aids over the J&J logo in a story titled "Ouch!"—asking if J&J can still be trusted after more than fifty recalls in fifteen months.[8]

Ouch, indeed. Here is a partial list of recent challenges facing the company:

- Recalls of Tylenol, Motrin, Rolaids, Benadryl, children's medications, artificial hips, heart medications, and more

- Takeovers of three J&J manufacturing plants by U.S. regulators and closure of another

- Thousands of lawsuits filed against the company

- Criticism about a deceptive "phantom recall" of Motrin

- A suit for wrongful termination by a former vice president, alleging he was dismissed for raising safety concerns

- $70 million to settle cases involving the Foreign Corrupt Practices Act, with allegations of paying kickbacks to secure business

- Allegations of marketing drugs for unapproved uses and overstating benefits

According to Robert Khuzami, director of the division of enforcement for the U.S. Securities and Exchange Commission, "J&J chose profit margins over compliance with the law by acquiring a private company for the purpose of paying bribes, and using sham contracts, off-shore companies, and slush funds to cover its tracks."[9]

"This is a real American tragedy," said University of Michigan professor Erik Gordon. "They really have blown one of the great brands." According to *Bloomberg Businessweek*, the firm's shares have been the third-worst performers in the Dow Jones Industrial Average since March 2009 and fell nearly 9 percent between 2010 and 2011 while the S&P 500 Health Care Index was rising.[10]

What happened? Observers have speculated widely on possible reasons:

- Sacrificing quality and safety in pursuit of short–term stock gains driven by growth, following an aggressive series of acquisitions

- Overly aggressive cost cutting, with operating margins rising from 17.7 percent in 1990 to 26.8 percent in 2010, an astonishing increase

- Too much decentralization in a company with 120 manufacturing facilities

- Deterioration of manufacturing procedures, including mislabeling and inadequate inspections and cleaning and maintenance practices

- Subpar training

William Weldon (who stepped down as CEO in 2012 but remains chairman) said that the criticism is overblown and that the main problems concern one company, J&J's McNeil Consumer Healthcare unit. Nonetheless, the company had more than twice as many major product recalls as Pfizer, the world's largest healthcare products company. Veteran industry analyst Ira Loss said, "I'm not familiar with another company that has had this many debacles in a very short period of time."[11]

Using our triple crown leadership practices, where might J&J have gone off track?

- Where was the steel leadership to demand adherence to the Credo? Has the Credo been gathering dust?

- Does J&J recruit and promote for integrity and fit with the Credo culture, as well as competence?

- Are the board, CEO, and officers serving as stewards and making defensible decisions about short- versus long-term tradeoffs?

- Is the company, with its sprawling network of manufacturing facilities, aligned?

- Are management goals and metrics too financially oriented, without sufficient attention to ethical practices?

- Are the firm's processes, such as quality control, compliance, and ethics, sufficiently rigorous?

- Are the communication loops robust enough for leaders to know about and take action on issues?

The healthcare industry is fraught with peril. Mistakes happen; people die; lawsuits and adverse publicity result. But the company's recent track record is unacceptable. J&J, an enduring institution founded in 1886, once an iconic example of triple crown leadership, has lost its stature.

Dr. Dan Sweeney, director of the Institute for Enterprise Excellence at the University of Denver, told us: "My suspicion is the Credo culture didn't get moved across new generations of executives." It appears that J&J leaders put revenue growth and earnings ahead of doing the right thing, and they failed to find a sustainable balance between short-term performance pressures and long-term ethics, reputation, and investment considerations. Based on their public statements, some company leaders seem to be in denial about that imbalance.

The lesson of J&J's breakdown is that when one of the three Es (in this case, "excellent") dominates, the odds of a fall increase dramatically, regardless of prior reputation or performance.

Toyota

In 2010, Toyota Motor Corporation became the world's largest automaker (by production), an extraordinary accomplishment for a company that was fourth largest in 1970. The company had built a stellar reputation for quality and long-running financial success in the brutally competitive auto industry. Its share price surged from around $50 in 2002 to more than $130 in early 2007.

Ultimately, something happened on the way to the top. As early as 2002, there were concerns about Toyota's quality. In 2005, the company had more vehicles recalled than sold, according to a high-ranking official.

Toyota's legendary quality was slipping.

By August 28, 2009, it had slipped too far. At 6:35 p.m., a California 911 operator received an emergency call from a man in a Lexus (a Toyota brand) on Highway 125 near San Diego: "Our accelerator is stuck . . . we're in trouble . . . there's no brakes . . . we're approaching the intersection . . . hold on . . . hold on and pray . . . pray . . ."[12]

The driver was an off-duty officer in the California Highway Patrol. He died in the crash, along with his wife, daughter, and brother-in-law. The incident brought widespread attention to thousands of complaints about unintended speed control issues.

Ultimately, a National Highway Traffic Safety Administration report, written in conjunction with NASA engineers, pointed to driver error, "sticking" accelerators, and a design flaw that allowed accelerators to become trapped in floor mats, but no electronic flaws.[13]

Meanwhile, millions of recalls for quality and safety concerns badly damaged the company's reputation and financial performance.

The company's market capitalization fell more than 40 percent from its 2006 value. In 2011, the company dropped out of Interbrand's annual list of the top ten global brands.[14] What happened?

To understand the breakdown, we need to start with what got Toyota to the top. For decades, Toyota had been synonymous with quality. The "Toyota Way" of operating, developed and refined over seventy-five years, draws upon two pillars: respect for people and continuous improvement. It also emphasizes continuously solving the root causes of problems and focuses on organizational learning, people development, and long-term thinking.

The Toyota system of just-in-time production and lean manufacturing has been widely hailed and emulated. Toyota's guiding principles emphasize clean and safe products. Its corporate culture embraces creativity, teamwork, harmony, integrity, mutual trust, and responsibility.

Corporate training programs seek to educate people in the Toyota culture and traditions. Company leaders emphasize employee health and safety, and they offer fitness and work-life balance programs to employees.

Toyota uses an extensive consensus-building process to refine new ideas and debug products. The company has for a long time used the famous "andon cord," which employees can pull to stop the production line if they suspect a problem.

Toyota has embraced sustainability, earning Interbrand's top global green brand ranking in 2011.[15] The company subscribes to the Global Earth Charter and spent large sums to develop some of the first hybrid vehicles before there was a proven market for them.

There is much to admire in these practices. However, as Jim Lentz, president of Toyota Motor Sales USA, told us, "Sometimes your greatest strength can become your greatest challenge. In our case, we knew we had great quality, so perhaps we didn't spend enough time and attention continuing to improve it."

We also spoke to Toyota critics. Many feel the company was not responsive to their concerns or sufficiently focused on safety. At some point, things got out of control. Something changed. Observers have speculated widely on the causes of the problems, including:

- Overemphasis on becoming the world's number one automaker

- Too much cost cutting to boost profitability

- Engineers insulated from marketplace feedback

- Overly centralized decision-making with functional silos that create barriers

- Reluctance to report bad news up the chain of command

- Legal and financial concerns about taking responsibility and admitting liability

- A board composed entirely of Japanese men, none of them independent, all company insiders[16]

Ultimately, the company recalled about nine million vehicles.[17] Toyota halted production for a week to divert parts to repair the cars of customers already on the road. In one case, federal safety regulators rebuked the firm for issuing an "inaccurate and misleading" statement.

Akio Toyoda, who took over as president and CEO in late 2009, publicly assumed responsibility for the company's actions. Testifying before the U.S. Congress, he said:

> Toyota has, for the past few years, been expanding its business rapidly. Quite frankly, I fear the pace at which we have grown may have been too quick. I would like to point out here that Toyota's priority has traditionally been the following: First: Safety, Second: Quality, and Third: Volume. These priorities became confused, and we were not able to stop, think, and make improvements as much as we were able to before . . . We pursued growth over the speed at which we were able to

develop our people and our organization . . . I regret that this has resulted in the safety issues described in the recalls we face today, and I am deeply sorry for any accidents that Toyota drivers have experienced.[18]

This public testimony, acknowledging responsibility and apologizing, is an important part of Toyota's quest to get back on track.

Toyota suffered great damage from these events. Where did it go off track?

- After decades of spectacular success, did it take its reputation for quality for granted?

- Did the company focus too much on short-term financial performance driven by growth?

- Was the board too insulated and deferential to company leaders?

- Where were the steel leadership and ethical fortitude to demand that employees raise and address suspected safety problems?

- Where were the stewards who would pull the andon cord on violations of Toyota's culture of character?

- Were insufficient processes in place to ensure safety and quality?

- Were communication loops missing, thus preventing quality alerts from reaching the right people?

Today, Toyota is making progress in getting back on track. According to Lentz, the company has:

- Assigned a thousand engineers to work on component design and quality before parts go into vehicles

- Appointed a chief quality officer and chief safety officer for North America

- Developed Swift Market Analysis and Response Teams to conduct onsite inspections of vehicles of concern

- Established six product quality field offices to support resolution of complaints

- Enhanced its computer system to mine more sources, including customer complaints, government data, and warranty claims

- Become the first full-line automaker to offer a package of six key accident avoidance technologies as standard equipment on every new vehicle

Toyota made the same mistake as J&J: letting one of the three Es dominate the others. The quest to be number one in volume (excellent results in the short term) trumped safety and quality concerns (the ethical and enduring imperatives). Dr. Sweeney at the Institute for Enterprise Ethics told us, "The new generation was quite taken by the prospect of being the world's largest automobile company. They were going to get bigger than General Motors, and they did."

Fortunately, Toyota leaders do not appear to be in denial. They admitted their mistakes and appear to be correcting them. Only time will tell what happens with Toyota's quest. In the wake of the devastating earthquake and tsunami in Japan in 2011, Toyota managed to rebuild one of the most complex supply chains in the world in about ninety days. Clearly, Toyota has tremendous capabilities.

SIGNS OF BREAKDOWNS

Organizations do not break down before emitting warning signs. Normally, the financial signals, such as revenue declines, shrinking margins, slowing inventory turns, and deteriorating working capital ratios, are *lagging* indicators. *Leading* indicators are more important because leaders can address them before the financials go south. Using our triple crown framework, what are some early warning signals of potential breakdowns? See Figure 7.1.

Figure 7.1   **Early Warning Signals**

Triple Crown: Three Es

- Focusing too much on strategy shifts and tweaking processes instead of accountability for results
- Letting complacency creep in
- Cutting ethical corners when the pressure is on
- Not building ethics into day-to-day processes and decisions
- Falling prey to short-termism and failing to find creative ways to address both short- and long-term interests

Head and Heart

- Neglecting integrity, cultural fit, and emotional intelligence in selection and promotions
- Failing to be rigorous with people selection
- Failing to invest adequately in developing people

The Colors

- Not seeking input from everybody in the organization regarding the colors (purpose, values, vision)
- Focusing on drafting the statements instead of inculcating the colors into the enterprise and daily decisions

Steel and Velvet

- Leaders staying in their comfort zones and not flexing between the hard and soft edges of leadership
- Excessively tight controls
- Leaders being too soft because they want to be liked

(continued on next page)

Figure 7.1 **Early Warning Signals** (continued)

Stewards

- Excessive deference to the top leaders

- Leaders assuming they must make all the decisions and have all the answers

- Failure to tap into the potential of people

- Reluctance to challenge authority or step out of functional roles

- Boards out to lunch about culture, ethics, and sustainability

Alignment

- Constantly changing priorities

- Poor communication and secrecy, with people operating in silos

- Insufficient understanding of how efforts across the enterprise fit together

- Lack of discipline and follow-through

WHAT TO DO WHEN IT BREAKS DOWN

Our greatest glory is not in never failing,
but in rising up every time we fail.

—**Ralph Waldo Emerson,** American author

All organizations suffer breakdowns at some level or at some time. The only question is how they respond when hit. The easy way out? Doing whatever it takes to make your numbers?

We have seen that people can perform extraordinary accomplishments. The late Steve Jobs of Apple was far from perfect as a leader, in our view, but he often refused to accept that something could not be done. "Leadership," he once said, "is about inspiring people to do things they never thought they could." The examples are legion, from insisting on "insanely great" products again and again to convincing the CEO of Corning Glass that Corning's especially strong "gorilla glass" could be manufactured in the vast quantities needed for the iPhone.[19]

Triple crown leadership sometimes entails constructively challenging people to do what they think is impossible. Often they produce astonishing results.

When the challenge is to make the numbers in the short *and* long term, *and* to do it ethically, while operating sustainably and honoring obligations to all stakeholders, that is when people really dig in and find the best way, a new way, and refuse to settle for the easy way out. We agree with Cory Booker, the dynamic mayor of Newark, New Jersey, who said, "You can't surrender to the options before you. There's always another way." *Triple crown leaders find another way.*

As you encounter the initial signs of breakdown, you will need courage to face up to the obstacles and face down the critics. Whoever said "Don't listen to your critics" was wrong. Your critics can give you important insights into what you may be missing. Listen to them. Engage with them. Then do what you think is right. While you cannot avoid breakdowns, the real issue is how you respond to them, becoming stronger in the broken places, as Hemingway said.

CHAPTER SUMMARY

No organization—not even the most prestigious of institutions—is immune from breakdowns. Normally, leading indicators flash the warning signs. One or more of the practices we have outlined have gone off track. In many cases, leaders focus too much on one of the three Es while neglecting the others. When breakdowns occur, leaders must take significant actions—avoiding denials and not abdicating responsibility to others—in order to salvage the quest and regain momentum.

Practical Applications

1. Does your organization have a rock-solid commitment to being excellent, ethical, and enduring?
2. Does one of these considerations dominate the others?
   a. What should you do to restore a proper balance?
3. To what extent is your organization infused with triple crown leadership?
   a. How can you infuse it further?
4. Do you see signs of potential breakdown in your organization? What are they?
5. To what extent does your organization have a culture that welcomes raising concerns?
6. Are you prepared to raise alarms before things go awry? How and when?
7. If your organization is hopeless when it comes to excellent, ethical, and enduring performance and impact, should you find another place to work?
   a. What is stopping you?

CHAPTER EIGHT

TURNAROUNDS

The signature of the truly great versus the merely successful is not the absence of difficulty, but the ability to come back from setbacks, even cataclysmic catastrophes, stronger than before.

—**Jim Collins,** bestselling business author and consultant, in *How the Mighty Fall*

The raid on the Rocky Flats nuclear site near Denver produced bone-chilling results: more than a hundred tons of toxic plutonium waste and numerous "infinity rooms," sealed to prevent entry because the radioactivity readings inside were off the radiation scale. ABC News's *Nightline* ominously called Building 771 "the most dangerous building in America." The nation was stunned.[1]

From the 1950s through the 1980s, Rocky Flats produced seventy thousand plutonium triggers for the U.S. nuclear arsenal. This top-secret complex, occupying three million square feet in eight hundred buildings, was surrounded by razor wire, patrolled by armed guards with shoot-to-kill authority, and armed with surface-to-air missiles. At its peak, the site employed more than eight thousand unionized workers who were proud of their patriotic role in America's defense.

Their accomplishments, however, came with a menacing cost: radioactive barrels leaking in open fields, windborne contaminated soil, onsite fires, and alarmingly high radioactivity levels. All dangerously close to more than a million people.

After the 1989 raid by the FBI and EPA, the workforce was demoralized. Thousands were paid by the government at a cost of over $500 million per year to sit around as officials tried to figure out what to do. No large toxic nuclear weapons site like Rocky Flats had ever been scrubbed and closed.

In 1995, Department of Energy (DOE) officials, who oversaw nuclear weapons production, decided to clean up Rocky Flats, estimating that the task was so complex with so many unknowns that it would cost over $37 billion and take a minimum of sixty-five years.

Given egregious problems with previous contractors, DOE awarded a five-year, $3.5 billion contract to Kaiser-Hill in 1995 to start the cleanup of Rocky Flats. Kaiser-Hill was a joint venture between two firms, but one partner declared bankruptcy, and Kaiser-Hill operated as a wholly owned subsidiary of the other partner, CH2M Hill (a privately held and employee-owned engineering firm). Since the cleanup project was unprecedented, enormous, and so risky, many outsiders believed it was doomed to fail.

Kaiser-Hill was willingly stepping into a turnaround that was a black hole. Under previous contractors, there had been environmental protests, safety violations, lawsuits, guilty pleadings, unprecedented fines, and allegations of a cover-up.

Nancy Tuor, now CH2M Hill's group president and executive sponsor for sustainability, who became CEO of Rocky Flats in 2003, told us that when Kaiser-Hill leaders arrived, they found a "bankrupt culture of strained relations, mistrust, and lack of leadership." Workers sat around and played card games or read newspapers, waiting for people to tell them what to do. The workforce "had forgotten how to succeed. Nobody would look you in the eye. Nobody would smile at you."

Kaiser-Hill leaders were skeptical of the official government cleanup estimates of sixty-five years and $37 billion. Bob Card, CEO of Kaiser-Hill in 1995, said, "How can this possibly take so long? It's not a project; this is a career. Our children will retire before it's done." Under his leadership, Kaiser-Hill put together a skunk works team of veterans and fresh faces charged with assessing what could be done with $5 billion over five years. Eight weeks later, after working day and night, the team creatively reported that with $7 billion and seven years the site might be safely "mothballed," consolidating and entombing the waste onsite.

Though this approach was rejected, the bold thinking behind it dramatically changed the mindset at Rocky Flats, leading to a new vision: "Make it safe; clean it up; close it down." Kaiser-Hill executives became evangelists for the new vision. They had to reengage the same workers who knew they were working themselves out of jobs, reestablishing trust with all stakeholders from workers and the three unions to community groups, DOE, and Congress.

Executives demolished the infamous "Mahogany Row" administration building, where managers had presided for decades. They dispensed with executive parking. Tuor converted a trailer into her office, working in jeans and boots, eating her meals off trucks alongside the crews. Executives ditched their ties and went into the "hot buildings" in bubble suits alongside workers.

In 1996, DOE cut its estimate of the cleanup costs to $17.3 billion, and Kaiser-Hill estimated completion by 2015. In 1997, DOE announced an accelerated closure schedule with a target completion date of 2006 and cost of $7 billion.

In 2000, DOE awarded a new $3.96 billion contract to Kaiser-Hill, based on its accumulated expertise with the cleanup work. The new contract set the goal of closing Rocky Flats by December 2006, with the waste safely transported to other sites. Among other rigorous cleanup standards, the government specified a level of residual plutonium of 651 picocuries per gram of dry ground soil.[2] Later, through negotiations among the various stakeholders, this target was reduced to fifty picocuries.

Cleanup of the contaminated area was to be supervised by DOE in accordance with a Rocky Flats Cleanup Agreement and under the oversight of the EPA and the Colorado Department of Public Health and Environment.[3]

DOE now felt that Kaiser-Hill understood the cleanup issues and had the accumulated experience to carry out this closure project well ahead of the previous estimates. However, even the U.S. General Accounting Office (now the U.S. Government Accountability Office) cited a 1 percent probability of successful closure by 2006, subsequently raising that estimate in 2001 to 15 percent.

Criticism of Rocky Flats was swirling at the time. Some distrusted DOE, given its supervision of prior contractors and poor history of self-regulation. Records of what had happened on the site in prior years were sealed under government order, and many remain sealed to this day, raising fears and frustrations. Some critics wanted more stringent standards, as low as thirty-five picocuries per gram.

When Kaiser-Hill managers emphasized the deadlines in the schedule-driven contract, which had financial incentives for speed and performance, employees groused that schedule was trumping safety. In response, management took down all the signs with the schedule targets and said, counterintuitively, "Don't worry about the schedule. Do everything right the first time, and the schedule will take care of itself." The paramount objective, Tuor told us, became a "safe and compliant closure." Safety became an ethical commitment.

As safety improved, productivity increased exponentially. By working safely, the company avoided duplication and delays, saving time and money.

There was also a hard edge to the leadership at Rocky Flats. Tuor and her team had to change out many of the old managers under the previous contractors. They brought in new leaders with unique skills, but some of them became casualties as well due to character issues. "The cost of their egos," Tuor explained, "was at some point overriding the value of their contributions."

Managers focused on engaging the entire workforce, "fostering leadership at all levels of the organization." Previously bitter and disengaged people became central players. Workers pioneered a new chemical decontamination technique and other safety innovations. According to Tuor:

> Many of the problems had to be solved at the floor level. We had a scheduler who was trying to get waste out of the upper floors of buildings on narrow stairs. She was on an airplane one day and saw how they cater things up to the airplane door on a moveable platform. We implemented her solution immediately. We had a worker who was laboriously dismantling equipment and putting the parts into large containers. At home he figured out how to build reusable boxes. With the scrap from every ninth box, we could make a tenth box. He couldn't get anyone to listen. He insisted I look. The next day we had a ceremony for him and handed him a $2,500 check.

When problems occurred, rapid-response teams deployed into the hot zones, getting endangered employees out and resolving issues quickly. Six months before scheduled closure, Tuor learned about a neglected pile of waste, with significant schedule and budget implications. Instead of pointing fingers, a crew member simply said, "We got it, Nancy," and the team took care of it.

Tuor told us, "We had differences of opinion; sometimes we closed the door, and people would just fight. But when it came time to make a decision, I made the call, or Bob Card [the CEO preceding Tuor] made the call, and you knew everybody in that room was going to do it."

The company launched creative job transition and retraining programs, enlisting the unions, government regulators, and local chambers of commerce as partners. The governor wrote a letter to all the major industries in Colorado extolling the skills of the workforce that would be available to them upon closure of Rocky Flats.

Kaiser-Hill completed its new contract in 2005, fourteen months ahead of the revised schedule and more than $500 million under budget. Importantly, company leaders decided to share the financial gains with the workforce. Over the ten-year closure, Kaiser-Hill paid out over $100 million in incentives to employees, nearly 20 percent of its total project profits. The actual closure results were far better than the early estimates and even substantially better than the revised estimates.

The final soil measurements on site met the fifty picocuries per gram target and were thirteen times better than the initially proposed standard of 651 picocuries. The closure project earned numerous awards from federal and state agencies and plaudits from elected officials.

In their book about the Rocky Flats cleanup, authors Kim Cameron and Marc Lavine concluded: "Within the scope of the cleanup agreement that was negotiated, the performance of Kaiser-Hill remains extraordinary in its timing, cost, quality, and outcomes."[4] Notwithstanding heated debates about nuclear weapons and their environmental impacts, the cleanup of Rocky Flats—especially in the wake of prior problems and with a demoralized workforce—was an impressive turnaround accomplishment.

After the cleanup, the company held a closing ceremony at the Denver Convention Center. Tuor recalls, "I've never been in a room so electric. They were so proud of the job they did. We created a culture of respect where average people produced extraordinary results. We grew and changed into different people. It was not about me; it was about them. It was the job of a lifetime."[5]

James Howland, one of the co-founders of CH2M Hill (the parent company of Kaiser-Hill), wrote a *Little Yellow Book* of company values and principles in 1982, which is still distributed to all employees today. Snippets include "Integrity is the prerequisite to employment," "Spread the returns around," and "Dream flamboyantly." CH2M HILL has since made both the Ethisphere Institute's list of the World's Most Ethical Companies and *Fortune*'s 100 Best Companies to Work For list for years, growing in revenue from $1 billion in 1995 to $6.36 billion in 2011, and winning high-profile, joint-venture contracts for the London Olympics, Panama Canal expansion, and construction of the world's first zero-waste, zero-carbon city in Abu Dhabi. The company's Colorado campus, which has been awarded a LEED (Leadership in Energy and Environmental Design) rating, connects operations on five continents with smart technology—all without executive dining rooms or reserved parking.

TRIPLE CROWN TURNAROUND LEADERSHIP

As we see from the Rocky Flats example, the five triple crown leadership practices are all applicable to turnarounds:

1. *Head and heart*. Picking people with the right skill sets, as well as character, emotional intelligence, and cultural fit.
2. *The colors*. Committing to uphold a new (or reaffirmed) purpose, values, and vision. Shared values are especially critical in a contentious turnaround because of all the emotions swirling.

3. *Steel and velvet*. Flexing between the hard and soft edges of leadership, anchoring on the shared values and taking the necessary casualties. Leaders should invoke steel to hold people accountable for the priorities and values but be careful not to squelch the initiative of potential leaders in the ranks.

4. *Stewards*. Unleashing multiple leaders empowered by the colors to act as stewards of the culture of character. Most turnaround successes cannot fairly be attributed to genius leaders making brilliant decisions.

5. *Alignment*. Achieving peak performance through disciplined, collaborative alignment, with clear action plans, accountability mechanisms, and feedback loops.

TURNAROUND ADAPTATIONS

In applying these triple crown practices, leaders must make adjustments that reflect the distinctive circumstances of turnarounds. To outline the required adaptations, we draw from our experience and that of our interviewees, about a dozen of whom had navigated turnarounds.

First, though, bear in mind that not every enterprise can or should survive. Some are hopelessly flawed, obsolete, or damaged. Others, however, have extraordinary people, unique capabilities, and valuable resources. If it is not too late, they may emerge stronger than ever.

In addition, there are different kinds of turnarounds: flips, back-to-normals, and rebirths. Leaders doing a flip sometimes provide a valuable service, saving a company from ruin and then selling it to or merging it with a stronger entity. Alternatively, the goal of the turnaround may just be to get back to business as usual.

Our focus is not on flips or back-to-normals but rebirths. Rebirth turnarounds, like a Phoenix rising from its own ashes, are the ultimate proving grounds for the triple crown quest. They make it possible to rediscover what is unique and worthwhile about organizations and what their people are made of. They can reignite passions and aspirations, taking the organization into new realms of performance and impact.

Turnaround leaders seeking a rebirth must be crystal clear with stakeholders about their ultimate aims, outlining the assets they intend to resurrect and setting appropriate expectations for the amount of time it will take.

The Turnaround CEO. Given the chaos of a turnaround, the selection of the leader at the top of the organization (we shall use the term "CEO") is critical. Many turnarounds begin with a new CEO, frequently an outsider, like Louis Gerstner at IBM. An accomplished insider with a new perspective can also be effective, as with Xerox. Sometimes a turnaround requires new leadership at the board level, as we saw with Tyco in chapter four.

Caution is necessary in selecting the CEO. Whoever enters the challenge of a turnaround as a self-proclaimed expert is delusional. "Chainsaw" Al Dunlap (infamous for ruthless turnarounds with massive layoffs at Scott Paper and Sunbeam) did not turn companies around so much as gut and strip them for a flip. Dunlap, also nicknamed "Rambo in Pinstripes," represents the antithesis of triple crown leadership. His legacy? Sunbeam descended into bankruptcy after a massive accounting scandal, with Dunlap fired and forced to pay millions to settle SEC lawsuits against him.

In a rebirth, by contrast, triple crown leaders launch the quest *in concert with compatriots*, believing that together they will prevail despite the long odds. The leaders must be simultaneously realistic about the circumstances, optimistic about ultimate success, and productively paranoid about the risks.

It is essential for the board and CEO to be in sync on the fundamentals of the turnaround. Even the best triple crown turnaround CEOs are likely to fail if they serve under business-as-usual or inept boards. It is critical to have alignment at the top, lest all the hard work be sabotaged by boardroom fiat.

Radical Focus. When you are nearly out of cash, your immediate vision is survival, as it was at Xerox, with the long-term vision waiting until stability has been restored. Leaders must ensure that necessary controls and processes are in place, focusing on making payroll before empowerment initiatives can begin.

Turnarounds take fierce discipline in personal and organizational time management. Leaders should expect to use more steel than velvet at the outset. Jim Unruh, chairman and CEO of Unisys Corporation, told us, "In a turnaround, you are forced more to the hard-edged side because there isn't time to build consensus. You have to make decisions and move on."

The turnaround CEO must mercilessly cast aside all manner of ideas and projects—some with real merit—to ensure a tight focus on one or two key priorities needed for survival. In the meantime, other priorities must wait.

The private equity firm backing the turnaround of Recognition Equipment had only one instruction for Bob as he moved to Texas: "Don't run out of cash." Indeed, to convince a bank to back their efforts, Bob and his partner Tom agreed to work for a dollar per year until achieving certain cash milestones, which took nine months.

When the board brought in Bob to lead the turnaround of Sensormatic (a billion-dollar security company), the firm was burning through cash at a rate of $100 million per year. Bob mandated a freeze on all hiring, capital purchases, and expenses not necessary for production. If people needed more supplies, they had to scavenge and improvise. Bootstrapping was the order of the day. He required daily cash balance reports and formed a rapid-action team to dispose of all inventory more than 180 days old in creative, nondisruptive ways. Bob announced that the company would allocate half the savings from quick wins to shore up cash balances, with the other half going into the necessary investments for other quick wins. Tough decisions were required: about 10 percent of the employee base was pared and about 10 percent of revenue was reduced as the company sold or closed unprofitable business lines.

Turnarounds demand focus on a few imperatives, with all else deferred. As circumstances improve, leaders flex to the velvet edge of leadership. Even with this radical focus, leaders should try to look beyond the current storm, seeking creative ways to position the organization to flourish once the storm has passed.

Communicating Reality and Confidence.   During a turnaround, stakeholders need to know what is going on, so constant communication is essential. The leader cannot hunker down in a bunker to do the work. The turnaround work is done through the people.

At Sensormatic, Bob blocked his calendar daily for time with customers, employees, vendors, and shareholders. Otherwise, the urgent incoming message stream would conscript his days.[6] The new CEO must be visibly present to employees and key stakeholders in one-on-one meetings, small-group sessions, and large forums—using all available technologies to enhance access.

Since people are stressed and worried as rumors fly, leaders must give people a sense of what is to come in the turnaround, blending both realism and confidence. For example:

> As you know, we are in a crisis. We have gotten off track. *(Acknowledge the major problems and be specific.)* We are addressing the immediate problems. *(Give a few specific examples, focusing on top priorities.)* Our organization has wonderful capabilities inherent in our people and products. Working together, we can not only survive but thrive. I am confident we can get through this and be stronger than ever if we work together and unleash your creative ideas. Let's now open up this session to your questions, concerns, and ideas.

It is essential to listen carefully and answer questions honestly in these sessions. People need to be heard, and they want answers:

> *Q:* "Will there be layoffs?"
>
> *A:* "Yes, unfortunately some layoffs are necessary to ensure the organization's survival."

Q: "Who, how many, when?"

A: "We don't know yet, but we will determine that within X days. We will treat people fairly and with dignity. Then we need to get on with rebuilding this great organization."

Psychological Stability.   In the turmoil of a turnaround, many people are demoralized, afraid, or angry. Many just want to dig a trench and protect themselves. Some feel betrayed, abused, or misled. Some are on the verge of panic. They have invested their time, ideas, and efforts into their work, only to face embarrassment and potential failure. Bloggers and reporters publish horror stories for all to see. Logo-inscribed baseball caps stay in the closet. Some people bail quickly because they have other opportunities. Many others are out looking for new jobs. Some just wait and see, not yet wanting to commit.

Therefore, the turnaround leader must establish not only financial stability but also what we call psychological stability. People need to be unfrozen, empowered to work on critical projects with confidence.

At Sensormatic, Bob found an effective vehicle to begin establishing psychological stability: an all-day senior staff meeting early in the turnaround. Running the meeting tightly to establish credibility, Bob focused on a handful of factors:

- *Ventilation.* To begin, Bob asked the attendees to identify *all* the problems and issues they could think of. They went around the table, with each person briefly stating one issue—whether major or trivial and without editorial comment—or passing. Bob sometimes had to keep emotions from boiling over. The process started slowly, with a few brave souls raising concerns at first and then all participants eventually chiming in. They stopped when everyone around the table had passed three times in a row. Hundreds of issues were raised, clearly written down on flip-chart paper, which was hung around the room. There it all was, the complete set of challenges, visible for all to see, from gripes about parking to warring factions and concerns about the board. This process took hours, but there was relief that people were finally talking about the elephants in the room.

- *Priorities.* The group then sorted the issues into topics (for example, financial, ethical, operational) and patterns (such as accountability lapses, conflict avoidance, and turf wars) and placed them into A, B, or C priorities, with spirited debate facilitated by Bob.

- *Projects.* Bob then enlisted volunteers to work on the A priorities. He noted that some people were silent, volunteering for nothing. The Bs were put into a holding area, awaiting progress on the As. The Cs were deferred. Bob requested that the volunteer groups submit weekly status reports to the senior staff on the A priorities, thereby establishing both transparency and accountability.

- *Values.* Bob then emphasized the need to operate by shared values. Otherwise, it would be too easy to revert to dysfunctional behaviors. Through open dialogue, the senior staff developed the values of leadership, integrity, teamwork, and excellence (forming the acronym LITE, which made the values easy to remember, as we previously reported). These words became the draft of shared values to be taken by a guiding coalition of volunteers to the whole organization for further input and refinement.

- *Amnesty.* To close the meeting, Bob noted there were many wounds in the room. People had legitimate grievances. However, progress would not be possible as long as people maintained vendettas. To move forward, everybody had to agree to amnesty for all prior sins. No one could hold grudges. Going forward, everyone would be held accountable for upholding the new shared values, and any significant breach would draw swift response.

"Agreed?" Bob asked, a steel question.

Everyone agreed.

This seminal meeting laid the groundwork for psychological stability. After such catharsis, people could stop looking backward and start looking ahead. Accomplishments at the meeting included ventilating issues, determining priorities, giving assignments, establishing shared values, and instilling a forward focus.

The Turnaround Team.   As he facilitated the ventilation meeting, Bob got a sense for who would be reliable officers in the stormy seas ahead and who would be deadweight or saboteurs. He supplemented these impressions with deep conversations with the officers, most often in their offices, to get a sense of their operating style. He spent every evening in one-on-one dinner meetings with officers to get to know them further.

Within a few weeks, Bob carefully picked the turnaround team, relying primarily on intuition. He separated the naysayers and misfits from the company in a respectful and fair fashion, working closely with human resources to ensure proper procedures were followed. Skill set, character, emotional intelligence, and buy-in with the new shared values were his criteria. Of twenty-five officers, one (the general counsel) kept the same job, twelve had new assignments, and twelve departed the organization. The new team committed to operate by the shared values and hold one another accountable for them. Trust began to build, and more people committed to the turnaround cause as they saw the progress and integrity at work.

Ventilating Outsiders.   Bob used a similar ventilation approach with Sensormatic's outside stakeholders, such as important customers angry about product delays and key vendors furious about late payments. He recalls requesting a fifteen-minute meeting with a large, critical customer, who had said he was ceasing to do business with Sensormatic. The purpose of the meeting was to understand the customer's issues, not to "sell" anything. Sensormatic's salesperson was most reticent to schedule the session. Bob insisted.

Bob listened carefully, saying nothing but writing down verbatim what the customer was saying. Fifteen minutes turned to an emotional thirty. When the customer stopped talking, Bob thanked him, sincerely apologized for the grievances, and started to read back the exact words the customer had said. Then the customer interrupted, unloading a new stream of invectives, which Bob again wrote down and again, after a pause, read back. After an agonizing hour, when the customer was finally finished, he realized that the CEO had really listened to him and written down his complaints. He felt understood, and perhaps even embarrassed by his outbursts. Bob then apologized again, thanked him again, noted how valuable his input would be to the turnaround, and rose to leave. The customer said, "Thank you for listening. Keep me apprised of your progress."

Bob and the sales team kept the customer informed of progress with several follow-up notes, showing how they had truly acted upon the problems he had identified. A year later, the business relationship was reestablished.

Operating Rhythm. A real risk in turnarounds is that the initial momentum fizzles, causing the enterprise to spiral down again. Old habits die hard. It takes time for people to adjust to new ways of operating. In the meantime, the bad news keeps coming. With much personnel turnover, there is mass confusion in some areas. Predictability is important, and so in order to maintain forward momentum, leaders must establish a persistent operating rhythm with accountability follow-ups. Daily, weekly, and monthly status report sessions and town hall meetings with employees are important.

It is essential to have an effective organizational structure with clear roles and responsibilities, reporting lines, and communication channels. The effort requires persistence. Group members have to hack away at the root causes of the problems, not symptoms. Together, they make slow and steady progress over time, reporting results and encouraging one another in regular sessions. Such feedback loops help foster alignment.

> *A river cuts through rock, not because of its power,*
> *but because of its persistence.*
> —**James Watkins,** author

Sanctuary. In turnarounds, leaders receive a barrage of body blows. The impacts of those blows can be devastating as they accumulate. Bob and his colleagues called turnarounds "organ donations" because they felt like they first gave a liver, then a spleen, next a lung, as still more hits came. They laughed at Murphy's law ("If anything can go wrong, it will") and quipped, "Murphy was an optimist." They scheduled some meetings in ten-minute increments and held others while waiting in line at the Department of Motor Vehicles to save time. Saturday staff meetings were not popular, but that was the only time when everyone was in town without customers or vendors to deal with.

To survive the punishment of turnarounds, Bob learned that he needed a daily time and place of sanctuary to refresh his mind and body. Harvard professor Ronald Heifetz and his colleagues advise leaders in crisis to find sanctuaries and to reach out to confidants for support and perspective. Leaders must not lose themselves in their role, taking the inevitable failures or attacks personally.[7]

CISCO'S TURNAROUNDS

Even with all these special adaptations, turnarounds often require midcourse corrections to adjust to changing circumstances. Stuff happens. Turnarounds flame out. Old problems resurface. New crises arise, requiring a new turnaround campaign.

Cisco Systems (a computer networking company) has experienced such ups and downs recently. Cisco, based in California's Silicon Valley, went from being the world's most valuable company in 2000 (with a $550 billion market capitalization) to the brink of disaster when the dot-com bubble burst a decade ago. Its revenues plummeted, its stock price plunged 68 percent in ten weeks, and the company took a $2.5 billion special charge to earnings to write down excess assets.

First, leaders stopped the bleeding. They laid off nearly 20 percent of the workforce. Longtime CEO John Chambers cut his salary to $1 and gave back two million of his six million stock options.[8]

Then Chambers and his management team set about reinventing the company. Moving beyond its historical focus on routers and switches, Cisco moved to intelligent network-enabled technologies such as cloud computing, smart electricity grids, virtual healthcare, and even consumer products. It went from pursuing a few new markets at a time to dozens—a head-spinning flurry of activity.

Cisco also redesigned its organizational structure to facilitate both innovation and execution, moving from a top-down, command-and-control behemoth to a radically decentralized team-of-teams enterprise. The new organization chart included a sixteen-member operating committee supported by twelve councils and forty-seven boards, all supported by temporary working groups. Chambers said, "Instead of ten people running the company . . . [we have] the top five hundred people running it today."[9] He said the goal was to spread Cisco's leadership and decision-making far wider than any large corporation had ever attempted.

Ironically, Chambers had to invoke steel leadership to impose velvet collaboration throughout the enterprise, telling people to get on board or be gone. "About 20 percent of my leaders didn't make the transition," Chambers recounted. "They were command-and-control, wonderful leaders but wanted to stay command and control and couldn't transition over."

To facilitate this collaboration, Cisco used its own alignment process called VSE, for vision, strategy, and execution. The goal was to drive flexible innovation that scaled by creating replicable processes, covering things like how to set up groups, evaluate their work, and make decisions. Using a common language, each group developed a five-year vision, two-year strategy, and ten-point execution plan.

Lynn Easterling, vice president and deputy general counsel, described it to us, "Every organization and individual has to have a VSE that aligns with the overall corporation's VSE. My boss's VSE is up here on my bulletin board."

Alongside the strategic and organizational changes, Cisco leaders initiated a cultural transformation based on new values: integrity, collaboration, change agents, and community.

Cisco invested heavily in its own internal talent development. The company launched Cisco University in 2003, using numerous electronic performance management, talent assessment, and leadership development tools for leaders, as well as executive coaching. Cisco's Action Learning Forum (ALF) is a rigorous sixteen-week program for high-potential leaders who, under the direction of faculty from MIT and Stanford, work on real Cisco business problems and present their recommendations to a Governance Committee. Since launching in 2007, ALF has generated billions of dollars in new value creation.[10]

Cisco consistently ranks high on the lists of most admired companies (2006–2011), most ethical companies (2008, 2010–2012), most innovative companies (2010), best global green brands (2011), best companies for leadership (2008–2010), best corporate citizens (2006–2011), best companies to work for (2006–2012), and more.

Despite this progress, Cisco is once again struggling and having to make midcourse corrections. Clearly, part of the challenge has been the global financial crisis and deteriorating conditions in many of Cisco's core markets. The company's sales growth has lagged its peer group in recent years. New products and markets pursued have yet to pay off as hoped.[11] Cisco's stock performance has suffered, trading in 2011 down to its 2002 levels and down 55 percent from its 2007 peak. Pressure is mounting for much better results.

Unfortunately, some of Cisco's pain has been self-inflicted. Bloggers have called Cisco's radical decentralization "insane" and "awful."[12] Senior execs reportedly spent about 30 percent of their time in meetings. Leaders may have overreached by attempting too many major changes, thereby diluting the focus, and by going too far with some reinventions. Not surprisingly, Cisco recently dismantled many of the councils and boards to accelerate execution, with Chambers admitting mistakes and the need for changes.[13]

Cisco survived its near-death experience a decade ago and radically transformed itself into a very different organization. Today, the firm is undergoing another turnaround—struggling to achieve better results, adjusting its strategy and tactics, while maintaining its new culture and overall approach.

CHAPTER SUMMARY

The triple crown turnaround is a rebirth, not only for the enterprise, but for the people who fight their way through it, becoming stronger and better in the process. A triple crown turnaround employs the five triple crown leadership practices—with adaptations. Critical success factors include selection of the right turnaround leader and turnaround team. Top leaders must be in sync and explicitly commit to a rebirth. They must institute radical focus while communicating both the reality of the situation and confidence about the future. Leaders must restore financial stability and establish psychological stability early in the process. They must instill an operating rhythm to maintain turnaround momentum, and they are wise to find sanctuary from the body blows. Over time, eyes previously averted in hallways look up, smiles appear, and incredibly capable people step up to execute and lead, creating a remarkable transformation.

Practical Applications

1. Have you clearly committed to a rebirth turnaround, not just a flip or business-as-usual turnaround?
2. Have you committed to all three Es (excellent, ethical, enduring), without one dominating the others?
3. To what extent have leaders allowed people to vent grievances and identify problems as a first step in establishing psychological stability?
4. Have leaders identified the one or two top priorities necessary for survival?
   a. Are there focused projects designed to address them?
5. Have you collaboratively established shared values to govern in the turnaround?
6. Have leaders granted amnesty for past problems?
   a. To what extent have people let go of their vendettas and hang-ups?
   b. What more needs to be done?
7. Have you carefully selected your turnaround team to build a culture of character?
8. Have you established open communication loops with all key stakeholder groups?
9. Does the organization have a strong operating cadence with accountability and follow-up to maintain momentum?
   a. What more should you do?
10. Are you taking care of yourself to ensure you can maintain the grueling pace?
    a. What else must you do?

CHAPTER NINE

STARTUPS

*Those who say it cannot be done
should not interrupt the people doing it.*
—Chinese proverb

n Secretariat's first race, a rival horse bumped him as they charged out of the starting gate, almost knocking him to the ground. Pinched back with no place to run, Secretariat fell far behind but then dug in to recover and finish fourth.

In his second race, he held back at the start to keep out of the crush of horses, then came from behind and won. That tactic became his modus operandi: a slow, safe start followed by a late surge.

In the Kentucky Derby, Secretariat again broke last out of the gates but then overtook Sham on the backstretch to win. In the Preakness, he broke last again but made his move on the first turn, surging from last to first and winning the race.

Belmont was different. His racing stable, seeing he was getting more comfortable with the start, devised a new strategy. Jockey Ron Turcotte pressed Secretariat for an opening surge, letting Big Red run with the leaders from the start and in the process setting a blistering pace, shocking the spectators. "Secretariat roared out of his rail post position like a demon possessed," wrote Marvin Drager.[1]

This strategy was a big risk. The conventional wisdom was that the Belmont Stakes—at a long one and a half miles—was about proper pacing and endurance, punishing its front-runners. In this case, the strategy paid handsome returns: Secretariat won by an astonishing thirty-one lengths and earned the Triple Crown trophy in one of the greatest athletic performances of all time, equine or human.

For Turcotte, the difference between Belmont and the prior races was like night and day. At Belmont, his goggles were clean all the way. He could see where he was going because Big Red led the field. In previous races, Turcotte had goggles caked with the dirt and mud kicked up by the horses ahead.

When launching a startup organization, the entrepreneur often has her goggles caked with mud too—mud from other horses already running in the race or from the chaos and confusion that accompanies launching. The entrepreneur needs to forge ahead—pivoting to the left and then right, sometimes hanging back and then surging forward—until she can find running room where, like Turcotte on Secretariat, she finally has a clearer view of the track. Of course, the extent of the visibility problem varies depending on whether the startup is replicating existing practices or pioneering new ones, and depending on what the industry and market conditions are like. But most entrepreneurs launch with muddy goggles.

MUDDY LAUNCH

Like Turcotte, Stephen Von Rump found himself mired in mud. He had been racing for venture financing and big, new customer accounts, but he was getting bumped around and could not see the path forward for his venture.

He and his wife, Paula, had relocated from their home in northern California to Västerås, Sweden, to launch a startup, Giraff Technologies. Giraff designs human-size robots that allow caregivers for the elderly to make virtual home visits via the Internet. Nurses and family members remotely visit a retiree in the home via a human-sized avatar on wheels equipped with a video screen. (Think Skype on wheels.) The company moved from Silicon Valley to "Robot Valley" (an enclave of robotic startups) in Sweden to penetrate the Scandinavian market as its beachhead.

Von Rump is a veteran of tough Silicon Valley startups, but Giraff was making his previous launches look like a breeze. As CEO, he had worked hard for months to line up a coalition of new Swedish investors. The company valuation in the investment term sheet was not as high as all the founders had hoped, but Von Rump and his board felt it was a good deal that would help Giraff move to the next level. The investors had sterling reputations, extensive contacts, and real belief in the company.

His founding co-owners rejected the valuation and wanted to push hard for a much higher number. Von Rump was torn. He understood their reasoning, but he knew the new Swedish investors were firm and not interested in negotiating. His co-owners refused to believe it. To them, everything was negotiable, and they insisted on playing hardball by inserting themselves into the process, pushing back, and seeking other investors. The investors in the original coalition became furious, and the deal blew up. Meanwhile, Giraff was running out of cash. Von Rump scrambled to salvage the deal, but the atmosphere was toxic.

When we spoke to Von Rump just weeks after surviving this ordeal, he was still reeling. His experience illustrates important points about building triple crown startups.

THE CHALLENGES WITH STARTUPS

Startups face three unique challenges that require leadership adjustments. The first is *extreme uncertainty*. Some startups vie for uncontested market space in tight niches with innovative offerings. When doing so, they lack visibility into what is likely to work. There is no history to build on, no clear path to follow. Even when competing in already contested market spaces, entrepreneurs cannot be certain about how to achieve sustainable competitive advantage or which business models will work. In both cases, their goggles are caked with mud. They lack vital information and clarity about how best to proceed. Yet they must act anyway, sometimes placing make-or-break bets with their limited resources.

The second problem for startups is *extreme time pressure*. Startups race to launch before their window of opportunity closes and before their cash runs out. The clock is ticking. Seed money is finite. Speed to market is essential. How to find time to plan, vet new recruits, and develop prototypes, let alone build a culture? Stress, pressure, and burnout are occupational hazards for entrepreneurs as they race to reach a seemingly endless series of critical milestones.

Third, startups operate with *extreme resource constraints*. In the early stages, they lack key people, money, hardware, software, systems, infrastructure, and more. Unlike established ventures, startups generally get little or no help from communities, governments, or even banks. They must rapidly recruit key people and allies, build or buy their technologies, develop processes, and raise funds, usually in multiple rounds. Many early-stage startups are considered too risky for bank loans and even too risky for venture capital funds, most of which finance more established ventures. For the early-stage startup, the game is bootstrapping—scavenging for all available resources to build the enterprise. Within these extreme resource constraints, founders must find ways to get traction in the market and make the necessary investments to position the venture for growth and future success. No wonder so many startups fail to reach escape velocity and crash, burning through their precious cash.

To avoid that common fate, entrepreneurs must be creatively persuasive and resourceful. A 2011 *Bloomberg Businessweek* feature story on Spotify, the Swedish music-streaming startup, described its founder as follows: "Daniel Ek is a Tom Sawyer: He finds fences that need painting, and he gets the world to pick up the brush . . . His central skill lies in talking other people into doing what he needs them to."[2] In 2012, *Forbes* dubbed Ek "the most important man in music" for his pioneering work on a free, Facebook-enabled platform "that could save the recording industry from piracy—and iTunes."[3]

The convergence of these three constraints—all related—can push entrepreneurs into compromising quality, abandoning ethics, and adopting an extreme short-term focus. The problems fall disproportionately on the shoulders of the founder. Many new ventures develop a case of "founder dependence," with everyone looking to the founder for decisions, solutions, and approval. As the enterprise grows, it can lead to "founder's syndrome," in which founders stay on too long or try to do too much when the venture has surpassed their capacities.

While these problems can be severe, startups do have certain advantages. For example, existing practices, systems, and processes do not imprison new ventures. They are free to make quick decisions and are not constrained by the layers of bureaucracy and complexity that burden large institutions. They also have a palpable excitement factor that allows them to recruit "true believers" who are passionate about the enterprise and its possibilities.

The five triple crown leadership practices apply to startups, but there are several areas that require adjustment.

BUILT TO LAST OR BUILT TO FLIP?

The first critical issue for entrepreneurs to resolve is *why* they are starting their venture. Will the enterprise be "built to last" or "built to flip"? Will they be what Randy Komisar calls "missionary" entrepreneurs, building something purposeful, impactful, and sustainable, or will they be "mercenary" ones, interested solely in personal wealth creation, status, and recognition? If the latter, fair enough, but it is critical to avoid falsely raising expectations among partners and employees who may have a different vision.

Our focus is not on mercenary entrepreneurs, although we respect their efforts and contributions (from job creation and product innovation to investor returns and economic development). Our focus is on the missionary, built-to-last entrepreneur who wants to build an outstanding organization—whether in the commercial or nonprofit sphere—that operates ethically and endures. Fortunately, purpose and profits are not mutually exclusive, and financial success is not incompatible with sustainability and social impact. (See chapter ten for more on this topic.)

In time, a built-to-last startup may conduct an initial public offering (IPO), merge with a compatible organization, or stay independent and grow organically and through acquisitions. But the reason it operates is to generate value and leave a lasting mark on the world. This sense of purpose at the outset colors many subsequent decisions and steps.

"KNOW THYSELF"

Socrates' admonition to "know thyself" is relevant to all leaders, but perhaps especially so to entrepreneurs. Founders are wise to reflect inward before building outward: What are your purpose and values? What is your vision for your life? What are the key goals in the different areas of your life? What is your tolerance for risk? What are you willing to give up to make your venture succeed? Do you intend to create a lifestyle venture, a simple small business, a transformational social venture, or a high-growth, take-the-world-by-storm company? What kind of culture do you want to establish? Will you pursue the triple crown quest? These questions will be answered, by either conscious choice or default. Excellent, ethical, and enduring organizations do not magically appear without conscious and persistent effort.

IP5280

We interviewed John Scarborough and Jeffrey Pearl, co-founders and managing partners of IP5280 Communications, a Colorado-based provider of hosted Voice over Internet Protocol and cloud-based communication services. They purposefully built their company culture, which they characterized as one of "adventure, winning, and pride," right from the start. According to Scarborough:

> We figured out long ago that having a vision of the culture you want to create must start from the very beginning. In most startups, the culture evolves haphazardly. That's a real shame. The culture should be well defined from the beginning. The culture and the business plan go hand in hand, because they help people understand the company's direction and how they can contribute. Culture is the underpinning for success.

When Scarborough and Pearl interview people, they ask questions about personal examples of pride, winning, and adventure. They ask about candidates' first work experiences and what they learned from them. They do deep reference checking, gauging the person's moral compass and fit with the company culture. Clearly, they recruit for heart as well as head. They also use a dashboard of key metrics both to keep the venture on track with critical milestones and to ensure alignment.

The company's revenues grew by 98 percent between 2008 and 2011, and profits have been consistent and robust. IP5280 ranks among the best companies to work for in Colorado and among the fastest-growing companies in the United States. According to Pearl, "We operate in a competitive environment, but it's exciting. There is a tidal wave of change occurring in the marketplace. There is a kind of magic in the office—a feeling of exhilaration, success, and fulfillment that you worked hard and the numbers are going up into the lights."

MegaPath acquired IP5280 in early 2012, with Scarborough and Pearl holding senior leadership roles in the company and every IP5280 employee keeping his or her job.

STAKEHOLDER FIT

Entrepreneurs should probe potential stakeholders carefully for fit. Established organizations already have a set of founders, board members, investors, customers, and vendors. The entrepreneur must decide who should be in each stakeholder set from the outset. These decisions can be crucial to future success.

Founders. Most people think of a solo entrepreneur when they think about startups, but often it is a partnership or founding team that launches ventures, as it was at Apple, Baidu, DropBox, Facebook, Google, H&M, HP, Infosys, KIPP, LinkedIn, Mayo Clinic, Microsoft, Share Our Strength, Skype, Spotify, Twitter, YouTube, Zynga, and countless others.

Some entrepreneurs spend hundreds of hours on market research and prototyping but jump into partnerships with hardly any thought or scrutiny. They rely only on gut feeling, or they choose to work with their buddies or the first people who come along. Effectively, they are jumping into a marriage without dating. Instead, potential partners should ask hard questions: Is there a fundamental fit among the founding partners? Do they like, admire, and respect each other? Do they

share a similar vision for the enterprise? Do they have compatible values and work styles? Can they be totally honest with each other? Do
they have complementary skills? Do they agree about the exit plan?

Big problems occur when fundamental fit is missing, as Von
Rump experienced at Giraff Technologies:

> There was a fundamental misalignment among the own-
> ers about fundamental values and vision. There was a conflict
> between, on the one hand, the passion for the business and what
> we are doing for the world and, on the other hand, the financial
> value. There was no common anchor point. The only resolu-
> tion, unfortunately, was to part ways.

Von Rump and the new investors negotiated an exit plan with
the founders, incurring the necessary casualties due to lack of agreement on the colors.

Board Members. When forming the board of directors,
entrepreneurs must determine the size of the board, the right balance
between inside and outside directors, the working relationship
between the board and management team, the frequency and length
of board meetings, the number and type of board committees, the
best person to serve as board chair, and board compensation. How
engaged will the board be with the venture: will it be a passive,
certifying, engaged, intervening, or operating board?[4] At worst, a
board can be a hassle and distraction, draining valuable time and
injecting politics and turf wars into the venture. In many cases, a
board is just a formality and does not add much value. At best, a
board can be an invaluable asset to the venture, providing critical
advice, mentoring, and oversight.

Investors. Entrepreneurs should also probe for fundamental fit
among possible investors. Entrepreneurs should expect that venture
capitalists and angel investors will perform extensive due diligence

on them before investing, but many entrepreneurs do not turn the tables and sufficiently scrutinize potential investors. Angel investor and venture capital deals typically come with aggressive return-on-investment (ROI) expectations that require lucrative and fast exits (via mergers or IPOs). Entrepreneurs must weigh their investor options carefully, lest they find people in critical positions of power who diverge with them on fundamental issues. What is their expected ROI and time horizon? How involved will they be with the venture, including board seats? What is their reputation? Do they share similar values and a common vision for the venture? Entrepreneurs are wise to consider the strings attached to investment deals.

As K12 (the online education startup where Gregg was a senior vice president) progressed through several financing rounds during its startup years, cash sometimes ran low due to customer payment delays or other factors. Fortunately, one of the key investors provided bridge loans to keep the venture afloat. Along the way, he also asked tough questions that nobody else dared to ask and provided wise counsel as the company navigated choppy waters. That investor added great value to the venture.

Customers. Some customers take advantage of startups, exaggerating their interest, delaying orders, or demanding extensive technical support and new bells and whistles. The best customers are early adopters willing to work with a startup, investing their own time and expertise to inform prototype and product development decisions. Not all startups have the luxury of being able to choose customers, but founders should recognize that not all customers are equal. Some come with heavy baggage and prohibitive costs. In some cases, entrepreneurs can reduce risk by diversifying their customer base, not becoming too dependent on a small number of customers.

Vendors. Founders should also scrutinize potential vendors for fit. Many vendors, especially large ones, are unsympathetic to the tribulations of a startup. Do they understand the venture's cash flow situation? Will they cut you off at a critical time when you most need components? Will they ship you second-rate material or skimp on technical support? Founders are wise to choose critical vendors only after extensive screening, then establish deep, open, and mutually beneficial relationships. They should outline what each party can expect and set up periodic senior management check-ins between the organizations to ensure alignment of interests and effective processes. Startups that take vendors for granted may not live to regret it. When Patagonia (the outdoor equipment company) entered the clothing market in the 1970s, it contracted with vendors in Asia for shirt production. The vendors' late shipments and poor quality almost bankrupted the firm.[5]

Vendor Woes

Gregg: In our early startup days at K12, we were racing to meet a hard deadline: the first day of school in August. On that day, K12 would start educating students all over the United States through innovative new virtual schools—with students doing self-paced, mastery-based lessons at home, supported by trained professional teachers working remotely and monitoring student progress online. The employees had been working day and night for months, designing the curriculum, building lessons and assessments, coding and animating them, and developing the digital infrastructure for the online lessons, assessments, attendance, and other school records. Meanwhile, all the online lessons had physical materials accompanying them, from history textbooks and vocabulary workbooks to science equipment, math manipulatives, and art supplies.

K12 was running three sprints at once: the online race (to design thousands of high-quality, research-based lessons), the offline race (to source and distribute thousands of boxes of instructional materials to individual students nationwide), and the marketplace race (to find partners, negotiate contracts for its affiliated virtual schools, and enroll students). All three were down to the wire as August arrived. We had been hiring people at a breakneck pace and praying that the online school would work as planned when our engineering team "flipped the switch."

To our surprise, it was boxes that almost killed us, not bits and bytes. We had been fretting more about the enormously complicated technical build, but it was old-fashioned packing and shipping that tripped us up. Our distribution vendor had served schools and districts for a century, shipping cases of books here and boxes of pens there, but we needed the company to pack and ship several boxes, each containing dozens of different items, to thousands of customers nationwide at their homes. The vendor had signed our contract, but it was set up for business-to-business, not business-to-consumer, distribution. K12's success in landing contracts and signing up customers overwhelmed the vendor's warehouse systems and staff. They could not keep up.

As a result, we couldn't get our boxes full of books, art tablets, magnifying glasses, and other school items to students fast enough. Some families got the wrong boxes. Others got the wrong stuff in their boxes. Others got boxes weeks or even months after school had started. We were getting calls from screaming-mad parents all over the country, and there was nothing we could do. We apologized profusely. We designed temporary online workarounds. We read our vendor the riot act. We even made plans to pack boxes and drive fleets of trucks ourselves.

It was a disaster. We weren't blameless. We had not planned sufficiently, built in extra time, or developed backup plans. We trusted too much and had not staffed adequately for oversight. It was a painful lesson about choosing the right vendor and coordinating with the company. It almost brought us to our knees.

Fortunately, we squeaked by, and K12 went on to thrive with rapid growth, a strong academic record, enthusiastic (and forgiving) customers, a successful IPO, and a positive impact on tens of thousands of students nationwide and eventually worldwide. When it came to key vendors, we learned valuable lessons about probing and planning.

EMPLOYEE FIT

In the world today, there's plenty of technology, entrepreneurs, money, venture capital. What's in short supply is great teams. Your biggest challenge will be building a great team . . . Focus on the team. Teams win.

—**John Doerr,** venture capitalist, Kleiner Perkins Caufield and Byers

We interviewed Andreas Ehn, co-founder and chief technology officer of Wrapp, a digital gift card service launched in Sweden in 2011 using mobile applications and social media. When asked about the keys to leading high-growth, technology-driven startups, Ehn told us, "If you can get only one thing right, it's recruiting. You need to find excellent people who are a good fit and outstanding in their fields. Everything else is secondary."

Recruiting is tough for startups because they have very little that is tangible at the outset, and they lack brand recognition. Founders must explain their vision and convince talented people to take a leap of faith, forgoing higher salaries and greater security elsewhere. They have to believe.

Complementarity. Entrepreneurs must go beyond recruiting people with head and heart. They need to recruit people whose skills augment their own. Technical founders who are weak in finance or sales, for example, should not just hire other techies. It is essential to have a detail-oriented person on the team—a point overlooked in many new ventures. Entrepreneurs should hire for the skills lacking on the team, while ensuring that new recruits share the dream, have integrity, and fit the culture. Entrepreneurs must build a complementary team, with people who enhance one another's capabilities, making a more balanced or complete whole.

Faster Cuts. Recruiting is not an exact science. Even the best organizations, without the time and resource constraints of a startup, make mistakes. Candidates put on their interview faces, sometimes feigning interest or exaggerating expertise. Bad hires are costly to startups, draining energy, momentum, and money. Some walk away with valuable intellectual property, trade secrets, or proprietary ideas. If there is no alternative position in the venture for a mistaken hire, the entrepreneur must face up to it quickly and part company. The startup has no time to reprogram people.

ALIGNMENT PIVOTS

Everybody has a plan till they get punched in the mouth.

—**Mike Tyson,** champion boxer

One of the biggest differences between startups and mature organizations concerns alignment. Entrepreneurs must align startups, but they must learn to "pivot" faster and further than established enterprises—rapidly changing direction in response to market feedback, competitive actions, and technology disruptions. Entrepreneurs must continually re-align as they iterate their way toward a business model that works. They must plan, but they must also be willing and able to abandon their plans and make new ones before missing the window of opportunity.

In *Getting to Plan B*, authors John Mullins and Randy Komisar quip, "What separates the men from the boys . . . is what they do when their first plan fails."[6] Startup success requires making many midcourse corrections. Many entrepreneurs these days do not even develop a business plan. Instead, they focus on pitching and prototyping to get market feedback, make necessary changes, and keep tweaking the model until it takes off.[7]

Ehn (also the former chief technology officer of Spotify) told us that both Spotify and Wrapp, like many other startups, made major pivots early on. Spotify, for example, initially planned to launch a streaming service that included both music and video but later abandoned the video plans after facing licensing challenges and determining the market was not ready. The Spotify founders also planned to offer only a free music-streaming service, backed by an advertising revenue model. After getting market feedback, they pivoted, adding a premium subscription service. They were then able to launch in seven European markets and the United States. By 2011, Spotify had 300 employees, 11.5 million registered users, rapid growth, and a lot of buzz.[8]

In *The New Entrepreneurial Leader*, Babson College professors and researchers emphasize the need for entrepreneurs to be "cognitively ambidextrous," shifting between "prediction logic" (acting based on analysis of known trends) and "creation logic" (devising options in the face of uncertainty).[9] They say the former is like assembling a puzzle from jigsaw pieces, and the latter is like designing a quilt from assorted fabrics. With prediction logic, entrepreneurs use existing tools, frameworks, and data to guide decision-making, identify optimal solutions, and mitigate risks. Unfortunately, entrepreneurs do not always have that luxury. While waiting for customer input or other data, the window of opportunity may close. Therefore, entrepreneurs must also use creation logic, an action-oriented approach focused on expanding the available opportunities through an iterative process of probes, pilots, and pivots—designing the venture as conditions continually change. Entrepreneurs must flex between the two sides, blending planning and analysis with intuition and innovation.

CHOOSING THE TRIPLE CROWN QUEST

In the swirl of a startup, with all its frenetic activity and pressure, entrepreneurs shape the culture either purposefully or by default. In the throng of daily decisions, patterns emerge that drive the venture in the future. How do the leaders make tradeoffs between the interests of employees, customers, owners, and others? Do they work to align those interests creatively? Do they build and invest in a culture of character? Do they keep their commitments? Do they develop their people? Do they build a foundation for long-term success even as they meet their short-term obligations? Do they choose the triple crown quest?

Early decisions lay the groundwork for the venture's future culture. What results are sought? How will they be achieved? What checks will be used to work through dilemmas and ensure ethical practices? What behaviors will not be tolerated? Will the venture operate sustainably? Will it give back to the community?

It is easy to get lost in the day-to-day details, but these decisions form the organization's culture over time. *Investments in people, culture, and leadership require discipline and foresight but pay big dividends.* Over time, acting in accordance with the organization's purpose, values, and vision becomes second nature to people throughout the venture.

According to Von Rump at Giraff, "Our long-term goal is to be a centerpiece of the smart home of the future. I use our weekly staff meeting to pull us back up and make sure that what we are doing is consistent with the ultimate goal. It is very easy for these things to slide off track." He gets valuable support and mentorship from his board, helping him maintain focus on the big picture while he is putting out fires.

Steve Mushero, co-founder and CEO of China NetCloud (a server management and cloud computing startup based in Shanghai), told us how he too must be a steward of the long-term perspective in the swirl of the startup:

> I am constantly telling our people, "Today we have twenty engineers and two hundred customers, but in a few months we'll have double that. When we have five hundred engineers, how are we going to do this?" The natural tendency is to think short term and solve today's problems. I spend almost all my effort dragging toward the long term: How are we going to grow? What are the systems, processes, and training we need to get to scale?

Mushero hires people who have no other daily responsibilities than developing plans and processes for the scaled company they envision in the future. He structures their bonuses around long-term growth milestones.

Ehn told us about the short- versus long-term tradeoffs in high-tech startups like Spotify and Wrapp. Faced with crushing deadlines, some engineers may be tempted to build suboptimal programs knowing they can fix them later. When those programs are fundamental to the platform, Ehn insists on investing the time and resources to do it right the first time. To do so, Ehn fights at the senior management team level for those scarce resources that also have other valid uses. "You build value in the company," Ehn told us, "by designing something to last" (the endurance imperative).

PATAGONIA

Canadian entrepreneur Yvon Chouinard built Patagonia after going to the junkyard and teaching himself how to forge metal like a blacksmith.[10] He loved the outdoors, including surfing, kayaking, falconry, fly fishing, and mountain climbing. After about a dozen years, the venture became the largest supplier of climbing hardware in the United States.

When Chouinard discovered that the company's steel pitons damaged the climbing rocks, he switched over to aluminum, even though steel pitons accounted for 70 percent of Patagonia's sales. It was a principled decision, based on his personal convictions about environmental stewardship. Chouinard decided to make all decisions as though Patagonia would be in business for a hundred years (the enduring imperative).

Patagonia was an early pioneer of maternity leave and onsite childcare. Chouinard created the now-famous "Let My People Go Surfing" flex-time policy for employees. Patagonia offers comprehensive health insurance, even to part-time employees. It donates 1 percent of sales to community and environmental groups. Its catalog was the first in the United States to use recycled paper. In 1994, it began to switch to organic cotton after conducting an environmental impact assessment and determining that regular cotton is too harmful due to the pesticides used to cultivate it.

These moves have been good for both the bottom line and the environment. For example, after changing packaging of Patagonia underwear from cardboard and plastic bags to a rubber band, the company saved $150,000 in packaging, reduced material consumption by twelve tons, and boosted sales by 25 percent. Its unprecedented corporate effort to recycle fabrics resulted in reduced production costs.

The privately held company now generates about $300 million in revenues and is widely recognized as one of the most ethical and environmentally responsible corporations on the planet.

Patagonia is not perfect. The company filed for bankruptcy after growing too quickly and running out of cash during a recession.[11] Chouinard acknowledges that he has made mistakes along the way, but the company employs many triple crown leadership practices: the staff at Patagonia hire carefully, recruiting what Chouinard calls "ensemble players," not stars who seek the limelight; they do extensive interviewing of candidates, where several staff members determine both skills and fit; and they evaluate decisions through the lens of ethics and sustainability. Patagonia employees are stewards of their shared values.

According to Chouinard, "In every long-lasting business, the methods of conducting the business may constantly change, but the values, the culture, and the philosophies remain constant . . . We have made many mistakes during the past decade, but at no point have we lost our way for very long."[12]

For Patagonia, clarity about values and culture from the beginning, with consistent follow-through, has been a critical success factor.

CHAPTER SUMMARY

When launching new ventures, entrepreneurs get muddy goggles from the chaos and confusion of launching or the competitive scrum around them. They race forward anyway, often at breathtaking speed, with limited visibility into where they are going.

Because they face extreme uncertainty, time pressure, and resource constraints, most startups do not survive. Some that do survive compromise their integrity and long-term vision along the way.

Triple crown leadership practices, adjusted for the unique challenges of startups, can help entrepreneurs avoid that fate.

How? Commit to create a triple crown organization that is built to last, not to flip. Purposefully shape a culture of character. Recruit for complementary skills and cultural fit, vetting your partners, employees, board members, customers, and vendors before working with them. Face up to it when you make bad hires. Make quick pivots. Passionately pursue your dream, and make it reality.

Practical Applications

1. Is your startup built to flip or built to last? Is it mercenary or missionary?
2. What are you doing to build an excellent, ethical, and enduring organization?
   a. What more should you do?
3. Do you refuse to take ethical shortcuts even when the pressure is on? What methods do you use to help?
4. Have you clearly defined your personal purpose, values, vision, goals, and risk tolerance?
   a. What more should you do?
5. To what extent have you defined your desired culture?
   a. What steps are you taking to build it?
6. Are you recruiting for people with complementary skills as well as head and heart?
   a. What more should you do?
7. How are you vetting your partners, board members, investors, customers, and key vendors for fundamental fit?
   a. What more should you do?
8. How are you pivoting when midcourse corrections are needed?
9. Are you parting quickly with mistaken hires?
10. To what extent are you positioning the venture for long-term success and scale even as you meet your short-term obligations?
11. Is the venture true to your dream?
    a. What are the most important things you need to do to make it so?

CHAPTER TEN

SOCIAL IMPACT

Make sure you aren't riding an old horse in a new race.

—**Cheryl Matthynssens,** entrepreneur
and counselor

Gary Erickson was about to become rich, and it was making him sick.

A young entrepreneur from northern California, Erickson had founded a bakery while living in his garage with little more than his two prized possessions, a bike and trumpet. He loved everything about the outdoors—hiking, camping, and long bike rides through the mountains. After accompanying a friend on a grueling daylong bike ride—what Erickson calls his "epiphany ride"—he came up with the idea for a better-tasting energy bar. He named it Clif Bar after his father, and the bakery eventually turned into an energy bar company. He worked hard with his business partner and his wife, Kit Crawford (who also worked at the company), to make it a resounding success.

After several years of exciting growth, though, they were under tremendous pressure. The industry was consolidating. Nestle, a $50 billion powerhouse, bought Power Bar, and Kraft bought Balance Bar. There was downward pricing pressure on energy bars; and the owners, stressed out and fearing they could not compete against the mega-companies, struck a deal to sell the company for three times the prior year's revenue—a home run.

But something bothered Erickson, who wrote about the day of the sale in his book, *Raising the Bar*:

> Monday, April 17, 2000, and I was about to become a very rich man. Today my business partner and I would sell Clif Bar Inc., our company, for $120 million. . . . I'd never have to work again. But instead of feeling excited, I felt nauseated constantly and hadn't slept well in weeks.
>
> Attorneys . . . had worked feverishly all weekend. Head honchos flew in from the Midwest to finalize the details. Finally it was late Monday morning, and I stood in the office waiting to go out and sign the contract. Out of nowhere I started to shake and couldn't breathe. I'd climbed big mountains, raced bicycles, played horn in jazz concerts: I handled pressure well, so this first-ever anxiety attack took me by surprise. I told my partner

that I needed to walk around the block. Outside, as I started across the parking lot, I began to weep, overwhelmed. "How did I get here? Why am I doing this?" I kept walking. Halfway around the block I stopped dead in my tracks, hit by an epiphany. I felt in my gut, "I'm not done," and then "I don't have to do this." I began to laugh, feeling free, instantly. I turned around, went back to the office and told my partner, "Send them home. I can't sell the company."

Erickson bought out his partner, paying her $55 million over time by leveraging the company with debt financing, and he and his wife threw their hearts and souls into taking Clif Bar to the next level and restoring the initial magic.[1] Erickson said, "I wanted to create a place where people had fun, worked hard, and felt that their work had meaning."

With a focus on nutritious and organic foods and drinks, Erickson and Crawford, as co-owners and co-CEOs, rebuilt Clif Bar around "five aspirations": sustaining the company's brands, business, people, community, and the planet. Crawford explained: "The interconnectivity of the five aspirations empowers our people, because it creates a decision-making framework which encourages people to look at their responsibilities from a variety of perspectives. It allows them to explore, create, and launch ideas that are in tune with the company's priorities."

The company bases employee performance reviews on the five aspirations, including each aspiration individually and how employees balance all five together. Crawford told us:

> Our approach to leadership is about staying true to our values as a company and creating a culture that inspires and motivates our people to bring those values to life . . . We challenge each other to do better—to make better food, to reduce our company's impact on the planet, and to give back to the community. We have a community that embraces hard work, creativity, and

play. It's a group of people who share similar values and a common vision.

To have a positive impact on its workers, Clif Bar offers flextime, sabbaticals, and an elaborate wellness program, including paid workout time for employees and an in-house fitness center with climbing walls, yoga classes, and several full-time personal trainers. The company offers nutritional counseling, massage, and life coaching to employees.

Many executives would consider these unnecessary expenses. To Erickson and Crawford, they are critical investments. "Inspired people," says Erickson, "are a company's most valuable resource."

Clif Bar also has a longstanding commitment to the environment, as demonstrated by its staff ecologist and impressive new solar-powered facility—the first 500-kilowatt, "smart" solar array in North America. Clif Bar offers financial incentives ($1,000 per person annually) to employees for making energy-efficient home improvements, commuting by bicycle, taking alternative transportation, and purchasing high-mileage hybrid or biodiesel vehicles.

Clif Bar has managed all this with a double-digit compounded annual growth rate and a long list of employment, diversity, and sustainability awards, including making *Inc.*'s list of the fastest-growing companies in the United States and *Forbes*'s "breakaway brands," in both cases for multiple years.

Of course, pressures remain. Industry competition still takes a bite, and the number of competitors has increased. But Clif Bar leads the market in several retail channels and continues to look to its aspirations and enduring commitments to keep it in shape.

As Clif Bar illustrates, social impact is not just for nonprofits, nor is it only about stewardship of resources and attention to external stakeholders. It can mean creating a quality workplace—with powerful effects on personal development and economic security.

Bright Horizons Family Solutions has also created a great place to work. The company is the world's leading provider of employer-sponsored childcare and early education. Founded in 1986, Bright Horizons serves about seventy thousand children each day at ninety Fortune 500 firms. As of 2012, the company had made *Fortune*'s 100 Best Companies to Work For list for thirteen years. No other company in this space has achieved it even once. It has also earned awards from *Inc., Working Mother, Diversity,* the Corporate Equality Index, and more.

Mary Ann Tocio, president and chief operating officer, told us, "Our culture is built on passion for what we do. We are in this business to make a difference in the lives of children, and we're also smart about the fact that it is a business. Profit is our oxygen line."

Bright Horizons is a social impact organization, focusing on the young children in its care, its people, *and* profit.

SOCIAL IMPACT ORGANIZATIONS

Today, many people are debating the proper role of the three traditional organizational sectors—business, government, and nonprofits—in society. A broader view about creating value for multiple stakeholders, which has been around for decades, is gaining momentum. A raft of ongoing social, economic, governmental, and environmental breakdowns has caused people to search for new models and call for fundamental changes in business and government. Some businesses are embracing what author Patricia Aburdene and others call "conscious capitalism" and variations thereof. Millions of people worldwide, with younger generations in the vanguard, are seeking new ways of working that take the best of the old world and leave the worst behind.

In horseracing terms, it is not just another race. A set of new races is emerging that has a new scoreboard, one that also measures "social impact"—going beyond solely financial returns (still critically important for many reasons, of course) to address social issues such as employee development, the environment, health, poverty, education, fair trade, human rights, disaster relief, and more. In short, some leaders commit to positive social impact as well as financial viability and success.

Today, many different kinds of organizations are pursuing social impact: nonprofits, foundations, social ventures, impact investors, and socially responsible businesses. New organizational forms are emerging, including for-benefit enterprises (B corporations), community interest companies (in the United Kingdom), low-profit limited liability companies (L3Cs), flexible-purpose corporations, and more. Boundaries between sectors are fading. Writing in *Harvard Business Review* in 2011, social entrepreneur Heerad Sabeti argued that for-benefit ventures "can fill the gaps created by the failure of the three-sector model [business, government, and nonprofits]."

Social impact organizations have some unique advantages, such as community goodwill, volunteer help, and tax advantages in some countries. Social impact organizations also tap into the desire of many for meaningful work—a powerful talent recruitment and retention force.

Teach For America (TFA), for example, has recruited 33,000 teachers since 1990 to work in underresourced urban and rural public schools. Among college seniors, TFA is a hot commodity. In the 2010–2011 school year, 18 percent of Harvard University seniors and 16 percent of Princeton seniors applied to TFA. TFA is one of the top recruiters at over a hundred colleges in the United States. It recently had 48,000 applicants for 5,300 teaching positions. TFA has ranked recently in the top ten of *Bloomberg Businessweek*'s Best Places to Launch a Career list. In 2011 and 2012, TFA was named one of *Fortune*'s 100 Best Companies to Work For.

On the other hand, social impact organizations also face two major challenges that require some flexing in the five leadership practices.

Resource Constraints

First, while all organizations confront resource constraints, social impact organizations often face them in the extreme, detracting from their ability to serve their target populations. Because of these resource constraints, many social impact initiatives never achieve

financial sustainability. Like hamsters on a treadmill, they perpetu-
ally scramble for resources, with the risk of burning out their people
through extreme overload. Still others reach a certain level of impact
but hit a ceiling and never scale the enterprise.

In corporations, social initiatives compete for resources with
other parts of the business. For nonprofits, the ongoing need to raise
money can be a big drain on service provision and quality. Many
foundations are conservative and risk averse when it comes to grants,
focusing on funding discrete programs instead of building organizational infrastructure and capacity to deliver services, programs, and
products. Some nonprofits are overly dependent on a small number
of funders. Such donor dependence can raise conflicts between nonprofits and donors, sometimes causing the former to stray from their
core (a common phenomenon called "mission drift").

There are also fewer capital markets for investment and research
and development in the social sector, though some "impact investors" and venture philanthropies are now emerging to rectify that
deficiency.

Venture Philanthropy: Creating Leverage for Social Impact

Echoing Green is a nonprofit investor in next-generation social entrepreneurs. It provides
seed funding, training, consulting, and networking, sponsoring successful social enterprises like Teach For America, City Year, Jumpstart, and more. Echoing Green has invested
over $30 million in seed grants to more than five hundred social entrepreneurs in forty-two
countries on five continents. Five years after completion of their Echoing Green fellowship,
leaders of sponsored organizations raised more than a billion dollars, the equivalent of
forty-four times their initial Echoing Green seed investment. Echoing Green also measures
its fellows' idea diffusion, the extent to which others adopt their approaches.

New Profit, Inc., is a nonprofit venture philanthropy fund that centers around two
mutually reinforcing sets of activities. New Profit provides multiyear financial and strategic support to a portfolio of innovative social entrepreneurs and their organizations,
while also pursuing a range of strategies to help create an environment in which all
social innovators may realize their full potential for impact. Vanessa Kirsch, founder and

managing director, told us, "New Profit is interested in building a movement of social entrepreneurs and changing the world."

Measurement Challenges

Second, there is the challenge of measurement. While measuring the financial bottom line can be relatively straightforward for businesses, measuring social impact can be elusive. The consequences can be problematic, including inattention to results (focusing instead on intention, effort, and process) as well as dispersion of efforts (without clear metrics and data to manage to). Fortunately, Ashoka, Acumen Fund, and others are developing innovative ways to measure what they call "social return on investment," but these measures are still works in progress.[2]

The SEED Foundation: A New Breed of Schools[3]

Everybody knows that boarding schools are for children of privilege raised in leafy suburbs. Everybody, that is, except Eric Adler and Rajiv Vinnakota, who one day discovered they had the exact same idea.

Separately, they had both envisioned a college-preparatory, public boarding school for underserved children in urban cities. In 1998, they gave up their lucrative management consulting careers and launched The SEED Foundation, which created the first urban public boarding school in the United States in the nation's capital. They worked for sixteen months without salary.

SEED offers an academic, social, and life skills curriculum to prepare students for college and beyond. The students—mostly minority students from low-income communities, 75 percent of whom enter the schools performing below grade level—live in dormitories five days a week, and the school encourages parents to volunteer to maintain a strong school-home connection. The students are inculcated with the idea that they will go to college from the time they enter the school.

SEED built its first school on the foundation of an abandoned, torched public school. The four buildings on the Washington, D.C., site include an academic building, a gym, a cafeteria, and dormitories where faculty provide round-the-clock supervision.

Adler and Vinnakota had to marshal resources to bend reality to their vision, including staging elaborate fund-raising campaigns and lobbying to change laws so that government funds could support their innovative urban, public boarding school model.

Now SEED operates public boarding schools in Washington, D.C., and Baltimore—with more in the works in other cities, including Cincinnati, Ohio. The schools receive two to three applicants for every available slot. To be admitted to The SEED School of Maryland, students must meet two of seven risk factors, including a record of truancy or suspension, a household below the poverty line, or an incarcerated immediate family member.

What are their results? According to the *New York Times Magazine*, the SEED school in Washington, D.C., "outpaces D.C. public schools in reading and math." Ninety-one percent of students who enter the ninth grade at SEED graduate from high school, and 94 percent of SEED graduates between 2004 and 2011 gained admission to four-year colleges and universities. Compared with their peers, three times as many SEED graduates complete college within six years.

While SEED has made impressive inroads against great challenges, the road was bumpy at times. Adler and Vinnakota encountered both of the challenges facing social impact organizations: resource constraints and measurement challenges. In terms of resources, they had to create a well-oiled fund-raising machine and lobby to change laws to cover the costs of room and board as well as teaching, supplies, and facilities in urban schools. As for measurement, SEED's success was dependent, not only on test scores and graduation rates, but on behavioral incidents, attitude changes, and school culture, which are harder to measure.

Of course, the team the men formed would be a key driver of success. The co-founders' biggest mistake was hiring people who were not good fits for some of the key leadership positions in the early years, with painful effects on their flagship school's performance, culture, and student retention. The problem was a function of two triple crown leadership practices—the team (recruiting process) and the organizational colors. Adler explained, "We made the mistake of assuming that people would share our values and our understanding of our mission. Over time, it became clear that was wrong. People don't just naturally share those things, so we became more aware of needing to clearly and immediately communicate our beliefs and establish a culture at the school."

In response, they started vetting candidates more thoroughly and doubled down on the colors. "The definition of an organization with integrity," Adler told us, "is one that does what it says it does. If you say you're there for kids, you must be there for kids.

If you say that you're going to provide a rigorous education, you must actually do it." Essentially, their ethical commitment to excellent performance would also help them endure by attracting students and families, quality educators, foundations, donors, government funds, and more, helping SEED achieve financial sustainability and perhaps impact more children by expanding to new areas.

TRIPLE CROWN SOCIAL IMPACT

Unfortunately, not every social impact organization can overcome the challenges of resource constraints and measurement challenges. As we have seen, those challenges can wreak havoc on organizations, causing new problems:

- *Mission drift.* Straying from core aims due to countervailing pressures from funders or others

- *Fund-raising treadmill.* Endlessly chasing donations and resources, often at the expense of program offerings and quality

- *Donor dependence.* Becoming overly reliant on a small number of funders

- *Financial instability.* Continually cutting back and making adjustments to shore up a precarious financial position

- *Leader dependence.* Becoming overly reliant on the efforts or talents of a charismatic leader

- *Inattention to results.* Focusing on intention, effort, and process instead of important outcomes

- *Dispersion of efforts.* Wasting time and resources due to lack of alignment about goals, strategies, and processes, caused by measurement challenges

Fortunately, there are things leaders can do to mitigate these painful ripple effects. We now turn to what needs special emphasis in the five triple crown leadership practices to address these common problems:

1. *Head and heart.* Working for social impact is a commitment of the heart. It taps into people's values and desire for meaningful work. This heart focus can become problematic if taken too far. While many enterprises focus on the head and neglect the heart when recruiting (as covered in chapter two), many social ventures make the opposite mistake. To achieve the impacts they seek, they must ensure people have experience, knowledge, qualifications, and skill sets necessary to get the job done. Otherwise, they will drag the organization down, making others pick up the slack. In recruiting and promoting people, social impact organizations cannot confuse passion for the work with the skill sets required. They need both.

2. *The colors.* Social ventures are mission driven, but as we showed earlier, they encounter powerful waves that can lead to mission drift. The financial pressures can take the organization far out at sea, as leaders try to placate critical funders with a different agenda. As a result, leaders must be fanatical about their organizational colors (purpose, values, and vision) and willing to forgo resources that put the colors at risk. Here, a long-term perspective is essential. If key funders or other partners are pressuring the venture away from its core, imagine how those pressures will intensify over time as the relationship deepens. Better to address those tensions early in the process. When an organization has coalesced collaboratively around a common purpose, shared values, and an inspiring vision, it becomes much better prepared to resist mission drift.

3. *Steel and velvet.* In some social ventures, their good intentions and noble aspirations become a velvet lovefest. People bask in the sunlight of the cause and avoid conflict. A culture of complacency can ensue when leaders fail to step up and hold people accountable for results: "Bill is a great guy. He cares about our work. He puts in long hours and wants to make a difference." Meanwhile, Bill is not getting the job done, and the venture is languishing. For the sake of the cause and all its desired impacts, leaders must flex to the steel edge of leadership when necessary to drive results. Too many social ventures suffer from a glut of velvet and dearth of steel.

4. *Stewards.* There are many charismatic leaders with larger-than-life personalities in the social sector. They exhibit great passion and infectious energy. In some cases, those strengths overwhelm others, leading them to defer too much to the executive director or CEO. Many social ventures need more leadership from the whole stable and less reliance on the horse. They must diversify and distribute the leadership throughout the enterprise. The importance of stewardship in social ventures cannot be overemphasized. We have seen too many executive directors and senior management teams throw up their hands and defer to the board on critical matters, even when the board's exposure to the issues and tradeoffs is limited. It is also essential to diversify the donor base so that one stakeholder does not dictate a direction incompatible with the colors. Ideally, all the funders will support the colors and become stewards themselves of the culture of character.

5. *Alignment.* Given the measurement challenges in the sector, leaders must pay particular attention to the Alignment Model. They must develop measurable goals with focused action plans and accountability milestones, and they must systematically gather data to track progress. They must cre-

ate robust feedback loops to communicate progress to all relevant stakeholders. And they must systematically define, gather, and review metrics of both financial and social impact, including qualitative and quantitative factors.

As we have seen, many leadership flexes are required for social ventures, given the need to create both financial sustainability and impact. Such a task is hard enough as it is, much less for organizations that aspire to large-scale impact. We now turn to one such venture, Ashoka, designed not just to make improvements but to change entire systems.

Ashoka: Social Impact at Scale

The job of a social entrepreneur is to recognize when a part of society is stuck and to provide new ways to get it unstuck. He or she finds what is not working and solves the problem by changing the system, spreading the solution, and persuading entire societies to take new leaps. Social entrepreneurs are not content just to give a fish or teach how to fish. They will not rest until they have revolutionized the fishing industry.

—**Bill Drayton,** founder and CEO, Ashoka

Ashoka is the world's largest association of leading social entrepreneurs. Founded by Bill Drayton in 1980, the social venture now has more than three thousand Ashoka Fellows (social entrepreneurs with bold and innovative solutions who receive support from Ashoka) in seventy-five countries across seven continents. In the beginning, Drayton saw firsthand the problem of resource constraints and risk-averse funders. "For the first five years of Ashoka," he said, "I could not get one public foundation in the United States to support us with one cent."[4]

Drayton, soft-spoken and reflective by nature, demonstrated fierce commitment in gathering the necessary resources. With a 2012 annual budget of more than $50 million from different sources, including individuals, entrepreneurs, and companies, Ashoka invests strategically in scouting talent, spotting emerging trends, connecting people, and leveraging its network of social entrepreneurs to amplify their collective impact. Almost

90 percent of Ashoka's revenue goes to programs, with administrative and fund-raising expenses at about 10 percent.[5]

Ashoka focuses its work on three levels:

1. **Social entrepreneurs.** Identifying and investing in exceptionally promising social entrepreneurs
2. **Group entrepreneurship.** Engaging communities of entrepreneurs and developing patterns of effective collaborations designed to transform entire fields
3. **Sector infrastructure.** Creating needed infrastructure, such as access to financing, bridges to other sectors, and frameworks for partnerships that deliver social and financial value

Ashoka has rigorous selection criteria for its staff, with four key elements: staff members must have proven entrepreneurial quality, belief in Ashoka's "everyone a changemaker™" vision, emotional and social intelligence, and exceptional ethical fiber. (The organization employs similar criteria for its Fellows.) Drayton learned these elements the hard way. He said Ashoka's worst mistake was compromising on hiring criteria during its first period of rapid growth, in which it grew 45 percent a year for five years. (Recall the need to sufficiently vet candidates, admittedly tougher when growing rapidly.) The consequences were severe, including a weakened culture and flat revenues for several years.[6]

Ashoka looks for people who can work effectively in decentralized teams. In a proper team, Drayton told us, "Every single person takes initiative. Every individual is a changemaker, but the team also functions as a unit. The individual strength is the group. The group strength is the individual."

By eliciting leadership from the whole stable, Ashoka amplifies its impact. Drayton envisions "a system that empowers everyone to be powerfully good . . . organizations whose critical factor for success is to what degree they help their team's teams be brilliant." Noting that it also entails ethical fortitude, he calls it a "values-based entrepreneurial community."

Addressing the measurement challenge, Ashoka developed its own pioneering impact assessment system. It measures the systemic pattern-change impact (on a continental scale) of the Ashoka Fellows by evaluating whether others have replicated their ideas, whether they have changed government policies (more than half have done so within five years of launch), and whether their ventures are national pacesetters in their respective fields.

> By designing Ashoka to work on multiple levels, Drayton has made it a steward for
> the social sector itself—working on the sector and not just in it.

It is one thing for nonprofits like the SEED Foundation and Ashoka to take on the social impact challenge, but how does it work when for-profit companies make the attempt, given their unique pressures and constraints? Author Rosabeth Moss Kanter points the way forward in a 2011 *Harvard Business Review* article:

> Great companies work to make money, of course, but in their choices of how to do so, they think about building enduring institutions . . . the value a company creates should not just be in terms of short-term profits or paychecks but also in terms of how it sustains the conditions that allow it to flourish over time . . . great companies are willing to sacrifice short-term financial opportunities if they are incompatible with institutional values . . . Articulating a purpose broader than making money can guide strategies and actions, open new sources for innovation, and help people express corporate and personal values in their everyday work.

Making such changes is a tall order in today's competitive global economy—and not for the faint of heart. Next we look at Indra Nooyi's bold attempt to guide PepsiCo through such a transformation, from an ordinary company to a pioneer of social impact—a tremendous and sometimes precarious challenge.

PepsiCo: Reinventing a Corporate Giant

Nooyi joined PepsiCo in 1994 and directed global strategy for more than a decade. She was named president and CFO in 2001 and CEO in 2007. In concert with the board and leadership team, she set out to reinvent the beverage giant into a beacon for socially responsible business. Under her leadership, the company adopted a new mantra: "performance with purpose."

In the Foreword to Stephen M. R. Covey's *Smart Trust*, Nooyi wrote, "While excellent operating performance had always been the lifeblood of PepsiCo, in order to make our work sustainable it was vital to add a real sense of purpose to our performance. We articulated three planks—human sustainability, environmental sustainability, and talent sustainability—that together laid out the roadmap for PepsiCo's future."

PepsiCo's mission is to be "the world's premier consumer products company focused on convenient foods and beverages . . . (striving for) honesty, fairness, and integrity." In 2008, Nooyi told *Fortune International*, "Companies today are bigger than many economies. We are little republics. We are engines of efficiency. If companies don't do [responsible] things, who is going to? Why not start making change now?"

Senior Vice President Larry Thompson said, "The corporation's values should be integrated into the normal channels of decision making . . . managers throughout the organization should understand the values and be empowered to make ethically sound decisions."[7]

Though many people still think in terms of the famous Coke versus Pepsi rivalry, in many ways Pepsi is moving beyond the cola wars. As of several years ago, PepsiCo's revenues come more from food than from beverages. The company now offers not only soda but also bottled water, organic tea, energy drinks, chips, cereal, oatmeal, rice, and more through brands like Gatorade, Tropicana, Frito-Lay, Quaker, and others.

One of PepsiCo's goals is to move away from sugary drinks and salty snacks and increase the company's portion of "good-for-you" products, such as nuts, oats, and fruit juice, from about $10 billion to $30 billion. By 2015, it seeks a reduction in salt in some of its biggest brands by 25 percent. By 2020, it seeks a reduction in added sugar to its drinks by 25 percent and in the amount of saturated fat in certain snacks by 15 percent.

The company also has aggressive goals relating to water-use efficiency, recycled packaging, reductions in solid waste to landfills, sustainable agriculture practices, support for local farmers, and more. Its SunChips brand pioneered the first compostable chip bag.

For employees, PepsiCo created a HealthRoads wellness program that arms them with information about their health via confidential, personal health records and assessments created by a third-party vendor, WebMD. The program includes counseling and health coaches to help employees stay healthy and help the company reduce healthcare costs. Meanwhile, the company has ranked among the world's most admired, ethical, and sustainable companies for many years.[8]

While PepsiCo's actions and ambitions are impressive, the company has stumbled in some areas. For example, there were allegations that traces of pesticide were found in Pepsi and Coke drinks in India in the early 2000s, as well as accusations that PepsiCo drained aquifers in areas affected by water scarcity. There has been criticism of Tropicana's marketing makeover and of the relaunch of Gatorade. The company's financial hedging strategies did not work out as intended and left PepsiCo with big bills for its commodities. As a result, even though its revenues and net income increased, PepsiCo's share price was essentially flat between 2006 and 2011. PepsiCo lowered its profit outlook twice in 2011 and lost market share in the soda business to Coca-Cola.[9] There have been recent calls for the company to break up into separate food and drink companies, an idea that PepsiCo officials have so far rejected.

The dilemma for PepsiCo is clear: how do you navigate these short-term performance challenges while maintaining the long-term vision of a sustainable company? In the age of an obesity epidemic and increasing attention to health and fitness, how do you reinvent a giant soda and snack company into a responsible corporation fit for the age? The pressures on Nooyi and her team are tremendous. How they navigate these tradeoffs among their 190,000 employees in 190 countries will determine whether the enterprise succeeds in its triple crown quest.

CHAPTER SUMMARY

More and more organizations of different kinds and across sectors are committing themselves to creating positive social impact alongside sustainable financial performance. Their efforts are not about running social impact initiatives in parallel with financial strategies—and diluting them both. They are devising new strategies for an economic engine that combines financial returns and social impact into a coherent and mutually beneficial whole. Leaders must address special challenges as they do so, including resource constraints and measurement challenges, emphasizing certain aspects of the triple crown leadership practices.

Practical Applications

1. To what extent is social impact built into your organization's purpose, values, and vision?
   a. What changes are needed?

2. To what extent is social impact a genuine organizational priority—built into the culture and strategy of the enterprise?
   a. What more should you do?

3. To what extent is your organization experiencing the following problems: mission drift, fund-raising treadmill, donor dependence, financial instability, leader dependence, inattention to results, and dispersion of efforts?
   a. Which are the biggest problems, and why?
   b. What leadership practices will you employ to address them?

4. Does your team have a good balance between head and heart?

5. To what extent are the organizational colors at risk due to financial and other pressures?

6. Do your leaders flex well between steel and velvet? What about you?
   a. Is there too much of one and not enough of the other?

7. To what extent does the organization inspire leadership from its whole stable?

8. Which people, departments, or stakeholders are not aligned with your social impact priorities?
   a. What will you do to address the misalignment?

9. Are your social impact initiatives financially sustainable? What changes are needed?

10. Are people throughout the organization stewards of your desired social impact, or are the efforts only a top-down mandate or side project?
    a. Who are the stewards?
    b. What do they do?

11. Is the enterprise aligned to achieve both financial return and social impact, with resources allocated appropriately, metrics, and communication loops to determine progress?
    a. What more should you do?

12. What more can be done to make financial viability and social impact mutually reinforcing?

CHAPTER ELEVEN

SNAPSHOTS

*Leadership involves the courage to practice
an art never completely mastered.*

—Author unknown

n this chapter, we take a snapshot look at the leadership practices of three organizations—Infosys, KIPP, and Google—to see how they are doing on the triple crown quest. None of them has mastered the art of leadership, of course, but all have made substantial progress in building excellent, ethical, and enduring organizations. We draw lessons from their successes, failures, and current challenges.

INFOSYS[1]

In 1981, N. R. Narayana Murthy met with six colleagues in his tiny apartment in Pune, India, hatching out a plan for a high-tech startup. Thinking big, they debated whether to try to become number one in India in terms of market share, job creation, or market capitalization. Murthy had something else in mind, something more in the spirit of the triple crown quest: aiming to become India's most respected company.

Murthy explained how respect would flow from being a values-based company: delivering on promises, treating employees fairly, operating with transparency and accountability, upholding all laws, and creating goodwill in society. With such values-based practices, he argued, "revenues, profits, and market capitalization would follow."

With only $250 in seed capital, they knew it was the longest of long shots. But they made it their commitment, with Murthy as their leader and "chief mentor."

Thirty years later, how is Infosys faring on its quest?

Today, the Infosys headquarters in Electronic City in Bangalore comprises fifty buildings on eighty acres. Its business is information technology (IT): next-generation, technology-enabled business solutions that range from IT outsourcing to software—competing against Wipro, Tata, Satya, IBM, and Accenture. Infosys pioneered the "global delivery model," now emulated by many, serving customers twenty-four/seven with India as the hub and with spokes at multiple worldwide locations.

In 2011, Infosys had revenue of $6.8 billion, a market capitalization over $29 billion, and cash reserves exceeding $3 billion (not a bad return on a $250 investment). Its three- and five-year return on assets and cash flow as a percentage of revenue far exceeded that of its peer group, while its year-over-year sales growth remained high and competitive. In the past five years, Infosys was among the world's fastest-growing large companies (*Fortune*), most respected companies (Reputation Institute), and best companies for leaders (*Fortune*).

Indian leader Mohandas Gandhi deeply influenced Murthy. He follows Gandhi's practice of leading by example, never asking people to do something that he has not already done himself. His example and moral authority have deeply influenced the Infosys leadership approach. In 2011, he told a *Harvard Business Review* interviewer, "A good company must go beyond following the law. Ethical behavior transcends legal compliance: It's about satisfying your conscience, whereas legal compliance is about satisfying the authorities."

Infosys's credo is "Powered by intellect, driven by values." Its shared values are client value, leadership by example, integrity and transparency, fairness, and excellence (C-LIFE).

During his thirty-year tenure before his recent retirement, Murthy addressed all new employees, reinforcing the company's values. C-LIFE sessions are mandatory for new employees. "Infy" TV and Radio spread messages about the values, and employees with ethical questions have access to designated contact points. Leaders are measured on C-LIFE, among other attributes, and given feedback to help instill the organizational colors and encourage more people throughout the enterprise to become stewards of the culture of character.

Infosys has invested heavily in leadership development, recognizing that leadership from the whole stable works better with sufficient resources and planning. Dr. Jayan Sen, lead principal at the Infosys Leadership Institute (ILI), told us the company focuses on developing leadership through an approach based on evidence, relevance, and rigor. ILI supplements its own team with outside leadership experts to create compelling programs.

In promotion decisions, panels of three senior leaders assess candidates based on the Infosys leadership model. For the top 760 leaders in the firm, there are focused leadership development programs. Leaders are assessed on the Infosys leadership dimensions, including ethics and integrity, and customized development plans are created for the senior-most 250 leaders. These development plans are based on robust experiences, interpersonal development, and formal learning and development efforts.

Each leader is assigned a more senior mentor, who is outside the chain of command, and a Leadership Institute executive coach to ensure personalized development. Infosys also leverages the strengths of these senior leaders by having them teach others via live and video sessions of the "Leaders Teach Program."

Infosys has built one of the world's largest learning campuses in Mysore, ninety miles from Bangalore. The Narayana Murthy Center of Excellence was founded on the premises that "our company is our campus, our business is our curriculum, and our leaders are our teachers."

New inductees to Infosys go through a rigorous twenty-three-week training program with batteries of tests on subjects ranging from Java programming to team building, interpersonal communications, and cross-cultural sensitivity. Infosys normally selects less than 1 percent of its applicants (compared with the U.S. Ivy League universities, which normally select 5 to 10 percent).[2]

Infosys goes to great lengths to explain and interpret its values in everyday business terms that its employees can understand. Leaders encourage employees to raise values questions at quarterly open house meetings. Infosys has a whistleblower program and a grievance review board.

In a country struggling with corruption, Indian business leaders encounter ethical dilemmas and integrity challenges. For example, companies that sell software to banks are often asked by bank officials for a reciprocal deposit—nothing illegal but not quite right in the eyes of Infosys. When Infosys imported its first computer to Bangalore in

1984, a customs official requested a bribe, which the firm ignored. Infosys paid a duty ten times higher than normal, borrowing the money to pay the higher fee. It took six years to recover the funds through a protest process. Similarly, Infosys paid a 40 percent premium for its Bangalore headquarters land after refusing to pay a bribe.

The government used to levy a duty of 135 percent on imported software packages. Infosys's rivals manipulated their invoices to pay lower duties. While lawyers advised that such actions were not illegal, Infosys leaders refused to operate in a gray area. Infosys once fired a valued project manager for fudging a $40 taxi bill. Even board members have paid heavy penalties for minor infractions.

When asked in a 2011 *Harvard Business Review* interview about whether Infosys worried about competitive disadvantage from such actions, Murthy responded:

> It takes time to benefit from putting values first. You feel the pain immediately and you reap the gains only in the long run . . . It took just a few years for corrupt officials to stop approaching us for favors. Because of Infosys' ethical image, our clients entrusted us with increasingly bigger projects. Our values have thus become our advantage, gaining us larger revenues, top-flight talent, and great investors and earning us the respect of governments and societies.

Infosys values its stable of leaders. It promotes what it calls collective thought leadership, emphasizing the complementarity of multiple views and leveraging the outcome of many people's passionate efforts. Infosys calls itself a noisy democracy, with widely distributed leadership and openness to hearing everyone's voice.

Like all organizations, Infosys has had its ups and downs, as well as occasional lapses. In the early years when the company was still small and unknown, one of the founders left, and the others debated whether to sell the business for $1.5 million. Murthy expressed confidence in the company's prospects and offered to buy them out. One by one, they pledged to stay, and Murthy said, "Let this be the last time we talk about selling our company under duress."

In 2003, Infosys was having internal troubles that were showing up on employee surveys, a surprise since it had been topping "best employer" lists. Its rapid growth over the previous decade had led to misinformation, discontent, and lack of trust.

In 2008, the company faced a leadership crisis, as people were "being rushed into jobs for which they were unprepared due to rapid growth," according to *Bloomberg Businessweek*. In response, company leaders transferred about 15 percent of employees to positions with lesser authority, because they judged them likely to fail in their current roles.

In 2011, Infosys leaders launched the largest reorganization in the firm's history, defining new structures, roles, and job descriptions to reposition the company toward creating client value and around innovating new solutions.

Notwithstanding these issues, Infosys has prospered and looked for ways to promote positive social impact. The nonprofit Infosys Foundation was established in 1996 to support the underprivileged in India, focusing on education, health, rural development, and the arts. The company's 1996–1997 annual report states, "The only hope for a stable society is for the corporations and the 'haves' to realize their social responsibilities towards the less fortunate." At Infosys, that means being environmentally conscious, improving corporate governance, and contributing to disaster relief.

Murthy told *Harvard Business Review*, "Maximizing shareholder value is essential . . . [otherwise] we won't be strong and will not be able to serve any stakeholders. However, we must maximize shareholder value legally, ethically, and fairly . . . The best index of a corporation's success is its longevity, which comes from living in harmony with society."

Like all firms, Infosys has had occasional lapses, but the company has made building an excellent, ethical, and enduring organization a top priority.

KIPP

Mike Feinberg and David Levin were clueless. They had entered the teaching profession right out of college through Teach For America with great expectations; but, like so many first-year teachers, they were struggling. Levin found his tires slashed in the parking lot.

It is a common story. Levin talks about the "blame game" in tough urban schools: "Parents blaming teachers, teachers blaming parents, colleges blaming high schools, high schools blaming middle schools, middle schools blaming elementary schools."[3] Feinberg and Levin had no interest in the blame game. They just wanted to be good teachers.

Enter Harriett Ball. At over six feet tall, she was a veteran of inner-city classrooms. She was a magician who could make jaded, antsy, and disruptive kids disappear and in their place summon bright, eager, and dedicated pupils. With her wildly popular classroom chants, she had figured out how to thrill children with the sense of accomplishment that comes from mastering complex arithmetic via fun, frequent, and rhythmic repetition.[4] She took Feinberg and Levin under her wing; Feinberg later called her "God's gift to the classroom."

With the help of Ball and other master teachers like Rafe Esquith, Feinberg and Levin honed their craft and started performing their own classroom magic. In 1994, they started the Knowledge Is Power Program (KIPP), named after one of Ball's chants: "You gotta read, baby, read. You gotta read, baby, read. The more you read, the more you know, 'cause knowledge is power." Levin called it "traditional education for the hip-hop generation."

Fearless or naïve—probably both—they took on all the challenges of urban schools: disengaged parents, burned-out teachers, peer pressure, poverty, apathy, drugs, and gangs. They resolved to do whatever it took for their students to succeed—no shortcuts, no excuses.[5]

When district bureaucracy got in the way of finding a suitable facility for the growing program, Feinberg sat on the rear bumper of the superintendent's car and waited for hours. When the superintendent finally showed up, he could see that this crazy teacher wouldn't take no for an answer.

Feinberg got what he wanted.

With time, KIPP was defying the long odds of urban schooling and showing that poor kids could learn and achieve to impressively high standards, just like any other children. It could have ended there, but then Scott Hamilton, a longtime education reformer, entered the picture. Hamilton first heard about KIPP through his wife, Stacey Boyd, a charter school educator in Boston. He was working for the family foundation of Doris and Donald Fisher, co-founders of Gap Inc. (the specialty clothing retailer), which was looking to invest in a promising educational model that could be expanded nationally. Thinking big, Hamilton developed a vision to scale KIPP into a national network.

In 2011, the KIPP network had 109 schools in twenty states, enrolling more than 33,000 students.[6] By most objective measures, it has been wildly successful. The average KIPP student enters fifth grade at the thirty-third percentile in reading and the forty-fifth percentile in mathematics, as measured by national, norm-referenced assessments. After three years in KIPP, these students perform at the fifty-seventh percentile in reading and the eightieth percentile in math—remarkable increases.[7] Nationwide, more than 85 percent of KIPP students are eligible for the federal free or reduced-price meals program (an indicator of poverty), and 95 percent are African American or Latino.

The founders built the KIPP program on five pillars:

1. High expectations
2. Choice and commitment
3. More time in the classroom
4. Power to lead
5. Focus on results

As KIPP grew, it was crucial to make sure that its schools were succeeding beyond just high test scores and other static measures of academic achievement. KIPP keeps a close eye on the overall health of its growing network of schools by asking six "essential questions":

1. Are we serving the children who need us?
2. Are our students staying with us?
3. Are KIPP students progressing and achieving academically?
4. Are KIPP alumni climbing the mountain to and through college?
5. Are we building a sustainable people model?
6. Are we building a sustainable financial model?

As of 2011, 36 percent of students who completed a KIPP middle school at least a decade ago had a bachelor's degree, versus 8 percent for similar students nationwide. Since KIPP began, 95 percent of students who finished the eighth grade at KIPP have graduated from high school, and more than 84 percent have enrolled in college.[8] KIPP students have a higher college completion rate than the average of all students across all income levels nationwide.

There are many contributing factors to KIPP's excellent results, but leadership plays a pivotal role. According to Richard Barth, CEO of the KIPP Foundation, "It's pretty simple—strong school leadership is the key . . . Great principals lead great schools and attract great teachers who are committed, results-oriented educators who put kids on the path to a college degree."

The KIPP Foundation—which selects, trains, and supports the KIPP school principals; provides research and analysis; and supports excellence, innovation, and sustainability across the network—is fanatical and systematic about leadership development. Along with its prestigious yearlong Fisher Fellows program for KIPP principals, it offers five other leadership development programs, all based on the homegrown KIPP School Leadership Competency Model.

KIPP places a premium on recruiting people who have all the right leadership "stuff," including a deep conviction that all students can excel, personal integrity, and fit with the KIPP culture.

KIPP's culture begins with its organizational colors. According to Mazher Ahmad, former chief people officer of the KIPP Foundation, "Our purpose, our values, our vision: those are the things that drive our regions, executive directors, school leaders, teachers, staff members, and students. It's what drives everybody every day. There's never a day when people working at KIPP question why they wake up and go to work. Everyone knows we are here to help kids."

"As an organization," Ahmad told us, "we are focused on building character at all levels." Walk into any KIPP school, and you will see common characteristics: college banners on the walls, games, mottos, and chants, not to mention dedicated teaching. KIPP has carefully crafted a culture of character. The greatest sin in a KIPP classroom is hurting or teasing other students. Jay Mathews captured KIPP's approach in the title of his book, *Work Hard. Be Nice.* Feinberg and Levin might add: No excuses. No shortcuts.

KIPP focuses not just on its leaders at the top but also on its whole stable of school leaders, teachers, and staff. KIPP treats its school leaders like independent franchisees, not branches of a central office. It uses a distributed leadership model, giving people what they call "the power to lead" (one of KIPP's five pillars). "We give school leaders the freedom to make decisions," Ahmad told us. "They are the closest to the action."

Most distinctive of all, KIPP looks for leadership, not just from its management team or board, but also from another group. According to Ahmad:

> We learn the most about leadership from our students. We ask them to put in long hours. We ask them to live by values that may be foreign to them. We ask them to exemplify excellence day in and day out. It's through their example that we see the power and the potential for what impact this can have on the world . . . It's really the little KIPPsters who are the true leaders and who will change this world for the better.

KIPP's clarity about its top priorities is a powerful alignment mechanism, with clear metrics and feedback loops that leave nowhere to hide in KIPP's no-excuses culture. The result is an organization that has done what some thought impossible—and then replicated it across the country with consistently high quality. U.S. Secretary of Education Arne Duncan said in *Bloomberg Businessweek* that KIPP has elicited "remarkable results from students." Other knowledgeable observers have called KIPP a "platinum brand," an "urban triumph," and a network with "the most promising schools in America." The *Washington Post* described KIPP as "the most successful charter school network in the country."

Of course, KIPP has made mistakes. It has its share of detractors and controversy. Critics call it the "Kids in Prison Program," a reference to the long days and strict norms. Others have criticized KIPP's attrition rates, alleging that average test scores may be higher due to a large number of students leaving KIPP schools. (An independent evaluation by Mathematica Policy Research in 2010 did not find higher attrition rates at KIPP.) In a couple of cases, KIPP leaders made the (steel) decision to remove the KIPP name from schools that failed to meet its standards. Despite the criticisms, KIPP's successes are difficult to deny, given independent observations over time on standardized tests.

KIPP's vision is that "one day all public schools will help children develop the knowledge, skills, character, and habits necessary to achieve their dreams while making the world a better place." Will the network continue to improve its results over time, operating with integrity while continuing to grow? According to Ahmad, "The culture is evolving so that KIPP can become an enduring institution. In this phase of development, we're focusing on how we get things done—the behaviors and processes required to get the results and sustain them over time."

No excuses, no shortcuts—perhaps a fitting chant for the triple crown quest? The KIPP approach is not about finding a superior curriculum or pedagogy (though the program certainly seeks the best available tools). Rather, it is about scouting a phenomenal team of leaders with head and heart and palpable commitment to the organization's colors, and then helping them create a culture of character and unleash the tremendous potential of educators and students in their schools.

GOOGLE

Google's ascent has been breathtaking: scaling from a dorm room search engine project called "BackRub" in 1996 to a global juggernaut with $29 billion in revenue, 32,000 employees, and a market capitalization of more than $200 billion in early 2012.[9] How does Google do in terms of being an excellent, ethical, and enduring company?

In 2011, Stephen Levy of *Wired* magazine called Google's advertising system "the most successful Internet commerce product in history."[10] One of Google's mantras is, "Great just isn't good enough." The startup took only six years to reach $1 billion in revenues, a decade faster than Microsoft.[11] In recent years, Google was ranked as the world's most valuable brand (*BrandFinance*), the world's most reputable company (*Forbes*), and the world's most innovative company (*Fast Company*).[12] It also made a number of other "best" lists for multiple years, including 100 Best Companies to Work For (*Fortune*) and the World's Most Admired Companies (*Fortune*).

Google's return on assets and year-over-year sales growth for the past seven years are significantly higher than its peer group average, and its cash flow as a percentage of revenue is even with its peer group average. Its stock price has soared, going from $85 per share when first floated in 2004 to between $473 and $642 in 2011. Google's financial results have been impressive.

The founders, Larry Page and Sergey Brin, named the company after a mathematical term ("googol") for the number one followed by a hundred zeros. They think big. The firm's innovation practices—such as "intelligent fast failure" and "20 percent time" for engineers to work on projects of their own choosing—have been influential outside the Googleplex.

Despite these successes, there are concerns, starting with overdependence on its advertising business model. Some wonder whether Google is a one-trick pony. While the company has had major product winners like Gmail and Google Maps, it has also had duds like Google Buzz and Google Health. It was slow to adapt to Web 2.0 and competition from Facebook, Apple, and Amazon.

Google attracts considerable scrutiny due to its high-profile success but also due to its own lofty ambitions. In an "owner's manual for shareholders" when Google conducted its initial public offering in 2004, co-founder Page wrote:

> Google is not a conventional company . . . Our goal is to develop services that significantly improve the lives of as many people as possible. In pursuing this goal, we may do things that we believe have a positive impact on the world, even if the near term financial returns are not obvious . . . As a private company, we have concentrated on the long term, and this has served us well. As a public company, we will do the same . . . Don't be evil. We believe strongly that in the long term, we will be better served—as shareholders and in all other ways—by a company that does good things for the world even if we forgo some short-term gains.[13]

Living up to these aspirations has not been easy. There is no shortage of criticism, from allegations of anticompetitive behavior to concerns about the scanning of out-of-print books, insufficient transparency, and insufficient controls on data collection and privacy. Google entered China despite its government censorship of Internet use but then later withdrew, calling it "the worst moment in our company."[14] Today, Baidu leads the Chinese search market.

Author Jeff Jarvis examines whether Google is living up to its values. He asks, "Is Google evil then? On balance, I don't think so. But its day is still young. At least Google is trying to be good."[15]

Google appeared on the list of the World's Most Ethical companies in 2008, 2009, and 2010. On principle, Google refuses to issue quarterly forecasts or earnings guidance in order to avoid short-term pressures. Google has launched high-profile philanthropic and sustainability initiatives—some through its influential charitable arm, Google.org. Google was listed on the 2010 CSR Index (Reputation Institute) and was named one of the World's Most Sustainable companies (Corporate Knights), in part for supporting renewable energy, geothermal power, energy from seawater, and a commitment to make the Googleplex carbon neutral.[16]

What practices have Google leaders employed to achieve their lofty goals? Google is famous for seeking top talent. Candidates must pass the difficult screens of hiring councils. According to Executive Chairman (and former CEO) Eric Schmidt, "We select people who want to change the world." Judy Gilbert, Google's former director of talent (and now director of people operations, YouTube), told us about Google's interview checklist, including not just technical chops, but also assessments of leadership, emotional intelligence, and "Googliness," or fit with the culture. Managers factor integrity and leadership into promotion decisions.

Google's director of staffing began a project a few years ago to identify factors that could distinguish between good and bad hires. He learned that Google managers had been looking too narrowly at résumés, focusing too much on education records and scores. After analyzing hundreds of traits that make good employees, he realized that some of the hidden gems about people—the kinds of things that reflected their character, heart, and fit—were at the bottom of the résumé in the "activities and interests" section, and so he and his fellow Googlers started reviewing résumés "upside down."[17]

Google is famous for its "ten things we know to be true" philosophy, a proxy for its organizational values. According to Gilbert, leaders at the company regularly consider, debate, and act upon the values. According to Schmidt, "If people in the organization understand the values of the company, they should be able to self organize to work on the most interesting problems. And if they haven't . . . you haven't built a shared value culture."[18]

Google has a collaborative style, but leaders exercise tough-minded positional authority when necessary. When he was CEO, Schmidt said, "The role of the leader is often, not to force the outcome, but to force execution."[19] Gilbert told us, "We want people to develop a range of influence skills. Sometimes you're going to be soft. Sometimes you're going to be hard and tell them, 'This is how it's going to be.'"

Google has a rich tradition of stewardship, starting with its founders, who stepped back and handed over the leadership reins to a seasoned veteran when they hired Schmidt as CEO for a number of years to provide "adult supervision." In terms of corporate governance, two-thirds of the Google board must be independent directors, and every board member stands for reelection annually.

"At Google," says Gilbert, "I've seen everyone become leaders. It's not just a label we slap on 'senior' people. It's not just about leadership in the traditional sense of authority. There is a strong emphasis on earning followership." Google uses panels of co-workers as judges to screen and rank all sorts of matters, from new development projects and quality parameters to new hires and promotions.

The company favors small teams, frequently three to seven people, and gives them precise objectives and short deadlines, often as little as six weeks. John Doerr, a prominent venture capital investor, convinced the leaders to adopt "OKRs" (objectives and key results) to align the organization as it scaled so rapidly.

How does someone like Judy Gilbert feel about working at Google? She says:

> I'm in an environment where there are unbelievably smart,
> capable people working on some of the hardest problems in

the world. They feel empowered to actually do something and make really big changes. That raises the bar for what I'm going to accomplish on a given day. I feel privileged to be part of this organization, and I want to be earning my seat in it.

Google's accomplishments are due to many factors, including its business model, technology, and innovations, but the company's leadership dynamic powerfully shapes all these factors. Bernard Girard, author of *The Google Way,* wrote that the company "represents the invention of a new management model—and calling it revolutionary is no exaggeration." Leadership expert Gary Hamel has called Google "a modern management pioneer."[20]

Co-founder Larry Page took over from Schmidt as CEO in 2011 and faces numerous challenges, such as getting the large firm to act like the fast-moving startup of its early days, catching up with Facebook in social media innovation and buzz, retaining key talent, and chopping lackluster projects. Page is flexing to more steel leadership than Schmidt usually did: "More wood behind fewer arrows," as he said to analysts in 2011.[21]

Overall, Google has achieved impressive results but faces challenges. Questions loom: Will the company address privacy and antitrust issues and complaints sufficiently? What will happen with Android, Google+, Google Play, and other high-profile new initiatives? Will Google reignite its revenue growth and stave off fierce competition from Facebook, Apple, and Amazon?

Google is still young, but in Internet years it risks becoming an aging giant. Will it continue to forgo short-term gains in order to generate long-term value and impact? When asked recently about the company's biggest threat, CEO Page answered in one word: "Google."[22]

So it is with all organizations on the triple crown quest.

SNAPSHOTS OF THE QUEST

We offer Infosys, KIPP, and Google as examples of organizations that are employing many triple crown leadership practices. Their efforts to build excellent, ethical, and enduring organizations are ongoing but instructive. We cite them here not as reigning triple crown champions, but as impressive enterprises that have much to teach us about the triple crown quest—including both admirable practices and pitfalls. They do not always succeed, but their efforts and approaches are notable.

Our intent is not to create a list of great organizations. *Triple Crown Leadership* is about a quest, not a list. It is about chasing perfection, knowing it can never be attained—at least fully or permanently—but seeking it still. Leadership is, indeed, an art never completely mastered, but we can learn from organizations on the quest.

CONCLUSION

AT THE POST

We know what we are, but know not what we may be.

—William Shakespeare

The bugle sounds, signaling that the horses and jockeys are at the starting post. The crowd goes quiet. Movements at the starting gate unfold in slow motion. The jockey adjusts his goggles and checks his boots in the stirrups. He listens to his horse breathing and gazes down the track. Anticipation swells as he awaits the starting bell. He squeezes the reins, feeling well-worn leather, and exhales. The race of his life is about to begin.

So it is with us and our own leadership races.

At the outset of this book, we asked some questions: What kind of leadership does it take to build excellent, ethical, and enduring organizations? How can we lead ventures for both high performance and positive impact on all stakeholders? How can we avoid breakdowns in performance, integrity, and sustainability?

Throughout these pages, we have seen powerful answers from leadership in action at many different organizations. Though the quest for the crown is sometimes murky, many leaders are lighting the path.

This quest for excellent, ethical, and enduring organizations may be the defining leadership challenge of our age. Will we rise to the occasion? We can, but we need a different brand of leadership better suited to our age.

We said *Triple Crown Leadership* is not another success study. Our journey has been in "quest land," not "list land." We sought leadership practices that promote the three Es: excellent, ethical, and enduring. The quest is ongoing. Some enterprises enter the triple crown zone for a while, then fall back, only to try again. The nobility is in the struggle.

No doubt the quest is hard, sometimes excruciatingly so. If you publicly commit to such aspirations, people will scrutinize your every move. If you fall short of excellence, the critics—often those who never attempt to lead—are quick to point fingers. If you commit to act ethically, some people will judge your every move against impossible standards. If you commit to build long-term value and ensure sustainability, you will surely face pressure to do more to boost your numbers today.

Do you think you can lead without adversity and setbacks? Leadership involves pushing through painful circumstances, devising innovative solutions for complex problems, and sometimes choosing between unpalatable alternatives. Values collide. You must navigate through the minefields.

Triple crown leaders undertake these challenges. They are realists *and* idealists, steel *and* velvet, disciplined *and* creative, leaders *and* followers, willful *and* humble. They use both head *and* heart. They create value for today *and* tomorrow.

WHY TRIPLE CROWN LEADERSHIP?

Why should people commit to triple crown leadership—to building excellent, ethical, and enduring organizations?

- We need better leadership if we are to address the challenges of our age.

- People can achieve incredible feats when they commit their hearts and work together toward a common purpose they believe in.

- We do not have to accept yesterday's methods.

- We need not choose between excellent, ethical, and enduring: with a certain kind of leadership, we can foster all three in ways that reinforce each other.

THE PARAMOUNT QUEST

New leadership imperatives are emerging today. People want organizations to live up to their values and aspirations. They look for excellent, ethical, and enduring leadership. They seek sustainable practices and positive social impact. They want challenge, connection, fun, pride, and accomplishment at work. They want their life and work to have meaning.

We believe the timeframe of focus must shift from the next quarter to the next quarter century. During Harvard Business School's centennial celebration, Harvard University president Drew Gilpin Faust identified the kinds of leaders Harvard aspires to develop: not those focused only on material rewards, or even those aspiring to be the best, but those who want to build cathedrals—serving a great purpose and connecting people to something deeper. That means educating leaders who make a difference *for* the world and not just *in* it.[1]

The foremost leadership task in the quest is committing the organization to the three Es. It is time to place the triple crown quest at the top of the leadership priority list, from the executive suites and boardroom to the shop floor and workstations.

We see powerful movement in this direction from some pioneering organizations around the world. Many thought leaders have documented elements of this phenomenon. Our hope is that we have added insights to this chorus with *Triple Crown Leadership*. See Figure C.1 for a summary of triple crown leadership.

How does it feel to work in organizations that are thriving with their ultimate aims? Here is what some of our interviewees said:

> **Steven Rothstein, Perkins School for the Blind:** "It was so exciting, so energizing, so inspiring."

> **Bob Hatcher, MidCountry Financial:** "They regularly walk up to me now and say, 'I'm proud to be a part of this company because of the values.'"

> **Nancy Tuor, CH2M Hill (Rocky Flats):** "I can't tell you the amount of personal satisfaction that came out of it. Every day was so much fun. They were proud. They were happy. This thing had new life. It was glowing . . . It was certainly the job of a lifetime."

Figure C.1   **Triple Crown Leadership Summary**

**Triple Crown
Leadership**

Make building an excellent, ethical, and enduring organization the overarching priority. Recognize that the three Es are interrelated and mutually reinforcing over time.

- **Excellent.** Achieving exceptional results that have significant, positive impacts on stakeholders.

  Average people produced extraordinary results.
  —**Nancy Tuor,** Rocky Flats (CH2M Hill)

- **Ethical.** Acting with integrity, paying attention to *how* the results are achieved.

  *I will go the board and tell them we had no sales this month
  rather than have one sale that is not right.*
  —**Harvey Wagner,** Quovadx

- **Enduring.** Standing the test of time and operating sustainably.

  The short-term focus has blown up.
  —**Bill George,** Medtronic

Triple crown leadership is not about a charismatic hero or happy-talk collaboration.

Triple crown leadership requires a group performance from many leaders.

Triple crown leadership develops and protects a culture of character.

Triple crown leadership minimizes breakdowns.

Triple crown leadership rejects the easy way out and finds another way forward.

The Five Triple Crown Leadership Practices

1. **Head and heart.** Recruit for, develop, and reward personal character, emotional intelligence, and cultural fit as well as skills and expertise.

> *I want to make sure they fit with our values and culture.*
> **—Ursula Burns,** Xerox

2. **The colors.** Collaboratively set an inspiring purpose, values, and vision and then bring them to life to build a culture of character in the organization.

> *My most important job is to articulate clearly*
> *and consistently what the values of the institution are.*
> **—Shirley Tilghman,** Princeton University

3. **Steel and velvet.** Get beyond your natural leadership style, flexing between the hard and soft edges, depending on the people and situation, but always anchored in the shared values.

> *Sometimes you have to be a wartime general;*
> *sometimes a peacetime general.*
> **—Lorrie Norrington,** eBay

4. **Stewards.** Empower people to act and lead by the shared values, encouraging them to step outside their traditional roles and be stewards of the culture of character.

> *Leadership is all about trusteeship.*
> **—Dr. M. N. Channabasappa,** Siddaganga Institute of Technology

5. **Alignment.** Collaboratively align the organization up, down, and around to reach a state of peak performance.

> *My role is to try to get everyone in the organization aligned.*
> **—Tony Hsieh,** Zappos.com

The five practices are all interrelated, overlapping and reinforcing each other.

YOUR RACE

I always wondered why somebody didn't do something.
Then I remembered. I was somebody.

—Lily Tomlin, actress

No matter what your burning issues are, better leadership can be one of the keys to breakthrough progress. The leadership practices we have outlined are not rocket science, but following them takes hard work, courage, and persistence. As you prepare for your race, here is our racing charge to you:

- Believe in the great potential of your colleagues—and figure out ways to unleash it.

- Role-model the behavior you wish to see in others.

- Build trust by trusting smartly, being worthy of trust, and honoring your commitments.

- Step up and lead, regardless of where you are in any organizational hierarchy.

- Keep your ego in check: recognize your weaknesses and learn to admit mistakes and ask for help.

- Know yourself, including your purpose, values, vision, personality, and leadership style.

- Take care of yourself by building in rituals of renewal and sanctuary.

- Make a binding commitment to triple crown leadership.

The bugle sounds at the post. The anticipation is electric. At the clang of the bell, mounts and riders charge forward from the gates, muscles flexing, dirt flying in the mayhem. After a surge of powerful opening strides, they enter a sublime flow, unleashed at last to race the way they were intended. It is magnificent to behold.

Leadership is a choice we can all make. Triple crown leadership is a bold and worthy choice. We commend it to you. You know what kind of leader you are now. What kind of leader might you be?

We wish you Godspeed on your quest.

APPENDIX

ABOUT THE RESEARCH

If we knew what it was we were doing,
it would not be called research, would it?

—Albert Einstein

This book draws upon many inputs: our own experience, encompassing leadership roles in different sectors and industries, as well as our consulting work, teaching, and board service; our interviews with business, social, and government leaders around the world; the leadership literature; our research; independent ranking systems; and the input of leadership experts and colleagues.

In the book, we cite many "thought leaders" and draw on concepts such as adaptive leadership, authentic leadership, emotional and social intelligence, level five leadership, participative management, servant leadership, shared leadership, Theories X, Y, and Z, transformational leadership, and more. We reviewed numerous books, articles, and studies, including a meta-review of eleven studies of high-performance organizations conducted over the past twenty-seven years.[1]

We draw upon the work of the Aspen Institute, Babson College, Business for Social Responsibility, Center for Creative Leadership, Center for Public Leadership, Ethisphere Institute, Globally Responsible Leadership Initiative, Harvard Business School, Kauffman Foundation, Kravis Leadership Institute, Leader to Leader Institute, McKinsey and Company, Net Impact, Santa Clara University's Markkula Center for Applied Ethics, Social Venture Network, Stanford University's Center for Social Innovation, Teleos Leadership Institute, TruePoint Center, University of Denver's Daniels College of Business and Institute for Enterprise Ethics, Vail Leadership Institute, and more.

We conducted preliminary research on more than two hundred organizations, looking at qualitative and quantitative factors such as organizational history and background, financial performance, evidence of impact, significant awards or other recognition, evidence of ethical or unethical behavior, sustainability and corporate social responsibility (CSR) practices, turnaround status, and other evidence of leadership practices. Then we conducted deeper research on the organizations that looked most promising in terms of results, impact, ethics, endurance, and sustainability. The research was mostly qualitative and not empirical.

We interviewed CEOs (or the equivalent, such as executive directors in nonprofit organizations), senior managers, and board members in the following organizations (including publicly traded corporations, privately held firms, turnarounds, startups, social ventures, and education, government, and military organizations) in eleven countries:

1. Advanced Micro Devices (AMD): Thomas McCoy, Former Executive Vice President, now Chair of Integrated Legal Strategies, O'Melveny & Myers
2. Ashoka: William Drayton, Founder, Chairman, and CEO
3. Baltimore City Schools: Dr. Andres Alonso, CEO
4. Bright Horizons Family Solutions: Mary Ann Tocio, President and COO
5. CH2M Hill: Nancy Tuor, Group President, Executive Sponsor for Sustainability
6. China Net Cloud: Steve Mushero, Co-founder, CEO, and CTO
7. Cisco Systems: Lynn Easterling, Vice President Law and Deputy General Counsel
8. Clif Bar and Company: Kit Crawford, Co-owner and Co-CEO
9. Coleman Corporation: Tim Daniel, Former Vice President, Sales, Special Markets
10. DaVita: Joe Mello, COO Emeritus
11. Delta Electronics: Yancey Hai, Vice Chairman and CEO
12. DuPont Corporation: John Krol, Former Chairman and CEO
13. eBay: Lorrie Norrington, Former President, eBay Marketplaces
14. Echoing Green: Cheryl Dorsey, President
15. French Air Force: General Jean Fleury, Chief of Staff
16. General Electric (GE): Ben Heineman, Former Senior Vice President for Law and Public Affairs

17. Giraff Technologies: Stephen Von Rump, CEO and Co-founder
18. Google: Judy Gilbert, Former Director of Talent, and now Director of People Operations, YouTube; and Therese Lim, Senior Associate, Global Communications and Public Affairs
19. Greensburg GreenTown: Daniel Wallach, Founder and Executive Director
20. Greensburg, Kansas: John Janssen, Former Mayor
21. Habitat for Humanity International: Elizabeth Crossman, Chair of the Board
22. Infosys Technologies: Dr. Jayan Sen, Lead Principal, Infosys Leadership Institute
23. Institute for Enterprise Ethics: Dr. Daniel Sweeney, Director
24. IP5280 Communications: John Scarborough and Jeffrey Pearl, Former Managing Partners and Co-founders
25. Jockeys' Guild, Inc.: Terry Meyocks, National Manager
26. KIPP Foundation: Mazher Ahmad, Former Chief People Officer
27. Mayo Clinic: Dr. Leonard Berry, Distinguished Professor of Marketing, Texas A&M University, and Dr. Kent Seltman, Marketing Division Chair Emeritus, Mayo Clinic
28. Medtronic: William George, Former CEO, now Harvard Business School Professor
29. MidCountry Financial Corporation: Robert Hatcher, President and CEO
30. Modern Technology Solutions: Philip Soucy, Co-president and CEO
31. Nack, William, Author and Journalist
32. National Thoroughbred Racing Association: Alex Waldrop, President and CEO
33. Neusoft Corporation: Dr. Liu Jiren, Chairman and CEO
34. New Profit Inc.: Vanessa Kirsch, Founder and Managing Director

35. North Castle Partners: Charles Baird, Managing Partner
36. Northrop Grumman: Dr. Ronald Sugar, Former Chairman and CEO
37. OMV: David Davies, CFO
38. Perkins School for the Blind: Steven Rothstein, President
39. Pitney Bowes: Michael Critelli, Former Chairman and CEO
40. Princeton University: Dr. Shirley Tilghman, President
41. Quovadx: Harvey Wagner, Former President and CEO
42. Qwest Communications: Edward Mueller, Former Chairman and CEO
43. Secretariat.com: Leonard Lusky, President
44. Share Our Strength: Bill Shore, Founder and Executive Director
45. Siddaganga Institute of Technology: Dr. M. N. Channabasappa, Director, and Dr. Manu Kulkarni, Professor Emeritus
46. Spotify: Andreas Ehn, Former CTO
47. Steinbeis Group: Franz Winterer, CEO and Managing Director
48. Strategic Air Command: General John Chain, Former Commander in Chief
49. The SEED Foundation: Eric Adler and Rajiv Vinnakota, Co-founders and Managing Directors
50. Toyota Motor Corporation: James Lentz, President, Toyota Motor Sales USA
51. Turcotte, Ronald, Triple Crown Jockey
52. Tyco International: Edward Breen, CEO, and Jack Krol, Former Chairman
53. Unisys Corporation: James Unruh, Former Chairman and CEO
54. University of Denver: Daniel Ritchie, Former Chancellor
55. Vanguard Group: John Bogle, Founder

56. Votorantim: Erik Madsen, CEO, and Felipe Lima, Former CFO, Votorantim Cement North America
57. Wrapp: Andreas Ehn, Co-founder and CTO
58. Xerox: Ursula Burns, CEO
59. Yale School of Management: Sharon Oster, Professor and Former Dean
60. Yum! Brands: Peter Bassi, Former Chairman, Yum Restaurants International
61. Zappos.com: Tony Hsieh, CEO

We sought to understand the leadership practices in these enterprises and gain insights about building excellent, ethical, and enduring organizations. Sometimes we were impressed with what we learned; other times, not. We did not set out to determine and rank a list of triple crown organizations.

To determine which organizations to interview, we incorporated a number of factors, including the research referenced above, reputable and objective rankings, and recommendations from trusted colleagues. We sought diversity in our interviews—both at the organizational level (for example, diversity of country, sector, industry, and organizational size and age) and at the individual level (for example, various leadership and functional positions, age, gender, race, and ethnicity).

Bob and Gregg conducted all the interviews. In a few cases, two people from an organization spoke to us together. Most interviews were conducted by phone, but some were conducted in person (sometimes including a site visit), and a few interviewees sent us written responses to our questions. In some cases, we went back to interviewees with follow-up questions. We recorded all interviews (with permission), transcribed the recordings (the transcripts exceed a thousand pages), and coded the text into more than thirty topics for analysis.

We used a common set of interview questions, with modifications over time as we learned from each interview, and we encouraged each person to focus on key points and guide the discussion to topics of special relevance to the person and his or her organization. We conducted additional targeted interviews as the book began to take shape, focusing on special cases such as turnarounds, startups, and horseracing.

We also reviewed the results of company ranking systems across major categories (for example, leadership, ethics, CSR, sustainability, workplace, and innovation). We looked at more than three dozen ranking systems. Sources included *Barron's, Bloomberg Businessweek, Fast Company, Forbes, Fortune, Newsweek, U.S. News & World Report,* Carbon Disclosure Project, Corporate Knights, CRD Analytics, Dow Jones, Ethisphere Institute, Governance Metrics International, Harris Interactive, Hewitt Associates, and more. Rankings included the World's Best Companies, Best Corporate Citizen Award, 100 Best Companies to Work For, Top Companies for Leaders, World's Most Innovative Companies, and many more. (Critics have noted that many ranking systems have drawbacks, such as an over-reliance on self-reporting and peer polling and a lack of transparency in their scoring systems.[2] In response, some ratings providers have made improvements.)

We then did further analysis, looking more closely at rankings that are global (not analyzing only a single country), that covered a span of five years or more, and that were most relevant to the topics in this book. After that winnowing process, we focused on three rankings: *Fortune's* World's Most Admired Companies, Ethisphere's World's Most Ethical Companies, and Corporate Knights's World's Most Sustainable Companies.

We compiled and analyzed those three rankings from 2006 to 2011. We found that twenty-seven companies made the most admired list all six years between 2006 and 2011 (including Cisco, GE, and Toyota), four made it five years, and another four made it four years. We found that thirteen companies made the most ethical list all five years between 2007 (this was the list's first year) and 2011 (including GE and Xerox), thirty-two made it four years (including Pitney Bowes), and twenty-seven made it three years (including CH2M Hill, Cisco, Google, and Zappos). We found that sixteen companies made the most sustainable list all six years between 2006 and 2011 (including Toyota), sixteen made it five years (including GE), and twenty-four made it four years.

Over those years (2006 to 2011), 415 companies made at least one of those three rankings at least once, sixty-five made two of those rankings at least once (including Cisco and Xerox), and fourteen companies made all three rankings at least once (including GE, Toyota, and Google). We then calculated a combined score, indicating the percentage of times the companies appeared on these three lists between 2006 and 2011 out of the total possible. We found that thirty-eight companies earned a combined score of 41 percent or higher (including Xerox and Google), with GE having the highest combined score (94 percent) of all companies, Toyota the second highest (80 percent), and Cisco in the top twenty.

We also performed additional, targeted financial analysis on more than two dozen public corporations and their respective peer groups. (Each firm has several companies in its industry peer group.) We analyzed all the companies that made all three of the rankings and many of the companies that made at least two of them—all in relation to their peer groups. We reviewed financial data over ten years (2001–2010) and focused on three indicators: (1) percentage return on assets (which we prefer to return on equity, because return on assets is a driver of shareholder value that filters out high-leverage organizations), (2) annual sales growth percentage (which reflects success in meeting customer needs), and (3) cash flow as a percentage of sales (since cash flow is much harder to manipulate, while net income can be influenced by accounting approaches). We compared the companies' performance with that of their industry peer groups, focusing on five-year and ten-year averages. With this approach, Google was the best of the lot. Clearly, there are many different ways to gather data and evaluate performance in these areas over time. There are drawbacks to each ranking system (and problems with combining them), but their value may increase over time as the metrics and measurement systems improve.

Our multifaceted approach of combining our experience with interviews and other research and analysis was helpful in illuminating leadership practices and the challenges of building excellent, ethical, and enduring organizations. Most research in this field addresses performance, ethics, or sustainability, but we are interested in how to excel in all three areas.

We acknowledge the limits of our approach. We did not set out to determine which organizations are great or more likely to succeed going forward. None of the organizations we looked at is flawless. There are always tradeoffs in these inquiries, with so many variables at play. Note, for example, differences between industries (growing versus stagnating), varying competitive dynamics and regulatory structures, different financial reporting systems across countries, and the challenges of measuring social impact. There are many factors that influence performance and impact, including leadership, culture, business model, strategy, execution, innovation, technology, marketing, intellectual property, size, structure, financing, governance, market trends, and even luck.

Our goal was to employ a reasonable approach for unpacking leadership lessons from a wide array of organizations and settings to supplement our own experience and thinking. We hope you find value in the final product.

Sport of Kings or Business of Knaves?

Jockeys could—and would—do anything to win . . . [they] grabbed hold of leading horses' tails or saddlecloths . . . joined arms with other jockeys to "clothesline" riders trying to cut between horses, formed obstructive "flying wedges" to block closers, and bashed passing horses into the inside rail. They hooked their legs over other jockeys' knees . . . they shoved and punched one another and grabbed another's reins.

—**Laura Hillenbrand,** *Seabiscuit*[1]

Much has changed since Laura Hillenbrand wrote about what jockeys would do to win in the early twentieth century, but thoroughbred horseracing still has both wonderful accomplishments and a dark side, much like other human endeavors.

Horseracing is popular worldwide, with over fifty countries reporting over 160,000 races and purses (the cash prizes won by the owners) worth over $4.4 billion in 2009.[2] Deloitte Consulting estimated that in 2004 horseracing had a total impact on U.S. gross domestic product of over $26 billion, generating over 380,000 full-time equivalent jobs and breeding more than four hundred thousand horses for the racetrack. Thoroughbred horseracing is big business.

Therein lies the crux of the challenge. Owners race horses for many reasons: money, fame, prestige, challenge, excitement, and more. Some owners are in it only for the money. Since recorded history, people have bet on races. Today, millions of fans enjoy horseracing's legalized gambling.

Not surprisingly, unethical behavior sometimes occurs. This sport of kings can sometimes be a business of knaves. Owners have falsified foal certificates, substituted ringers, raced horses too early or late in their lives, and run horses under false racing silks. Sometimes the cheating was farcical. In 1984, Australian owners substituted a ringer disguised with hair coloring and white paint. After the race, the paint started running down the horse's leg, exposing the fraud.[3]

Thoroughbred owners range from reprehensible to reputable. Contrast the crooked leadership of Calumet Farm with Penny Chenery's distinguished record: volunteering to serve in the Red Cross in Europe during World War II, becoming the unofficial "First Lady of Racing," receiving a merit award for her lifetime of achievements, serving as a worldwide goodwill ambassador, and advocating for the health and welfare of retired thoroughbreds.[4]

Jockeys were abused for many years, risking life-threatening injuries with no insurance, pressured into not unionizing, and chronically starving themselves to reduce their weight, taking laxatives or vomiting to reduce a few ounces, and worse. Some took bribes to win or lose races.

The Jockeys' Guild, which was founded by legendary jockey Eddie Arcaro, recites its successes: securing health and disability insurance, compulsory savings plans, safety helmets and padded vests, automatic deduction of mount fees from owners' accounts, on-track ambulances, workers' compensation coverage, and the Permanently Disabled Jockeys Fund.[5]

Some trainers or veterinarians have doped horses with performance-enhancing drugs or lied about equine injuries. Journalist Bill Nack told us:

> They weren't doing it for history. They were doing it for the money. The veterinarian was doing it because he gets paid by the owner to do it. The owner was doing it because he wanted the horse to win. Owners and trainers are under great pressure to run a popular horse. Fans give up their vacations to travel to a race and don't want to be disappointed. That pressure is hard to resist.

Human athletes often choose to compete when they are less than 100 percent, especially when the big event is on the line, but horses run when their owners or trainers decide.

Animal rights groups, like the American Society for the Prevention of Cruelty to Animals, have long criticized horseracing and lobbied for the proper treatment of the animals. People for the Ethical Treatment of Animals, an advocacy group, has criticized horseracing as "barbaric," calling it cruel and stating that it should be "eliminated entirely."[6]

We interviewed Alex Waldrop, president and CEO of the National Thoroughbred Racing Association (NTRA), who told us:

> Concerns about safety and integrity are industry-wide. No track is immune. The NTRA formed the Safety and Integrity Alliance in 2008 on the heels of the industry crisis resulting from the death of Eight Belles and the revelation that Big

Brown, the 2008 Triple Crown hopeful, was competing on steroids. We formed the Alliance and created an industry-wide code of standards. Today, fifty-five tracks [of ninety] have pledged to abide by the code. The NTRA, the Jockeys' Guild, and others are working hard to improve industry practices.

We interviewed Terry Meyocks, national manager of the Jockeys' Guild, Inc., which represents most U.S. jockeys. He told us:

Conditions have steadily improved since the Guild's inception in 1940. Since that time, the Guild has worked with various industry participants, such as the NTRA, to improve the safety conditions for both the jockey and the equine athletes. Currently, the Guild, along with others, is developing a study on jockey injuries. The Guild is continually working to improve the integrity and image of racing.

Industry leaders, such as Churchill Downs, Inc. (the company that owns several racetracks, including the one that hosts the Kentucky Derby), have embraced third-party testing of track surfaces, "supertesting" of horses (comprehensive tests for many banned substances at minute levels), age restrictions on horses, steroid bans, banning of unsafe horseshoes, low-impact riding crops, catastrophic injury insurance for jockeys, mandatory equine injury reporting, safety equipment improvements, and more.[7] Meyocks represents the Guild on the Racing Medication and Testing Consortium, which develops and promotes uniform rules, policies, and testing standards.

Thoroughbred horseracing is a wonderful sport, beset at times—like all sports—with challenges. We encourage industry officials and participants at all levels—from the owners and stewards to the jockeys and fans—to embrace triple crown leadership in proactively addressing the challenges.

FREQUENTLY ASKED QUESTIONS

1. *I'm not the CEO or executive director of my organization. What can I do about triple crown leadership?*

   A great deal. First, don't fall into the trap of assuming that leadership is only for people in positions of authority. Leadership is not about rank or title. It is a way of acting and thinking. At best, it is a group performance. (That is why we focus on "leadership" and not "the leader.") Triple crown leadership invites all people to step up and lead from where they are. Sometimes they lead, and other times they follow, letting others lead. All people should be stewards of the organization's "colors" (its purpose, values, and vision) and culture of character.

2. *My organization does not have triple crown leadership. What can I do to influence it to move in that direction?*

   Start by developing your own triple crown leadership. Focus on the three Es—excellent, ethical, and enduring—and role-model the five practices. Practice triple crown leadership with your team. Build it into your processes, discussions, and incentives. Identify key influencers or allies in the organization and work with them to identify two or three initiatives that can build momentum for triple crown leadership (such as changing the hiring process, piloting leadership development programs, and forming skunk works teams).

3. *My boss is not a triple crown leader. How can I influence my boss to embrace these practices?*

   Triple crown leadership often entails leading from below. Often, we can influence people deeply even when we work for them. Some leaders may be open to triple crown approaches but are not familiar with them or do not know how to proceed. Begin by developing your own leadership capacities and role-modeling the practices. Start showing results. Demonstrate ethical decision-making through dialogue and active debate. Raise long-term issues alongside the short-term imperatives and creatively look for ways to address them both. Achieve results ethically and sustainably, so your boss will want to know how you do it. Engage your boss in open, one-on-one dialogue, expressing your ideas and input thoughtfully while also listening to his or her ideas and concerns. Demonstrate that you are a productive and loyal team player. If you find the situation hopeless after your best efforts, move on and find an organization that fits your values and aspirations.

4. *How does* Triple Crown Leadership *fit with other books in the field?*

   We have learned a great deal from—and draw upon—books like *Built to Last, Good to Great, Great by Choice, In Search of Excellence, Supercorp, Higher Ambition, Sustainable Excellence, Authentic Leadership, True North, On Becoming a Leader, The Leadership Challenge, Servant Leadership,* and many more. We encourage you to read them. We are adding our own voices to the ongoing dialogue, based on our own experiences and research. We also see important differences. We are practitioners first. We focus on practice in the field but also draw upon research. *Triple Crown Leadership* is forward looking, calling people to the quest, not focused on past performance. *Triple Crown Leadership* also takes a multisector view, looking at business, social, government, and hybrid organizations.

We focus on leadership practices, not identifying a list of great organizations based on certain criteria. We also bring in many international examples and address synergies as well as tradeoffs between financial and social performance.

5. *I am considering joining an organization. How do I find out if it practices triple crown leadership and has a culture of character?*
Start by doing your homework. Look at the organization's web site, blogs, Facebook page, Twitter feeds, newsletters, annual reports, and sustainability and corporate responsibility reports. Search online for articles about the enterprise from reliable sources and bloggers. See if it makes any of the rankings (most admired, most ethical, most sustainable, most innovative, best places to work, etc.). Check out its financial performance versus its peers, or look for evidence of its financial viability and impact if it is a social enterprise. Perhaps most importantly, talk to people who work there (or did so recently) and ask for their candid insights. Visit the organization, even just as an outsider taking a tour if possible; talk to people; and walk around and get a sense of the "vibe." Ask your interviewers candid questions about how the organization approaches results, ethics, endurance, sustainability, and impact. If you have any doubts, move slowly. While you may feel pressure to take a job, recognize the consequences of working for the wrong organization on your health, happiness, and reputation, including the likelihood that you will have to make a change later.

6. *Even if an organization has values, the tough ethical questions are not easily answered. So, what is the benefit of your focus on shared values?*
Values are an important starting point. The process of debating, choosing, articulating, and inculcating organizational values can serve as an important anchor for the organization and help with decision-making. Most ethical problems occur when people do not stop and think about

the consequences of their actions or have no checks or controls on their behavior. Values can help with both. In cases where values collide, often the greatest benefit comes from engaging in dialogue with colleagues, viewing things from different perspectives, and examining all potential ramifications. Using such processes, you can make better decisions and instill a culture of character in the enterprise.

7. *Won't money spent on sustainability and corporate responsibility just detract from financial results?*
   It depends. Research on this topic is mixed. Today, we are much better at measuring financial performance than we are at measuring social performance. Some studies show a positive correlation; others do not. Researchers have not established a definitive causal link between the two at this point. We believe that it depends on which sustainability initiatives you choose (as some have high potential value in terms of reducing production costs, boosting revenues, or reducing risks, and others do not) and on how well you execute them. There is no magic formula. You must choose wisely, execute well, measure the right things, make adjustments, and more. But we advocate smart sustainability and social impact initiatives for two primary reasons: first, because it is the right thing to do and they are worthy in and of themselves (taking a multiple stakeholder perspective and looking at the big picture of organizations in the context of their communities and resources); and second, because they can boost results when done well. There is a moral case and a performance case for them, but it requires smart strategy, crisp execution, and effective leadership.

8. *Don't you need an extraordinary CEO to create an excellent, ethical, and enduring organization?*
   No doubt, the CEO (or executive director) is critically important. We do not believe that creating an excellent,

ethical, and enduring organization requires an extraordinary leader. We believe that it can be guided by an ordinary person at the top committed to an extraordinary quest, and further that it can only be achieved as a group performance with triple crown leadership pervading the organization. The very best CEOs know that great leadership is a group performance. Note, though, that bad CEOs can sabotage triple crown leadership. Triple crown leadership is hard enough as it is, and probably impossible with a CEO who undermines it. Boards must be stewards of the triple crown quest and ensure that the CEO is the right person for the job.

9. *Isn't ethical business just good for business?*
Over the long run, we believe it is. But ethical challenges are an occupational hazard of leadership, and leaders should be prepared to make difficult choices and to walk away from short-term financial value or increased performance when it requires unethical behavior. Sometimes there is a real tradeoff, and triple crown leadership requires steadfast upholding of the ethics imperative, sometimes at the expense of the performance imperative. Over time, such actions are likely to pay off in terms of enhanced reputation and loyalty from employees, customers, and vendors, as well as reduced risks of fines and penalties. But most importantly, it is the right thing to do. Triple crown leaders do not need a performance case for ethical behavior. They do it as a matter of integrity.

10. *Some of the organizations you interviewed or cited have had problems or breakdowns with at least one of the three Es (excellent, ethical, enduring). Doesn't that detract from your argument?*
Recall that *Triple Crown Leadership* is not a success study. Our intent was not to identify a list of triple crown organizations. Recall also that we specifically sought to interview

and research organizations that had experienced breakdowns and that had required turnarounds. Beyond that, all organizations struggle. The quest for excellent, ethical, and enduring organizations is ongoing. None of these organizations is perfect. The important point is how leaders respond to adversity and work to correct their mistakes.

11. *With your focus on ethical practices, what role do you think spirituality plays in triple crown leadership?*

We are both spiritual persons. Some of the organizations we interviewed (for example, Habitat for Humanity International and Siddaganga Institute of Technology in India) are strongly spiritual. In many other organizations we interviewed, individual leaders draw upon a spiritual perspective in their outlook and approach, recognizing that there is something beyond the self, beyond the ego, that matters. We see natural compatibility between triple crown leadership and a spiritual perspective, and we believe the former can benefit greatly from the latter.

12. *This quest looks impossible to achieve. Aren't these standards too high in today's turbulent world and competitive marketplace? Why even try?*

Remember that the point is to chase perfection, not to expect to achieve it. By raising our sights and our standards, we can achieve more than we thought possible because people, especially with the leadership we describe, can achieve extraordinary things. While we cannot expect to get everything right, we can expect to learn and grow in the endeavor, leaving a legacy we can be proud of. The world needs a different brand of leadership. We are up against grave challenges. We can and must do better.

ENDNOTES

INTRODUCTION

1. Announcer's call of the 1973 Belmont Stakes race, accessed on January 10, 2012, at http://www.secretariat.com/past-performances/belmont/.
2. A length is approximately 8 feet, so 31 lengths is 248 feet, or 76 meters.
3. Marvin Drager, *The Most Glorious Crown: The Story of America's Triple Crown Thoroughbreds from Sir Barton to Affirmed* (Chicago: Triumph Books, 2005), 192. All quotations in this section are from this book unless otherwise indicated.
4. "The Ten Greatest Horse Races of All Time," *The Observer Sport Monthly*, September 1, 2002.
5. Drager, *The Most Glorious Crown*, ix. The Kentucky Derby is one and a quarter miles (2.01 kilometers), the Preakness Stakes is one and three-sixteenths miles (1.91 kilometers), and the Belmont Stakes is one and a half miles (2.41 kilometers). The last U.S. Triple Crown win was in 1978, creating the longest drought in Triple Crown history. The term "Triple Crown" originally applied to an English, Irish, Scottish, or Welsh national rugby team that defeated all three of its opponents in a season. Many sports use "Triple Crown" to describe the act of winning the three most difficult events, including baseball, basketball, boxing, cricket, cycling, dog shows, golf, hiking, motor sports, rugby, skiing, snooker, surfing, and wrestling. In horseracing, the English Triple Crown predates the U.S. Triple Crown, and it has fewer winners as a percentage of the years run.
6. Jack Welch cited in Andrew Hill, "Sustainable Growth Is the New Incarnation of Capitalism," FT.com, May 17, 2011. See also "Jack Welch Elaborates: Shareholder Value," *Bloomberg Businessweek*, March 16, 2009; Steve Tobak, "Does Jack Welch Think Shareholder Value Is a Dumb Idea?" *BNET.com Blog*, March 24, 2009.

CHAPTER 1

1. Dr. Leonard Berry and Dr. Kent Seltman, *Management Lessons from Mayo Clinic: Inside One of the World's Most Admired Service Organizations* (New York: McGraw-Hill, 2008).
2. Dr. Kent Seltman quoted in Anne Lee, "How to Build a Lasting Brand," *Fast Company*, September 2, 2008.
3. Paul Roberts, "The Agenda—Total Teamwork," *Fast Company*, December 19, 2007.
4. Ezekiel Emanuel and Steven Pearson, "It Costs More, but Is It Worth More?" *New York Times*, January 2, 2012. See also John Noseworthy's letter to the editor, "Mayo Clinic's Investment," *New York Times*, January 3, 2012.
5. We distinguish between "excellent results" and the broader concept of "excellence," which includes a number of components. As mentioned in the Introduction, we

believe the concept of excellence can include things like ethics and endurance, but we draw them out in this book for special emphasis because they have been neglected.

6. Julia Kirby, "Toward a Theory of High Performance," *Harvard Business Review,* July–August 2005.

7. From 2001 to 2008, Princeton University was ranked first among national universities by *U.S. News & World Report.* In 2009, it ranked second. It has been ranked eighth among world universities by Shanghai Jiao Tong University.

8. *Built for Learning: A Unified Architectural Vision for the University of Denver* (Denver, Colorado: University of Denver, 2008).

9. The Markkula Center for Applied Ethics has outlined "unavoidable ethical dilemmas" for leaders, such as conflicting priorities between stakeholders, the challenge of honoring dysfunctional agreements of a predecessor, perceived conflicts of interest, loyalty to the team versus personal expressions of concern, and more. Over the centuries, philosophers and ethicists ranging from Aristotle to John Stuart Mill and Immanuel Kant have developed frameworks for resolving such conflicts of values (for example, utilitarianism, rights, virtues, communitarianism).

10. For example, see the interview with Dr. Max Bazerman, "Evaluating Your Business Ethics," *Gallup Management Journal,* June 12, 2008. Note the famous experiments by Stanley Milgram in the 1960s in which twenty-six ordinary people were asked to administer what they thought were electric shocks to people in another room for giving wrong answers. They all gave what they believed were very strong shocks in obedience to authority.

11. *Sources for the data points:* "2010 Global Fraud Study: Report to the Nations on Occupational Fraud and Abuse," Association of Certified Fraud Examiners, Austin, Texas, 2010. Survey participants estimated that the typical organization loses 5 percent of its annual revenue to fraud, including asset misappropriation, financial statement fraud, and corruption schemes. Sharon Allen, "The New ROE: Return on Ethics," *Forbes,* July 21, 2009; Shirley Li, "34 Percent of Employees Have Express Knowledge of Workplace Misconduct," *Inside Counsel,* December 13, 2011; LRN, "New Research Indicates Ethical Corporate Cultures Impact the Ability to Attract, Retain, and Ensure Productivity Among U.S. Workers," August 3, 2006, cited in Ronald Howard and Clinton Korver, *Ethics (for the Real World): Creating a Personal Code to Guide Decisions in Work and Life* (Boston: Harvard Business Press, 2008); Jeremy Meyer, "Students' Cheating Takes a High-Tech Turn," *Denver Post,* May 27, 2010; Carolyn Woo, "Cheating: You Have to Sweat the Small Stuff," *Forbes,* February 16, 2010.

12. AMD ranked among the World's Most Sustainable Companies (Corporate Knights) in 2007, 2008, 2009, and 2010, as well as among the Best Corporate Citizens (*Corporate Responsibility Magazine)* in 2006, 2007, 2009, 2010, and 2011.

13. Cited in Matthew Scott, "Is Your Company Building 'Integrity Capital?'" *Business Insider,* June 2, 2011.

14. "Ethical Companies Make More Money," *Environmental Leader,* November 29, 2006. See also Curtis Verschoor, "Ethical Culture More Important Than Ever," *Strategic Finance,* August 2007, 11.

15. Scott, "Is Your Company Building 'Integrity Capital?'"

16. John Graham, Campbell Harvey, and Shiva Rajgopal, "The Economic Implications of Corporate Financial Reporting," Duke University, January 11, 2005. See also Nelson Repenning and Rebecca Henderson, "Making the Numbers? 'Short-Termism' and the Puzzle of Only Occasional Disaster," Harvard Business School Working Paper 11-033 version 1.0, August 2010, 3.

17. Mariane Jennings, "The Seven Signs of Ethical Collapse," *CXO Europe*, April 2010.

18. Sheila Bair, "Short-Termism and the Risk of Another Financial Crisis," *Washington Post*, July 9, 2011.

19. Aspen Institute, "Overcoming Short-Termism: A Call for a More Responsible Approach to Investment and Business Management," September 9, 2009. See also Karen Kroll, "Short-Termism: On the Way Out?" *BigFatFinanceBlog*, September 15, 2009; Aspen Institute, *Long-Term Value Creation: Guiding Principles for Corporations and Investors*, June 2007; and Dean Krehmeyer, Matthew Orsagh, and Kurt Schacht, "Breaking the Short-Term Cycle," CFA Institute and Business Roundtable, 2006.

20. Simon Wong, "Seven Ways CEOs and Investors Can Promote the Long Term," *Harvard Business Review Blog Network*, September 29, 2011.

21. James Stewart, "Amazon Says Long Term and Means It," *New York Times*, December 16, 2011.

22. See also GuideStar, greatnonprofits.org, and other sources for different data points and pieces of the puzzle.

23. They also resonate with other phrases used today, including "conscious capitalism," "corporate citizenship," "sustainable excellence," "shared value," "social businesses," and more. Many today prefer the term "corporate responsibility" (CR) to CSR.

24. There are also moral obligations to help others in some cases, such as when a tsunami devastates a coastal town or an earthquake levels a city. Triple crown leaders leap to lend a hand, not content to sit on the sidelines when they know they can make a difference, even though such actions have costs. They are not hung up on philosophical debates about the proper roles of business, government, and nonprofits in society. They step up and act. In doing so, they reveal their organization's values in practice and help shape its character.

25. Joshua Margolis and James Walsh, "Misery Loves Companies: Rethinking Social Initiatives by Business," *Administrative Science Quarterly*, Volume 48, June 2003, 277. See also Marc Orlitzky et al., "Corporate Social and Financial Performance: A Meta-Analysis," *Organization Studies* 24, March 2003, 403–441; Archie Carroll and Kareem Shabana, "The Business Case for Corporate Social Responsibility: A Review of Concepts, Research, and Practice," *International Journal of Management Reviews*, 2010, 85–105; Nathan Washburn, "Why Profit Shouldn't Be Your Top Goal," *Harvard Business Review*, December 2009. The evidence is not yet conclusive. Recall also that correlation does not indicate causation. There are many measurement issues and questions. Much information is self-reported, and measuring systems are imperfect and in flux. Are high performers profitable because they operate sustainably, or are they able to afford to be sustainable because they are already high performers? Are some orga-

nizations good at getting high rankings versus actually operating sustainably? We need more and better information before we can draw firm conclusions.

26. David Kiron, Nina Kruschwitz, Knut Haanaes, and Ingrid von Streng Velken, "Sustainability Nears a Tipping Point," *MIT Sloan Management Review,* December 15, 2011.

27. "U.S. Execs: CSR Initiatives Do Boost the Bottom Line," *BusinessGreen.com,* November 24, 2008.

28. Author John Di Frances defines "corporate character" as "an environment where people do the right thing as standard operating procedure." See John Di Frances, *Reclaiming the Ethical High Ground: Developing Organizations of Character* (Wales, Wisconsin: Reliance Books, 2002). See also Rob Goffee and Gareth Jones, *The Character of a Corporation: How Your Company's Culture Can Make or Break Your Business* (New York: Collins, 1998); Tom Hill and Walter Jenkins, *Making Character First: Building a Culture of Character in Any Organization* (Edmond, Oklahoma: Character First Publishers, 2010); Frank Sherosky, *Perfecting Corporate Character: Lessons for 21st Century Organizations* (Clinton Township, Michigan: Strategic Publications, 1997); Peter Firestein, *Crisis of Character, Reputation in the Age of Skepticism* (New York: Union Square Press, 2009).

29. Lou Gerstner, *Who Says Elephants Can't Dance? Inside IBM's Historic Turnaround* (New York: Collins Business, 2002) 182.

30. Eric Sanders and Robert Cooke, "Financial Returns from Organizational Culture Improvement: Translating 'Soft' Changes into 'Hard' Dollars," *Human Synergistics White Paper,* 2011.

31. Barry Jaruzelski, John Loehr, and Richard Holman, "The Global Innovation 1000: Why Culture Is Key," *Strategy + Business,* Winter 2011, October 25, 2011.

32. Deidre Campbell, "What Great Companies Know About Culture," *Harvard Business Review Blog Network,* December 14, 2011.

CHAPTER 2

1. This story has been compiled from these sources: Laura Hillenbrand, *Seabiscuit, An American Legend* (New York: Ballantine Books, 2001); Ron Hale, "Seabiscuit vs. War Admiral: The Greatest Match Race of the Century," *About.com Horse Racing,* 1998, accessed January 29, 2012 at http://horseracing.about.com/od/history1/l/blseabis.htm.

2. Tom Smith cited in Hillenbrand, *Seabiscuit, An American Legend,* 44.

3. Charles Howard cited in Hillenbrand, *Seabiscuit, An American Legend,* 45.

4. Parker Palmer cited in L. J. Rittenhouse, "Leadership and the Inner Journey: An Interview with Parker Palmer," *Leader to Leader,* fall 2001, 27.

5. John Horan-Kates, *The Leader's Journal: Integrating Head and Heart* (Bloomington, Indiana: AuthorHouse, 2011), vii. See also http://www.vailleadership.org. *Full disclosure:* Bob is a former trustee of Vail Leadership Institute (VLI), chairman emeritus, and serves on the board of scholars. Gregg is a current trustee. VLI has been a longtime proponent of living and leading with "head and heart."

6. Bill George, *Authentic Leadership: Rediscovering the Secrets to Creating Lasting Value* (San Francisco: Jossey-Bass, 2003), 133.

7. Stephen M. R. Covey, *The Speed of Trust: The One Thing That Changes Everything* (New York: Free Press, 2006), 30. See also Stephen M. R. Covey and Greg Link, *Smart Trust: Creating Prosperity, Energy, and Joy in a Low-Trust World* (New York: Free Press, 2012).

8. A. G. Lafley, "The Art and Science of Finding the Right CEO," *Harvard Business Review,* October 2011.

9. Alan Lewis, "How My Company Hires for Culture First, Skills Second," *Harvard Business Review Blog Network,* January 26, 2011.

10. Tony Hsieh, *Delivering Happiness: A Path to Profits, Passion, and Purpose* (New York: Business Plus, 2010), 172. Nick Swinmurn founded Zappos.com, and Hsieh joined the company after investing.

11. Andrew Sobel, "What's So Special About Special Ops?" *Strategy + Business,* Issue 57, November 24, 2009.

12. Schumpeter (column), "The Tussle for Talent," *The Economist,* January 8, 2011.

13. Diane Brady, "Can GE Still Manage?" *Bloomberg Businessweek,* April 15, 2010.

14. Hewitt Associates and Human Capital Institute, "The State of Talent Management: Today's Challenges, Tomorrow's Opportunities," October 2008.

15. For more on this topic, see Bill George and Doug Baker, *True North Groups: A Powerful Path to Personal and Leadership Development* (San Francisco: Berrett-Koehler, 2011).

16. See Christopher Gergen and Gregg Vanourek, *Life Entrepreneurs: Ordinary People Creating Extraordinary Lives* (San Francisco: Jossey-Bass, 2008); Bob Aubrey, *Managing Your Aspirations: Developing Personal Enterprise in the Global Workplace* (Singapore: McGraw-Hill, 2011).

17. Here Drs. Kent Seltman and Leonard Berry, whom we interviewed, are referring to a comment from a former Mayo Clinic CEO. When asked about star physicians at Mayo, he said, "Mayo has a constellation in that I think that virtually everyone is a star. But there is no Big Dipper . . ." We quote Berry and Seltman with their permission. Berry and Seltman are authors of *Management Lessons from Mayo Clinic: Inside One of the World's Most Admired Service Organizations* (New York: McGraw-Hill, 2008).

18. Leonard Berry and Neeli Bendapudi, "Clueing in Customers," *Harvard Business Review,* February 2003, 102.

19. Paul Roberts, "The Agenda—Total Teamwork," *Fast Company,* December 19, 2007.

20. We recommend consulting with legal counsel and human resources officials and remaining mindful of privacy and legal restrictions when determining which questions to ask.

CHAPTER 3

1. The tornado was an EF5, or five out of five—the highest possible—on the Enhanced Fujita scale. In meters, a typical tornado is only about 150 meters across, but this one was about 2.7 kilometers wide and had wind speeds of over 320 kilometers per hour.

2. *Sources:* Lamar Graham, "The Greenest Town in America," *Parade,* April 19, 2009, 6; Bryan Walsh, "Turned Green by a Twister," *TIME,* February 3, 2008; Victoria

Witchey, "Rebuilding a Model of Sustainability and Hope," *Attribute* magazine, January 2009; Bryan Walsh, "Postcard: Greensburg," *TIME,* March 6, 2008; Frank Morris, "Tornado's Gifts: Greensburg Rebuilds, Revitalizes," *NPR.com,* May 4, 2008.

3. Frank Morris, "Kansas Town's Green Dreams Could Save Its Future," *NPR.com,* December 27, 2007; Walsh, "Postcard: Greensburg." Three other people lost their lives because of another tornado system around the same time.

4. Michelle Moore quoted in Graham, "The Greenest Town in America," 8.

5. Adam Andrews, "LEED Certifications: Platinum and Gold," *GreensburgGreentown.org,* July 11, 2011.

6. Many racing colors and patterns used today can be traced to medieval cities in Italy.

7. Linda Holbeche with Nigel Springett, "In Search of Meaning in the Workplace," Roffey Park, 2004.

8. Linda Hill and Kent Lineback, "The Fundamental Purpose of Your Team," *Harvard Business Review Blog Network,* July 12, 2011.

9. Medtronic: 100 Best Corporate Citizens (CR): 2010–2012; Best Companies to Work For (*Fortune*): 2007. Named to *Fortune*'s annual list of America's Most Admired Companies for the eleventh consecutive year and ranked number six in industry sector (March 2008).

10. Rosabeth Moss Kanter, *SuperCorp: How Vanguard Companies Create Innovation, Profits, Growth, and Social Good* (New York: Crown Publishing Group, 2009), 17, 57.

11. eBay: World's Most Admired Companies (*Fortune*): 2010–2012; World's Most Ethical Companies (Ethisphere): 2011, 2012; Best Companies to Work For (*Fortune*): 2008, 2009.

12. Rated by *Fortune* as one of the Top Ten Most Admired Healthcare Companies for the third year.

13. Steven Kaplan and Bernadette Minton, "How Has CEO Turnover Changed?" National Bureau of Economic Research, August 2008. See also "Leading CEOs: A Statistical Snapshot of S&P 500 Leaders," Spencer Stuart, February 2006.

14. James Kouzes and Barry Posner, *A Leader's Legacy* (San Francisco: Jossey-Bass, 2006), 108.

15. James O'Toole, "Doing Good Business: Leadership, Ethics, and Corporate Culture," in James O'Toole and Don Mayer, editors, *Good Business: Exercising Effective and Ethical Leadership* (New York: Routledge, 2010), 116.

16. David Weaver, Jr., CEO, South Plains Food Bank, Lubbock, Texas, cited in Share Our Strength's *Annual Report 2009.*

17. U.S. Department of Agriculture, *Household Food Security in the United States,* Economic Research Report Paper Number 108, Washington D.C., November 2010. See also http://www.globalissues.org/ and http://www.strength.org/.

18. Material in this section comes from our interview with Bill Shore as well as his book, *The Cathedral Within: Transforming Your Life by Giving Something Back* (New York: Random House, 1999).

CHAPTER 4

1. Doris Kearns Goodwin, *Team of Rivals: The Political Genius of Abraham Lincoln* (New York: Simon & Schuster, 2005).

2. Jim Collins, *Good to Great: Why Some Companies Make the Leap . . . and Others Don't* (New York: HarperBusiness, 2001), 52.

3. See, for example, Connson Locke and Cameron Anderson, "The Downside of Looking like a Leader," London School of Economics Doctoral Thesis/Dissertation, 2008.

4. Marvin Drager, *The Most Glorious Crown: The Story of America's Triple Crown Thoroughbreds from Sir Barton to Affirmed* (Chicago: Triumph Books, 2005), 166–169.

5. Lawrence Scanlan, *The Big Red Horse* (Toronto: Harper Trophy Canada, 2007), 71.

6. *Source:* Secretariat.com, accessed January 14, 2012, at http://www.secretariat.com/ spotlight/penny-chenery/.

7. See Bill George, *Authentic Leadership: Rediscovering the Secrets to Creating Lasting Value* (San Francisco: Jossey-Bass, 2003); Bill George with Peter Sims, *True North: Discover Your Authentic Leadership* (San Francisco: John Wiley & Sons, 2007).

8. The Myers-Briggs Type Indicator assessment is a psychometric questionnaire, based on the work of Swiss psychiatrist Carl Jung, designed to measure psychological preferences in how people perceive the world and make decisions. People use it for insights on their personality type. Insights Discovery System, also based on Jung's work, uses a four-color model to understand an individual's unique preferences and present a personality profile.

9. Our notion of steel, velvet, and flexing between them builds upon the work of others, such as Fred Fiedler's "contingency model" and its notion of situational favorableness and whether leaders are task oriented or relationship oriented. See Fred Fiedler, *A Theory of Leadership Effectiveness* (New York: McGraw-Hill, 1967). Tom Peters and Robert Waterman introduced the "tight-loose" paradox in *In Search of Excellence*. According to Jim Collins, a "level-five executive" brings to bear a paradoxical blend of personal humility and professional will. See Collins, *Good to Great*, 20. Joseph Nye, Jr., talks about soft power, hard power, and smart power. For Nye, hard power rests on inducements and threats, while soft power depends on shaping the preferences of others via charisma, persuasion, and example. See Joseph Nye, Jr., *The Powers to Lead* (Oxford: Oxford University Press, 2008), x.

10. There are notable instances of the co-CEO arrangement working well (see, for example, the SEED Foundation in chapter ten).

11. Noel Tichy and Warren Bennis, *Judgment: How Winning Leaders Make Great Calls* (New York: Penguin Group, 2007).

12. James O'Toole, *Leading Change: The Argument for Values-Based Leadership* (New York: Ballantine Books, 1995).

13. Drager, *The Most Glorious Crown*.

CHAPTER 5

1. Gregory Ferraro quoted in William Nack, "The Breaking Point," *Sports Illustrated,* November 1, 1993.
2. Gregory Ferraro, "The Corruption of Nobility: The Rise and Fall of Thoroughbred Racing in America," *North American Review,* 1992.
3. Often, leaders bound such empowerment with spending limits or other thresholds. In other ventures, like Zappos.com, there is greater operational freedom (for example, "use your best judgment to delight the customer").
4. This section draws upon an article we wrote: Bob Vanourek and Gregg Vanourek, "The Power of Leadership Trustees," *People and Strategy,* Volume 33, Issue 3, 2010.
5. Simon C. Y. Wong, "Boards: When Best Practice Isn't Enough," *McKinsey Quarterly,* June 2011.
6. "Brand Promise: What's Your Ethical Brand Value?" *Ethisphere,* November 2, 2009.
7. Raymond Gilmartin, "CEOs and Boards Need a Pact on How the Firm Will Be Run," *Harvard Business Review Blog Network,* October 28, 2011.
8. James Kouzes and Barry Posner, *A Leader's Legacy* (San Francisco: Jossey-Bass, 2006), 91.
9. "Open-Door Policy, Closed-Lip Reality," Corporate Executive Board, New York, 2011, 2.
10. David Novak cited in Tim Donnelly, "Leadership Lessons from the Man Behind the World's Biggest Restaurant Company," *Inc.,* January 9, 2012.

CHAPTER 6

1. Laura Hillenbrand, *Seabiscuit: An American Legend* (New York: Ballantine Books, 2001), 324.
2. Mihaly Csikszentmihalyi, *Flow: The Psychology of Optimal Experience* (New York: Harper Perennial, 1990), 3.
3. Örjan de Manzano et al., "The Psychophysiology of Flow During Piano Playing," *Emotion,* Volume 10, Issue 3, June 2010, 301–311.
4. Steve Donoghue cited in Hillenbrand, *Seabiscuit,* 80.
5. Paul Leinwand and Cesare Mainardi, "The Coherence Premium," *Harvard Business Review,* June 2010. See also Paul Leinwand and Cesare Mainardi, "Measuring Executive Frustration—and Going After the Big-Picture Cure," *SmartBlog on Finance,* March 21, 2011; and "Executives Say They're Pulled in Too Many Directors," *Booz.com,* January 18, 2011.
6. Steve Crabtree, "Getting Personal in the Workplace," *GovLeaders.org,* June 2004. See also James Harter et al., "Q[12] Meta-Analysis: The Relationship Between Engagement at Work and Organizational Outcomes," Gallup, August 2009; and Aon Hewitt, "Trends in Global Employee Engagement," June 2010.
7. Patrick Lencioni, *The Five Dysfunctions of a Team: A Leadership Fable* (San Francisco: Jossey-Bass, 2002), 188.
8. Stephen M. R. Covey, *The Speed of Trust: The One Thing That Changes Everything* (New York: Free Press, 2006), 19.

9. A "skunk works" refers to a group given a high degree of autonomy within an organization and tasked with difficult and important projects. The term was first widely used by Lockheed Martin in the 1940s for accelerated development work on new aircraft.

10. See Christopher Gergen and Gregg Vanourek, *Life Entrepreneurs: Ordinary People Creating Extraordinary Lives* (San Francisco: Jossey-Bass, 2008), 95–100.

11. Of course, Coca-Cola does not reveal its secret soft drink formula in its strategy summary. Some things should be kept confidential. But, we submit, limiting the key elements of the strategy to the upper echelons precludes alignment.

12. Jeffrey Hollender and Bill Breen, *The Responsibility Revolution: How the Next Generation of Businesses Will Win* (San Francisco: Jossey-Bass, 2010), 38. See also http://plana.marksandspencer.com/about.

13. The McKinsey 7S Framework is a management model that includes strategy, structure, systems, shared values, skills, style, and staff. Balanced Scorecard is a strategic performance management tool that includes vision and strategy, financial processes, internal business processes, learning and growth initiatives, and customer focus.

14. Jim Collins and Jerry Porras, "Building Your Company's Vision," *Harvard Business Review*, October 1996.

15. Lencioni, *The Five Dysfunctions of a Team*, 220.

CHAPTER 7

1. Ruffian's story is compiled from William Nack, *Ruffian: A Racetrack Romance* (New York: ESPN Books, 2007); and Jane Schwartz, *Ruffian: Burning from the Start* (New York: Random House, 1991).

2. The Filly Triple Crown is now the Triple Tiara of Thoroughbred Racing. It includes three U.S. horse races and is only open to three-year-old fillies. The three races are the Acorn Stakes, the Coaching Club American Oaks, and the Alabama Stakes.

3. Presley White, "Ruffian," *HorseFix*.com, undated, accessed January 16, 2012, at http://www.horsefix.com/pages/Famous%20Horses/famous-ruffian.htm.

4. The Triple Crown winners did finish in the money (first, second, or third) over 90 percent of the time.

5. Many said that if the race were longer, there is no doubt she would have won.

6. Unless otherwise noted, we derived the material in this section from Ann Hagedorn Auerbach, *Wild Ride: The Rise and Tragic Fall of Calumet Farm Inc., America's Premier Racing Dynasty* (New York: Holt Paperbacks, 1994).

7. Skip Hollandsworth, "The Killing of Alydar," *Texas Monthly*, June 2001.

8. David Voreacos, Alex Nussbaum, and Greg Farrell, "Johnson & Johnson: Ouch!" *Bloomberg Businessweek*, March 31, 2011. See also Susan Todd, "N.J.'s Johnson & Johnson Facing Shareholder Lawsuit over Recalls," *NJ.com*, December 22, 2010.

9. "SEC Says Johnson & Johnson to Pay More Than $70M in Settlement," *Bloomberg.com*, April 8, 2011.

10. Voreacos, Nussbaum, and Farrell, "Johnson & Johnson: Ouch!"

11. Ira Loss cited in Voreacos, Nussbaum, and Farrell, "Johnson & Johnson: Ouch!"

12. Bill Vlasic, "Toyota's Slow Awakening to a Deadly Problem," *New York Times*, February 1, 2010.

13. "U.S. Department of Transportation Releases Results from NHTSA-NASA Study of Unintended Acceleration of Toyota Vehicles," DOT 16-11, February 8, 2011, accessed January 16, 2012. Some of the critics disagree, and the debate continues.

14. Suzanne Vranica, "Public Relations Learned the Hard Way," *Wall Street Journal*, December 29, 2010; Drake Bennett, "Toyota Bets on Japan," *Bloomberg Businessweek*, May 9–15, 2011, 72.

15. Interbrand, "Best Global Green Brands 2011 Ranking."

16. See, for example, Alex Taylor III, "How Toyota Lost Its Way," *CNNMoney.com*, July 12, 2010; Matthew Phillips, "Toyota's Digital Disaster," *Newsweek*, February 3, 2010.

17. According to Lentz, the recalls were primarily for risk of floor-mat entrapment and slow-to-return or sticking accelerator pedals.

18. Akio Toyoda, "Testimony to House Committee on Oversight and Government Reform," Prepared Testimony of Akio Toyoda, President, Toyota Motor Corporation, to Committee on Oversight and Government Reform, U.S. Congress, February 24, 2010.

19. See Walter Isaacson, *Steve Jobs* (New York: Simon & Schuster, 2011), 38, 52, 117–120, 140, 145, 161, 175–176, 179, 185–186, 191, 226, 229, 235, 240, 454, 471–472.

CHAPTER 8

1. In addition to our interview with Nancy Tuor from CH2M Hill, our sources for this story unless otherwise indicated are Kim Cameron and Marc Lavine, *Making the Impossible Possible: Leading Extraordinary Performance—The Rocky Flats Story* (San Francisco: Berrett-Koehler, 2006) and Bob Darr, a DOE legacy support contractor at Rocky Flats, employed by the S. M. Stoller Corporation, an environmental consulting firm. For additional Rocky Flats details, see also Len Ackland, *Making a Real Killing: Rocky Flats and the Nuclear West* (Albuquerque: University of New Mexico Press, 1999).

2. A curie is an international measurement unit of radioactivity. A picocurie is one one-trillionth of a curie. According to the U.S. Army Corps of Engineers, one nanocurie, which is one one-billionth of a curie, is the amount of radiation given off by some consumer products, and a picocurie is roughly equivalent to background environment levels of radiation. See http://www.lrb.usace.army.mil/fusrap/docs/fusrap-fs-picocurie.pdf.

3. A Final Comprehensive Conservation Plan and Environmental Impact Study was conducted on the refuge lands (separate from the cleanup area) after the former buffer areas were assigned to become a wildlife refuge. That work led to a decision to convert portions of the site to a National Wildlife Refuge to provide habitat for wildlife species, including threatened or endangered species, and to protect rare prairie plant communities. Although the refuge was designed to provide moderate levels of visitor use on sixteen miles of trails and developed overlooks, currently there is no public access to the refuge due to lack of appropriations. See http://www.fws.gov/rockyflats/.

4. Cameron and Lavine, *Making the Impossible Possible*, 256.
5. In spite of these successes, some critics were not satisfied with the final soil and water quality levels established by DOE. During the course of the cleanup, there were some safety violations and DOE penalties levied on Kaiser-Hill. Note, however, that the number of safety incidents in 2005 fell by 80 percent (versus pre-1995 numbers) and to a level 75 percent below the construction industry average and half the DOE average. (See Cameron and Lavine, 25.) Others raised concerns about the payments of benefits to former employees whose employment ended before dates that would have entitled them to larger benefits. The FBI agent who led the raid on Rocky Flats joined other critics in objecting to the government's decision to seal the special grand jury files about the criminal investigation of the prior contractor, Rockwell International, and DOE employees. See Wes McKinley and Caron Balkany, *The Ambushed Grand Jury* (New York: Apex Press, 2004).
6. According to McKinsey data, visibility from the CEO or relevant business unit leader is an important success factor in transformations. "McKinsey Global Survey Results: Creating Organizational Transformations," *McKinsey Quarterly*, July 2008, 4.
7. Ronald Heifetz, Alexander Grashow, and Marty Linsky, "Leadership in a (Permanent) Crisis," *Harvard Business Review*, July–August 2009, 118. See also John Kotter, "Leading Change: Why Transformation Efforts Fail," *Harvard Business Review*, January 2007, 87; Bill George, *Seven Lessons for Leading in a Crisis* (San Francisco: Jossey-Bass, 2009).
8. Jennifer Chatman et al., "Cisco Systems: Developing a Human Capital Strategy," *California Management Review*, Winter 2005, 137.
9. "McKinsey Conversations with Global Leaders: John Chambers of Cisco," *McKinsey Quarterly*, July 2009.
10. Sylvia Ann Hewlett, "How Cisco Created Their Own Talent Incubator," *Harvard Business Review Blog Network*, October 20, 2009.
11. Adam Hartung, "Is Cisco a Value Stock? Skip It," *Forbes*, June 23, 2011.
12. Henry Blodget, "Has Cisco's John Chambers Lost His Mind?" *Business Insider*, August 6, 2009.
13. Rosabeth Moss Kanter, "Cisco and a Cautionary Tale About Teams," *Harvard Business Review Blog Network*, May 9, 2011.

CHAPTER 9

1. Marvin Drager, *The Most Glorious Crown: The Story of America's Triple Crown Thoroughbreds from Sir Barton to Affirmed* (Chicago: Triumph Books, 2005), 192.
2. Brendan Greeley, "She Sings, He Streams," *Bloomberg Businessweek*, July 18–July 24, 2011.
3. Steven Bertoni, "Spotify's Daniel Ek: The Most Important Man in Music," *Forbes*, January 16, 2012.
4. This framework for levels of board engagement comes from David Nadler, "Building Better Boards," *Harvard Business Review*, May 2004.
5. Yvon Chouinard, *Let My People Go Surfing: The Education of a Reluctant Businessman* (New York: Penguin Books, 2005), 39–40, 78.

6. John Mullins and Randy Komisar, *Getting to Plan B: Breaking Through to a Better Business Model* (Boston: Harvard Business Press, 2009).

7. Most venture capital funds, angel investors, and banks require a business plan, so this only works in certain cases and at certain points in the early stages of a venture.

8. Greeley, "She Sings, He Streams."

9. Danna Greenberg, Kate McKone-Sweet, and H. James Wilson, *The New Entrepreneurial Leader: Developing Leaders Who Shape Social and Economic Opportunity* (San Francisco: Berrett-Koehler, 2011).

10. *Source for this example:* Chouinard, *Let My People Go Surfing.*

11. Mullins and Komisar, *Getting to Plan B,* 103.

12. Chouinard, *Let My People Go Surfing,* 84.

CHAPTER 10

1. Scott Smith, "He Rides High with Clif Bar," *Investor's Business Daily,* July 13, 2009.

2. For examples of social impact measurement systems, see the SROI Method (SROI Network); Pulse (originally called the Portfolio Data Management System, used by the Acumen Fund); Social Evaluator BV (developed in the Netherlands); and Measuring Effectiveness (used by Ashoka). There are challenges with such systems, including self-reported data and potential sample biases due to attrition and response rates. There have also been gaps in data collection. Efforts like Charity Navigator, Guidestar, and GiveWell are now addressing such issues.

3. We based portions of this section on a March 2, 2001, article in the *Princeton Alumni Weekly* on Rajiv Vinnakota, 31–32.

4. Bill Drayton cited in David Bornstein, *How to Change the World: Social Entrepreneurs and the Power of New Ideas* (Oxford: Oxford University Press, 2004), 63.

5. *Source:* Charity Navigator, http://www.charitynavigator.org.

6. "Q&A with Bill Drayton, Founder of Ashoka," *U.S. News & World Report,* October 31, 2005.

7. Remarks of Larry Thompson at the State Bar of Texas Annual Meeting, June 16, 2006, accessed January 19, 2012, at http://ethisphere.com/the-tone-at-the-top -full-transcript/.

8. World's Most Admired Companies (*Fortune*): 2006–2012; World's Most Ethical Companies (Ethisphere): 2007–2012; Top Twenty Best Companies for Leadership (Hay Group): 2005–2008, 2010; 100 Best Corporate Citizens (CR): 2006–2012; Green Rankings (*Newsweek*): 2008, 2010; top companies for leaders in 2012 (*Chief Executive* magazine); and more.

9. Mike Esterl, "PepsiCo Board Stands by Nooyi," *Wall Street Journal,* January 13, 2012.

CHAPTER 11

1. Unless otherwise indicated, material on Infosys comes from Matthew Barney, editor, *Leadership @ Infosys* (New Delhi: Penguin Group, 2010), and an interview with N. R. Narayana Murthy by Anand P. Raman, "Why Don't We Try to Be India's Most Respected Company?" *Harvard Business Review,* November 2011, 80–86.

2. Julie Schlosser, "Harder Than Harvard," *CNNMoney,* March 17, 2006.

3. Dave Levin cited in Susan Headden, "Two Guys . . . and a Dream," *U.S. News & World Report,* February 20, 2006.

4. *Source:* Jay Mathews, *Work Hard. Be Nice: How Two Inspired Teachers Created the Most Promising Schools in America* (Chapel Hill, North Carolina: Algonquin Books, 2009), 34.

5. See, for example, the following: Dave Levin cited in Eddy Ramirez, "America's Best Leaders: Mike Feinberg and David Levin, Knowledge Is Power Program (KIPP)," *U.S. News & World Report,* November 19, 2008; Mike Feinberg cited in Bob Herbert, "A Chance to Learn," *New York Times,* December 16, 2002; Feinberg cited in Headden, "Two Guys . . . and a Dream."

6. KIPP is a national network of public charter schools focused on serving underserved urban schoolchildren. Free and open to all who choose to attend (space permitting), the schools are focused on academics and preparing students for college. KIPP launched initially with middle schools but later added elementary and high schools.

7. In 2010, Mathematica Policy Research released preliminary findings from the most rigorous and extensive study on KIPP schools to date: "We find that students entering these 22 KIPP schools typically had prior achievement levels that were lower than the average achievement on their local school districts. For the vast majority of KIPP schools studied, impacts on students' state assessment scores in mathematics and reading are positive, statistically significant, and educationally substantial. Estimated impacts are frequently large enough to substantially reduce race- and income-based achievement gaps within three years of entering KIPP." *Source:* Mathematica Policy Research, "National Evaluation of KIPP Middle Schools," June 22, 2010. Note that as public charter schools, KIPP schools typically only receive 60 to 90 percent of the operational revenues and none of the capital expenditure funds that district public schools get. (KIPP schools raise independent funds to cover the cost of their longer school day and year.)

8. Andrew Rotherham, "KIPP Schools: A Reform Triumph, or Disappointment?" *TIME,* April 27, 2011. See also the KIPP web site: http://www.kipp.org. For more information on KIPP results, see also Mathematica Policy Research, "National Evaluation of KIPP Middle Schools"; Angrist et al., "Who Benefits from KIPP?" NBER Working Paper Series, National Bureau of Economic Research, February 2010; SRI International, "San Francisco Bay Area KIPP Schools: A Study of Early Implementation and Achievement—Final Report," September 2008; Center for Research in Educational Policy, "Urban School Reform: Year Four Outcomes for the Knowledge Is Power Program in an Urban Middle School," University of Memphis, March 2008; Center for Social Organization of Schools, "Baltimore KIPP Ujima Village Academy, 2002–2006: A Longitudinal Analysis of Student Outcomes," Johns Hopkins University, June 2007; Augenblick, Palaich and Associates, "Opening Closed Doors: Lessons from Colorado's First Independent Charter School," September 2006; Musher et al., "Can an Intense Educational Experience Improve Performance on Objective Tests?" Summer 2005; Center for Research in Educational Policy, "KIPP Diamond Academy Year Three Evaluation Report," University of Memphis, October

2005; Center for Research in Educational Policy, "Analysis of Year Two: Student Achievement Outcomes for the Memphis KIPP Diamond Academy," University of Memphis, January 2005; Center for Research in Educational Policy, "Year One Evaluation of the KIPP Diamond Academy," University of Memphis, May 2004; New American Schools, "Evaluating Success: KIPP Educational Program Evaluation," October 2002.

9. Market capitalization information as of early April 2012.

10. Stephen Levy, "Larry Page Wants to Return Google to Its Startup Roots," *Wired,* March 18, 2011.

11. Rich Karlgaard, "Leadership Lessons from Google," *Forbes,* November 23, 2009.

12. Lancy Whitney, "Google Tops List of World's Most Valuable Brands," *CNET.com,* March 25, 2011.

13. Larry Page and Sergey Brin, "2004 Founders' IPO Letter from the S-1 Registration Statement," accessed January 2, 2012, at http://investor.google.com/corporate/2004/ipo-founders-letter.html.

14. Stephen Levy, *In the Plex: How Google Thinks, Works, and Shapes Our Lives* (New York: Simon & Schuster, 2011), 302.

15. Jeff Jarvis, *What Would Google Do?* (New York: Collins Business, 2009), 99–100.

16. Janet Lowe, *Google Speaks: Secrets of the World's Greatest Billionaire Entrepreneurs* (Hoboken, New Jersey: John Wiley & Sons, 2009), 223–232.

17. George Anders, "The Rare Find," *Bloomberg Businessweek,* October 17–October 23, 2011.

18. Eric Schmidt cited by James Manyika, "Google's View on the Future of Business: An Interview with CEO Eric Schmidt," *McKinsey Quarterly,* September 2008.

19. Schmidt cited by Manyika, "Google's View on the Future of Business."

20. Rob May, "Why Google May Not Be a Good Model for Innovation," *Business Pundit,* December 15, 2007.

21. Alexei Oreskovic, "Google CEO's Inner Circle: Meet the L Team, *Reuters,* December 16, 2011.

22. Claire Cain Miller, "Google's Chief Works to Trim a Bloated Ship," *New York Times,* November 9, 2011.

CONCLUSION

1. Remarks by Drew Gilpin Faust summarized in "Harvard and HBS: The Next 100 Years," Harvard Business School, Centennial Global Business Summit, October 14, 2008, accessed January 4, 2012, at http://www.hbs.edu/centennial/business summit/past-present-future/harvard-and-hbs-the-next-100-years.html. We note that Faust used the cathedral metaphor also used by Bill Shore in *The Cathedral Within: Transforming Your Life by Giving Something Back* (New York: Random House, 2001).

APPENDIX

1. Julia Kirby, "Toward a Theory of High Performance," *Harvard Business Review: The High-Performance Organization,* July–August 2005. See also Jay Jamrog et al., "High-

Performance Organizations: Finding the Elements of Excellence," *People and Strategy,* Volume 31, Issue 1, 29–38; Michael Raynor et al., "A Random Search for Excellence: Why 'Great Company' Research Delivers Fables and Not Facts," Deloitte Consulting, April 2009.

2. Here is a partial list of recent publications that address these topics: "Analysis: Sustainability Indexes Lack Own Transparency," *Reuters.com,* September 16, 2010; Christine Arena, "Top CSR Companies. Or Not," *ChristineArena.com,* March 17, 2010; Bill Baue, "Corporate Sustainability Ranking Gets a Face Lift," *Business Ethics,* February 3, 2010; CFO Research Services, *A Climate of Convergence: The U.S. Road to Global Reporting Standards,* CFO Publishing Corp., September 2008; McKinsey Global Survey Results, "Valuing Corporate Social Responsibility," *McKinsey Quarterly,* 2009; SustainAbility, *Rate the Raters Phase Two: Taking Inventory of the Ratings Universe,* October 2010; "When Pigs Fly: Halliburton Makes the Dow Jones Sustainability Index," *TriplePundit.com,* September 24, 2010.

POSTSCRIPT

1. Laura Hillenbrand, *Seabiscuit: An American Legend* (New York: Ballantine Books), 53.

2. Unless otherwise noted, the facts cited here are from the "2011 Online Fact Book," Jockey Club, accessed January 5, 2012, at http://www.jockeyclub.com/factbook.asp.

3. Glenn Davis, "Remembering Fine Cotton," *Racing and Sports,* August 15, 2004, accessed January 5, 2012, at http://www.racingandsports.com.au/racing/rsNewsArt .asp?NID=46668&story=Remembering_Fine_Cotton.

4. "Penny Chenery," *Secretariat.com,* undated, accessed January 5, 2012, at http://www .secretariat.com/spotlight/penny-chenery.

5. "Jockeys' Guild History, 1940 to Present," *JockeysGuild.com,* undated, accessed January 5, 2012, at http://www.jockeysguild.com/history.html.

6. "Horse Racing," *PETA.org,* undated, accessed January 5, 2012, at http://www.peta .org/issues/animals-in-entertainment/horse-racing.aspx.

7. Julie Koenig Loignon, "Churchill Downs Incorporated Racetracks Maintain Focus on Safety as Spring Racing Seasons Begin," Churchill Downs Inc., April 11, 2011, accessed January 5, 2012, at http://www.churchilldowns incorporated.com/our_company/company_news/2011/04/11/churchill_downs_ incorporated_racetracks_maintain_focus_on_safety.

ACKNOWLEDGMENTS

We extend thanks to all the people who helped with this book. Special thanks to our interviewees for their candid insights about their organizations and their own views on leadership. (They are listed in the Appendix.) Unfortunately, we could not include insights from all interviewees in the book.

Our own experiences are built on the insights and wisdom of many extraordinary colleagues and mentors over the years, to whom we offer our heartfelt gratitude. Our friends, colleagues, and students at the University of Denver, Royal Institute of Technology, Stockholm School of Entrepreneurship, and Colorado Mountain College have sharpened our thinking. The Vail Leadership Institute and its thought leaders have provided inspiration, fellowship, and a rich body of leadership thinking that has deeply informed our outlook. We are grateful to our colleagues and associates at various organizations, including Bob Aubrey, Terrence Brown, Art Currier, Larry Donnithorne, Peggy Curry, John Horan-Kates, Nick Kaye, Björn Larsson, Rasmus Rahm, and Martin Vendel.

We offer special thanks to our research assistants Sara McGlathery and Abby James, who have been responsive, professional, thorough, tireless, and a joy to work with. We also thank Naila Razvi for her cheerful assistance and professional interview transcriptions.

Numerous friends, colleagues, and experts were kind enough to take the time to review early drafts of the manuscript or certain chapters, challenge our thinking, and provide invaluable insights. They include Miguel Brookes, Dick Chandler, Bob Darr, Christopher

Gergen, David Gray, Dick Gyde, John Horan-Kates, Greg Kesler, Bill Kleh, Manu Kulkarni, Marty Linsky, Leonard Lusky, Stephen Martin, Elise Micati, Anne O'Leary, James O'Toole, Mike Petrilli, Dan Sweeney, Paul Thallner, and Steve Zimmerman. We also thank the others who provided help during the process, including William J. Bennett, Leonard Berry, Judith Briles, Kim Cameron, Katherine Carol, Peter Dougherty, Chester E. Finn, Jr., Bill George, Marc Lavine, Richard Leider, Neal Maillet, Kent Seltman, Peter Sims, Jeevan Sivasubramaniam, Malorie Stroud, and Myles Thompson. Lee Coburn, Tim Wright, Leah Gaultney, and their colleagues at Coburn Creative provided expert assistance with design, graphics, and the web site. Our friend Jamie Bailey did terrific photography work for our web site.

Our agent, Craig Wiley, was an enthusiastic, creative, and involved partner. He also came up with the idea for the book's title and provided helpful input on the manuscript. The professional help of the staff at McGraw-Hill has been terrific, led by Mary Glenn and including Pamela Peterson, Courtney Fischer, Laura Yieh, and Janice Race. Hearty thanks to our copyeditor, Judy Duguid, for her good work and to our publicist, Lori Ames, for helping us get the word out.

Finally, no undertaking like this could come to fruition without the support and encouragement of our life partners, June and Kristina (and of Alexandra and Anya, Gregg's daughters), to whom we are eternally grateful.

—Bob Vanourek and Gregg Vanourek

INDEX

ABOUT THE AUTHORS

Bob Vanourek has served as CEO of New York Stock Exchange companies during his thirty-year business career. As CEO (now retired), Bob guided Sensormatic (a $1 billion security company) and Recognition Equipment (a $250 million optical character recognition company) through successful turnarounds. Bob has served as group vice president and division president of two major divisions of Pitney Bowes (a $5 billion mail-stream company) and vice president and general manager of two divisions of Avery International (a $6 billion adhesives company). Bob has led businesses and teams that have won numerous local, state, and national awards, including a state-level Malcolm Baldrige Quality Prize and the Shingo Prize for Manufacturing Excellence (shortly after Bob left).

Bob is a dynamic and popular speaker on leadership and has written several book chapters and articles. He has taught leadership at the University of Denver and Colorado Mountain College and is chairman emeritus of the Vail Leadership Institute. Bob has served on the boards of and consults with numerous businesses and community organizations. He is a Baker Scholar graduate of the Harvard Business School, is a magna cum laude graduate of Princeton University, and served as an officer in the U.S. Army. Bob and his wife, June, have been married since 1963. They live in the Rocky Mountains of Colorado, where they won the Governor's Award for Volunteer Service. Bob and June have two sons, Scott and Gregg, and five grandchildren.

Gregg Vanourek is co-author of two other books: *Life Entrepreneurs* and *Charter Schools in Action.* He has written several book chapters and reports, as well as numerous articles for leading media outlets, including *Harvard Business Review* blogs and *Washington Times* columns. Gregg teaches at the Stockholm School of Entrepreneurship and the Royal Institute of Technology. Previously, he taught at the Euromed

School of Management, University of Denver, and Colorado Mountain College. Also previously, he co-founded New Mountain Ventures (an entrepreneurial leadership development company) and served as senior vice president of school development for K12 (an online education company) during its startup years. Previously, he helped to launch and served as vice president for programs at the Thomas B. Fordham Foundation (an education reform foundation) and research fellow at the Hudson Institute (a think tank).

Gregg is a featured speaker and consultant for clients worldwide. He is a graduate of the Yale School of Management, London School of Economics and Political Science, and Claremont McKenna College. He serves on the board of the Vail Leadership Institute. A native of California, Gregg lives in Sweden with his wife, Kristina, and two daughters, Alexandra and Anya.

Bob and Gregg Vanourek are father and son.

For more information, visit
http://www.triplecrownleadership.com

To contact the authors, email them at
authors@triplecrownleadership.com

Find them on Twitter here: @TripleCrownLead